The Magic Machine
A *Handbook of Computer Sorcery*

The Magic Machine
A Handbook of Computer Sorcery

A. K. Dewdney

W. H. Freeman and Company
New York

Library of Congress Cataloging-in-Publication Data

Dewdney, A. K.
   The magic machine: A handbook of computer sorcery / A. K. Dewdney.
      p.   cm.
   ISBN 0-7167-2125-2 (hardcover); 0-7167-2144-9 (paperback)
   1. Microcomputers — Programming.   2. Computer software.
3. Computer graphics.   I. Title
QA76.6.D5173 1990
794.8'1536 — dc20   90-31250
                                                                         CIP

Printed in the United States of America

1 2 3 4 5 6 7 8 9 0   V   9 9 8 7 6 5 4 3 2 1 0

Dedicated with respect and affection
to
John Francis Hart
Computer scientist and philosopher

Contents

○ Spell Three ○

Deus Ex Machina   105

○ Spell Four ○

Puzzling Landscapes   177

○ Spell Five ○

Mathemagical Movies   245

○ Spell Six ○

Battles of the Magi   281

Prologue

A "magic machine" can be understood as a machine that produces magical effects or one that operates by magic. For most people, the computer is both. Let this book then serve as a manual of magic, an entrée to the occult world of programming and to esoteric knowledge of the machine.

Taken from my Computer Recreations column in SCIENTIFIC AMERICAN magazine, here are topics ideally suited for sorcerers and apprentice sorcerers.

In the section "Order out of Chaos," there are spells for invoking the Mandelbrot set or an infinite number of its cousins, all called Julia. At the heart of chaos lie some simple iterative formulas. Placed in a program, the formulas come to life on the screen, producing "strange attractors" and even stranger creatures called biomorphs.

Being magical, the machine will certainly incarnate in different forms. In the section "Weird Machines," computers lurk in a monstrous assembly of Tinker Toys, lie quietly beneath the soil of the ancient island of Apraphulia, or vibrate at atomic frequencies in molecule-sized machines drifting through the human bloodstream! There are, moreover, machines that inhabit toy cars which gather at street lights and machines that make gold out of nothing. Here at last is the Philosopher's Stone. Or is it?

A section on artificial life brings new light to the magian imperative — to create a living organism. We cannot claim to have done this, but there are systems that grow like trees, imitate self-sustaining chemical reactions. An entire miniature universe called a cyclic cellular automaton produces strange, crystalline growths that compete for ever-diminishing resources. A little higher on the scale of being the evolution of feeding patterns in protozoa is simulated. Higher yet, there are humanoids attending a party, moving from guest to guest in an amusing quest for personal equilibrium.

Puzzles and wordplay, always a favorite in Martin Gardner's "Mathematical Games" column (the predecessor of "Computer Recreations"), sharpen the wizard's brain. How to escape the dread Minotaur in an actual reconstruction of King Minos' cruel labyrinth? Is there a formula for prime numbers? How does one turn around the train from Problemtown to Solutionville? In people puzzles, one has to think about what people think about other people to solve a problem. Words, of course, abound. Poetry and prose written by computers leave the muse out in the cold. But even the magic machine cannot solve Axel Thue's famous word problem!

In "Mathemagical Movies," simple programs produce striking effects, from a screenful of writhing worms to raindrops on a pond. Whoever thought we might someday watch balls bounce around inside boxes simulating air pressure? The Invisible Professor makes a nonappearance to draw enchanting curves with names like the lemniscate of Bernoulli and the witch of Agnesi.

Appropriately, the book ends with Battles of the Magi, wherein the forces of good and evil invade technology. There are machines that make codes but also machines that break them. There are programs that war within a computer's memory. The famous game of Core War gives way to a new and far more deadly struggle: computer viruses. By what magic will they be stopped?

Programmers will find ample material here to practice their arts. Some 28 programs are outlined in sufficient detail for readers of even moderate programing skill to bring their own screens to life. As always, the beginner is not left out. Here and there some simple programs will attract and reward the tyro.

Even with full knowledge of what goes on "behind the scenes," so to speak, the sense of magic will never quite leave us. The magic, after all, is ours. The computer only manifests what is in our minds, the home of enchantment.

ACKNOWLEDGMENTS

I owe much to the two editors I have worked with since the appearance of my previous collection of columns *The Armchair Universe*. Greg Greenwell, whose unfailing enthusiasm buoyed me up when I most needed it, kept me on track. Russell Ruthen's careful work continues to illuminate dark corners in my prose. Presiding over the process, Jonathan Piel, SCIENTIFIC AMERICAN's editor-in-chief, has watched this writer learning to view himself increasingly with his own editorial eye. The end result, still some distance off, will be worth the wait: a writer who can edit himself.

A special thanks to my computational assistant, his plurality, David Wiseman. "The Magi," as his friends call him, has converted many of the spells herein to actual programs. Frequently, he has been able to suggest improvements that prevented readers from becoming lost or confused. We owe much to his wizardry. I am also grateful to Alice Puddephatt, who proofread the text and prepared the index. A final thanks to Stephen Wagley, the editor at W. H. Freeman who has brought these pages meticulously to life.

A. K. Dewdney

A Word to Programmers and Apprentice Programmers

The pages that follow are packed with potential programs. By this I mean that some 28 programs are specified by means of algorithms — English-language descriptions of all the main ingredients required to write the programs and set them in operation on any magic machine worthy of the name.

Advanced practitioners of the art of BASIC, Pascal, C, or any other programming language will delight in a potpourri of clever programs that perform interesting feats, from plotting the Mandelbrot set to simulating bacteria, planning parties, and setting up a Core War system.

Beginners will find a special path already paved for them through the book and signposted below as a guide to what topics may best suit their skills, and how to develop those skills from almost any starting point, however humble. Consider the reader who has never programmed, for example, but owns a computer and has bought at least one "how-to" book that explains the basics — from turning on the machine to getting a system such as BASICA to blink its cursor in expectation of a program that said reader will (however haltingly) type in.

Even for such readers the path is clear: Start with WORMS, a program that is first laid out as an algorithm and then displayed as an actual working program (see below). The use of algorithms can then be practiced on programs even simpler than WORMS: the CIRCLE program outlined by the Invisible Professor, SLUICE1, a prime-finding program suggested by Old Yuke who pans for primes in the land of cold Northern Logic. There is also the fascinating but elementary chaos program called CHAOS1.

Not all algorithms are laid out in the same level of detail. Some will seem frustratingly vague to those who do not quite see what to do. Further practice is available here as well. Two potential programs, HODGEPODGE and BUGS, are specified as rather complete algorithms. The translation into working programs is not exactly line-by-line, but almost.

Programmers of all levels of experience will find all potential programs graded in difficulty, from E for easy and M for medium to H for hard. There is even one double-hard program (HH): the Core War system called MARS. A few programs are transitional, coded E/M for easy-to-medium or M/H for medium-to-hard.

Finally another dozen or more programs are implicit in puzzles, in tales, and in descriptions that are never spelled out algorithmically but are clear enough to cast in one's favorite code.

These are the 28 programs given as algorithms.

CHAPTER	PROGRAM	LEVEL OF SKILL
1 Mandelbrot Magic	MANDELZOOM generates Mandelbrot set	E/M
	RHOP detects cycles in iterative processes	E
2 Visions of Julia	JULIAZOOM generates the Julia set	E/M
4 The Strange Attractions of Chaos	CHAOS1 the simplest known chaotic system	E
	CHAOS2 the Hénon attractor	E

	CHAPTER	PROGRAM	LEVEL OF SKILL
5	Catching Biomorphs	BIOMORPH generates algebraic "life" forms	M/H
		POPCORN fractal forms laid out on a grid	E/M
10	Fractal Mountains and Graftal Plants	MOUNTAIN draws profile of a mountain	M
		PLANT L-system for generating a plant	M
11	Hodgepodge Reactions	HODGEPODGE cellular automaton that produces a self-sustaining reaction	M
12	The Demons of Cyclic Space	DEMON cellular automaton that evolves	M
13	Slow Growths	SLO GRO simulates natural clustering processes	E/M
14	Programmed Parties	PARTY PLANNER token people party on a computer screen	M/H
15	Palmiter's Protozoa	BUGS simulates protozoa hunting bacteria	M/H
18	Panning for Primes	SLUICE1 simple prime number generator	E
		SLUICE2 smart prime number generator	E

CHAPTER	PROGRAM	LEVEL OF SKILL
22 Special FX	WORMS draws worms that crawl on computer screen	E
	RAINDROPS draws raindrops on a pond surface	E
	STARBURST the view from a spaceship	E/M
23 Balls in Boxes	BOUNCE molecules in a box	M/H
	BLEND molecules diffuse	M
	BOOM nuclear chain-reactions	M
24 The Invisible Professor	CIRCLE draws circles	EE
	TSCHIRNHAUSEN draws Tschirnhausen's cubic curve	E
	HIPPOPEDE draws the Hippopede curve	E
	BOWDITCH draws all the Bowditch curves	E
26 Computers in the Crypt	DES the date encryption standard code	M
27 Core Wars	MARS the Core War operating system	HH

The Magic Machine
A Handbook of Computer Sorcery

Conjuring Up Chaos

Wh^{hat} visions are these that appear? The Mandelbrot set is etched, pixel by pixel, on the screen. On its edges, strange colors play amid fantastic filigrees. Infinite detail plunges in fractal regress to infinitesimal reaches. A myriad of Julia sets, each a delicate doily born of a single point in the Mandelbrot set, parade across the screen. And now, strange creatures called biomorphs appear, with radiolarian spikes and innards like the ectoplasm of algebra.

How were these visions conjured up? The spell is simple:

$$z \leftarrow z^2 + c$$

To use it, one does not really need to know that z and c are complex numbers; one only needs the incantation, a program that works the magic. And here are programs aplenty, one for each kind of vision.

All these manifestations represent one aspect or another of the topic called chaos. Certain dynamical systems, from double pendulums to global weather, are subject to the strange laws of chaos whereby a small perturbation in the system at one moment may (or may not) cause very large changes in the system in a surprisingly short time. The changes are deterministic but, because the effect is amplified by so many orders of magnitude, it is impossible to predict precisely by computer or in any other way.

To conjure up chaos, we do not need to set up a double pendulum or wait for a sharp exhalation on Sunday to produce a tropical hurricane on Tuesday. There are model systems and formulas for them that enable us to plot the shape of chaos. The simplest formula lurks in Chapter 4; it has a parameter which, when steadily changed, shows chaos creeping up on the model system until, suddenly, all is awry: Instead of settling into a comfortable equilibrium, the system swings wildly from state to state.

But chaos is dangerous. If things get out of hand, we may turn for relief to biomorphs, fractal plankton that inhabit an imaginary drop of water. They do not swim but stay anchored near the origin. The spell for the Mandelbrot set, when modified appropriately, calls for the biomorphs with their spikes, cilia, and flagella, and whose weird innards regress to astonishing levels of detail. What biology is this?

○ 1 ○

Mandelbrot Magic

The Mandelbrot set broods in silent complexity at the center of a vast two-dimensional sheet of numbers called the complex plane. When a certain operation is applied repeatedly to the numbers, the ones outside the set flee to infinity. The numbers inside remain to drift or dance about. Close to the boundary minutely choreographed wanderings mark the onset of the instability. Here is an infinite regress of detail that astonishes us with its variety, its complexity, and its strange beauty.

The set is named for Benoit B. Mandelbrot, a research fellow at the IBM Thomas J. Watson Research Center in Yorktown Heights, N.Y. From his work with geometric forms Mandelbrot has developed the field he calls fractal geometry, the mathematical study of forms having a fractional dimension. In particular the boundary of the Mandelbrot set is a fractal, but it is also much more.

With the aid of a relatively simple program a computer can be converted into a kind of microscope for viewing the boundary of the Mandelbrot set. In principle one can zoom in for a closer look at any part of the set at any magnification (*see* Color Plate 1). From a distant vantage the set resembles a squat, wart-covered figure 8 lying on its side. The inside of the figure is ominously black. Surrounding it is a halo colored electric white, which gives way to deep blues and blacks in the outer reaches of the plane.

Approaching the Mandelbrot set, one finds that each wart is a tiny figure shaped much like the parent set. Zooming in for a close look at one of the tiny figures, however, opens up an entirely different pattern: a riot of organic-looking tendrils and curlicues sweeps out in whorls and rows (*see* Color Plate 2). Magnifying a curlicue reveals yet another scene: it is made up of pairs of whorls jointed by bridges of filigree. A magnified bridge turns out to have two curlicues sprouting from its center. In the center of this center, so to speak, is a four-way bridge with four more curlicues, and in the center of these curlicues another version of the Mandelbrot set is found.

The magnified version is not quite the same Mandelbrot set. As the zoom continues, such objects seem to reappear, but a closer look always turns up differences. Things go on this way forever, infinitely various and frighteningly lovely.

Here I shall describe two computer programs, both of which explore the effects of iterated operations such as the one that leads to the Mandelbrot set. The first program generated Color Plates 1 and 2. The program can be adapted to run on personal computers that have the appropriate hardware and software for generating graphics. It will create satisfying images even if one has access only to a monochrome display. The second program is for readers who, like me, need an occasional retreat from infinite complexity to the apparent simplicity of the finite.

The word "complex" as used here has two meanings. The usual meaning is obviously appropriate for describing the Mandelbrot set, but the word has a second and more technical sense. A number is complex when it is made up of two parts, which for historical reasons are called real and imaginary. These terms have no special significance for us here: the two parts of a complex number might as well be called Humpty and Dumpty. Thus $7 + 4i$ is a complex number with real part 7 (Humpty) and imaginary part $4i$ (Dumpty). The italic i next to the 4 shows which part of the complex number is imaginary.

Every complex number can be represented by a point in the plane; the plane of complex numbers is called the complex plane. To find $7 + 4i$ in the complex plane, start at the complex number 0, or $0 + 0i$, and measure seven units east and four units north. The resulting point represents

---○---

COMPLEX-NUMBER ARITHMETIC

Two complex numbers are added by summing their respective real
and imaginary parts separately. In other words, the sum of the
complex numbers represented by $a + bi$ and $c + di$ is
$(a + c) + (b + d)i$.

The product of the two numbers is slightly more complicated. It is
$(ac - bd) + (ad + bc)i$. That formula can be applied in order to
derive a formula for the square of $a + bi$, which is $(a^2 - b^2) + 2abi$.
The square's real part is $(a^2 - b^2)$ and its imaginary part is $2ab$.

One further application of the multiplication formula yields another formula, one for the third power of $a + bi$. The real part of
$(a + bi)^3$ is $a(a^2 - 3b^2)$, and the imaginary part is $b(3a^2 - b^2)$.

---○---

$7 + 4i$. The complex plane is an uncountable infinity of such numbers.
Their real parts and their imaginary parts can be either positive or
negative and either whole numbers or decimal expansions.

Adding or multiplying two complex numbers is easy. To add $3 - 2i$
and $7 + 4i$, add the parts separately; the sum is $10 + 2i$. Multiplying
complex numbers is only slightly more difficult. For example, if the
symbol i is treated like the x in high school algebra, the product of $3 - 2i$
and $7 + 4i$ is $21 + 12i - 14i - 8i^2$. At this stage a special property of the
symbol i must be brought into play: it happens that i^2 equals $- 1$. Thus
the product can be simplified by collecting the real and the imaginary
parts: it is $29 - 2i$.

It is now possible to describe the iterative process that generates the
Mandelbrot set. Begin with the algebraic expression $z^2 + c$, where z is a
complex number that is allowed to vary and c is a certain fixed complex
number. Set z initially to be equal to the complex number 0. The square
of z is then 0 and the result of adding c to z^2 is just c. Now substitute this
result for z in the expression $z^2 + c$. The new sum is $c^2 + c$. Again
substitute for z. The next sum is $(c^2 + c)^2 + c$. Continue the process,
always making the output of the last step the input for the next one.

Strange things happen when the iterations are carried out for particular values of *c*. For example, here is what happens when *c* is $1 + i$:

first iteration $1 + 3i$
second iteration $-7 + 7i$
third iteration $1 - 97i$

Note that the real and the imaginary parts may grow, shrink, or change sign. If this process of iteration continues, the resulting complex numbers may get progressively larger.

What exactly is meant by the size of a complex number? Since complex numbers correspond to points in the plane, ideas of distance apply. The size of a complex number is just its distance from the complex number 0. That distance is the hypotenuse of a right triangle whose sides are the real and the imaginary parts of the complex number. Hence to find the size of the number, square each of its parts, add the two squared values, and take the square root of the sum. For example, the size of the complex number $7 + 4i$ is the square root of $7^2 + 4^2$, or approximately 8.062. When complex numbers reach a certain size under the iterative process I have just described, they grow very quickly: indeed, after a few more iterations they exceed the capacity of any computer.

Fortunately I can ignore all the complex numbers *c* that run screaming off to infinity. The Mandelbrot set is the set of all complex numbers *c* for which the size of $z^2 + c$ is small even after an indefinitely large number of iterations. The program I am about to describe searches for such numbers. I am indebted in all of this to John H. Hubbard, a mathematician at Cornell University. Hubbard is an authority on the Mandelbrot set, and he was one of the first people to make computer-generated images of it. The images in Color Plates 1 and 2 were made by Rollo Silver, publisher of *Amygdala*.

Hubbard's program has inspired a program I call MANDELZOOM. The program sets up an array called *pic*, which is needed for saving pictures. The entries of *pic* are separate picture elements called pixels, which are arranged in a grid pattern. Hubbard's array has 400 columns and 400 rows, and Heinz-Otto Peitgen's is even larger. Readers who want to adapt MANDELZOOM for personal use must chose an array suited to their equipment and temperament. Larger arrays impose a longer wait for the pictures, but they improve the resolution.

In the first part of MANDELZOOM one may select any square region of the complex plane to be examined. Specify the southwest corner of the square with the complex number to which it corresponds. Two variables in the program, *acorner* and *bcorner*, enable one to enter the real part and the imaginary part of the number respectively. Specify the length of each side of the square by entering a value for a variable called *side*.

The second part of the program adjusts the array *pic* to match the square of interest by computing the size of a variable called *gap*. *Gap* is the distance within the square between adjacent pixels. To obtain *gap* divide *side* by the number of rows (or columns) in *pic*.

The heart of the program is its third part. Here a search is made for the complex numbers *c* in the Mandelbrot set, and colors are assigned to the numbers that are, in a special sense, nearby. The procedure must be carried out once for every pixel; thus Hubbard's 400-by-400 array requires 160,000 separate computations. Assume the program is currently working on the pixel in row *m* and column *n*; the third part then breaks down into four steps:

1. Calculate one complex number *c* that is assumed to represent the pixel: add *n* × *gap* to *acorner* to obtain the real part *ac* of *c*; add *m* × *gap* to *bcorner* to obtain the imaginary part *bc* of *c*. It is not necessary to include the imaginary number *i* in the program.
2. Set a complex variable *z* (which has parts *az* and *bz*) equal to $0 + 0i$. Set an integer variable called *count* equal to 0.
3. Carry out the following three steps repeatedly until either the size of *z* exceeds 2 or the size of *count* exceeds 1000, whichever comes first:

$$z \leftarrow z^2 + c$$
$$count \leftarrow count + 1$$
$$size \leftarrow \text{size of } z$$

Why is the number 2 so important? A straightforward result in the theory complex-number iterations guarantees that the iterations will drive *z* to infinity if and only if at some stage *z* reaches a size of 2 or greater. It turns out that relatively many points with an infinite destiny reach 2 after only a few iterations. Their slower cousins become increasingly rare at higher values of the variable *count*.

4. Assign a color to *pic* (*m,n*) according to the value reached by
count at the end of Step 3. Display the color of the
corresponding pixel on the screen. Note that the color of a pixel
depends on only one complex number within its tiny domain,
namely the one at its northeast corner; the behavior of this
number then represents the behavior of the entire pixel.

The scheme for assigning colors requires that the range of *count* values
attained within the array be grouped into subranges, one subrange for
each color. Pixels for which the size of z reaches 2 after only a few
iterations are colored red. Pixels for which the size of z reaches 2 after
relatively many iterations are colored violet, at the other end of the
spectrum. Pixels for which the size of z is less than 2 even after 1000
iterations are assumed to lie in the Mandelbrot set; they are colored black.

It makes sense to leave the colors unspecified until the range of *count*
values in a particular square has been determined. If the range is narrow,
the entire color spectrum can then be assigned within that range. Thus
Hubbard suggests that in Step 4 only the value of *count* be assigned to
each array element of *pic*. A separate program can then scan the array,
determine the high and low values of *count*, and assign the spectrum
accordingly. Readers who get this far will certainly find workable
schemes.

The reader who does not have a color monitor can still take part in
black and white. Complex numbers for which z is larger than 2 after r
iterations are colored white. The rest are colored black. Adjust r to taste.
To avoid all-night runs the array can be, say, 100 rows by 100 columns.
Hubbard also suggests it is perfectly reasonable to reduce the maximum
number of iterations per point from 1000 to 100. The output of such a
program is a suggestive, pointillistic image of its colored counterpart (*see
illustration on the facing page*).

For other effective approaches which utilize a black-and-white monitor, see the Addendum which follows this chapter.

How powerful is the "zoom lens" of a personal computer? It depends
to some degree on the effective size of the numbers the machine can
manipulate. For example, the IBM PC uses the 8088 microprocessor, a
chip manufactured by the Intel Corporation designed to manipulate
16-bit numbers. A facility called double precision makes it possible to
increase the length of each number to 32 bits. With such double precision I calculate that magnifications on the order of 30,000 times can be

Pointillist, miniature Mandelbrot in monochrome.

realized. Higher precision software that in effect strings these numbers together can enhance the numerical precision to hundreds of significant digits. The magnification of the Mandelbrot set theoretically attainable with such precision is far greater than the magnification needed to resolve the nucleus of the atom.

Where should one explore the complex plane? Near the Mandelbrot set, of course, but where precisely? Hubbard says that "there are zillions of beautiful spots." Like a tourist in a land of infinite beauty, he bubbles with suggestions about places readers may want to explore. They do not have names like Hawaii or Hong Kong: "Try the area with the real part between .26 and .27 and the imaginary part between 0 and .01." He has also suggested two other places:

REAL PART	IMAGINARY PART
−.76 to −.74	.01 to .03
−1.26 to −1.24	.01 to .03

The reader who examines color images of the Mandelbrot set should bear in mind that any point having a color other than black does not belong to the Mandelbrot set. Much of the beauty resides in the halo of colors assigned to the fleeing points. Indeed, if one were to view the set in isolation, its image might not be so pleasing: The set is covered all over with filaments and with miniature versions of itself.

In fact none of the miniature Mandelbrots is an exact copy of the parent set and none of them is exactly alike. Near the parent set there are even more miniature Mandelbrots, apparently suspended freely in the complex plane. The appearance is deceiving. An amazing theorem proved by Hubbard and a colleague, Adrian Douady of the University of Paris, states that the Mandelbrot set is connected. Hence even the miniature Mandelbrots that seem to be suspended in the plane are attached by filaments to the parent set. The miniatures are found almost everywhere near the parent set and they come in all sizes. Every square in the region includes an infinite number of them, of which at most only a few are visible at any given magnification. According to Hubbard, the Mandelbrot set is "the most complicated object in mathematics."

Readers unable or unwilling to write the MANDELZOOM program may order one that runs on an IBM PC or other machines by consulting the List of Suppliers. This list also contains sources for slides and posters of the Mandelbrot set.

Confronted with infinite complexity it is comforting to take refuge in the finite. Iterating a squaring process on a finite set of ordinary integers also gives rise to interesting structures. The structures are not geometric but combinatorial.

Pick any number at random from 0 through 99. Square it and extract the last two digits of the result, which must also be a number from 0 through 99. For example, 59^2 is equal to 3481; the last two digits are 81. Repeat the process and sooner or later you will generate a number you have already encountered. For example, 81 leads to the sequence 61, 21,

41, and 81, and this sequence of four numbers is then repeated indefinitely. It turns out that such loops always arise from iterative processes on finite sets. Indeed, it is easy to see there must be at least one repeated number after 100 operations in a set of 100 numbers; the first repeated number then leads to a loop. There is a beautiful program for detecting the loops that requires almost no memory, but more of this later.

It takes only an hour to diagram the results of the squaring process. Represent each number from 0 through 99 by a separate point on a sheet of paper. If the squaring process leads from one number to a new number, join the corresponding points with an arrow. For example, an arrow should run from point 59 to point 81. The first few connections in the diagram may lead to tangled loops, and so it is a good idea to redraw them from time to time in such a way that no two arrows cross. A nonintersecting iteration diagram is always possible.

One can go even further. Separate subdiagrams often arise, and they can be displayed in a way that highlights some of the symmetries arising from the iterations. For example, the nonintersecting iteration diagram for the squaring process on the integers from 0 through 99 includes six unconnected subdiagrams. The pieces come in identical pairs and each piece is highly symmetrical (*see* illustration on page 12). Can the reader explain the symmetry? What would happen if the integers from 0 through 119 were used instead? Is there a relation between the number of unconnected pieces found in the diagram and the largest integer in the sequence?

Similar patterns of iteration hold for some of the complex numbers in the Mandelbrot set: for certain values of c repeated iterations of $z^2 + c$ can lead to a finite cycle of complex numbers. For example, the complex number $0 + 1i$ leads to an indefinite oscillation between the two complex numbers $-1 + 1i$ and $0 - 1i$. The cycle may even have only one member. Whether such cycles are found in a finite set or in the infinite Mandelbrot set, they are called attractors.

Each of the six parts of the iteration diagram for the integers 0 through 99 includes one attractor. Geometrically the attractor can be represented as a polygon, and the sets of numbers that lead into it can be represented as trees.

One way to find an attractor by computer is to store each newly generated number in a specially designated array. Compare the new number with all the numbers previously stored in the array. If a match is found, print all the numbers in the array from the matching number to

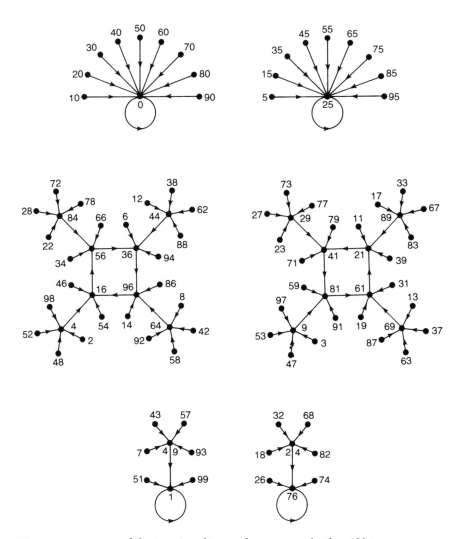

The six components of the iteration diagram for squaring the first 100 integers.

the number just created. The method is straightforward and easy to program. Nevertheless, it can take a long time if the array is large. An attractor cycle within an array that includes *n* numbers would take on the

There is a clever little program that will find an attractor much faster. The program requires not *n* words of memory but only two, and it can be encoded on the simplest of programmable pocket calculators. The program is found in a remarkable book titled *Mathematical Recreations for the Programmable Calculator*, by Dean Hoffman of Auburn University and Lee Mohler of the University of Alabama (*see* Further Readings). Needless to say, many of the topics that are covered in the book can be readily adapted to computer programs.

The program is called RHOP because the sequence of numbers that eventually repeats itself resembles a piece of rope with a loop at one end. It also resembles the Greek letter rho (ρ). There are two variables in the program called *slow* and *fast*. Initially both variables are assigned the value of the starting number. The iterative cycle of the program includes just three instructions:

$$fast \leftarrow fast \times fast \text{ (mod 100)}$$
$$fast \leftarrow fast \times fast \text{ (mod 100)}$$
$$slow \leftarrow slow \times slow \text{ (mod 100)}$$

The operation mod 100 extracts the last two digits of the products. Note that the squaring is done twice on the number *fast* but only once on the number *slow*. *Fast* makes its way from the tail to the head of the rho twice as fast as *slow* does. Within the head *fast* catches up with *slow* by the time *slow* has gone partway around. The program exits from its iterative cycle when *fast* is equal to *slow*.

The attractor is identified by reiterating the squaring process for the number currently assigned to *slow*. When that number recurs, halt the program and print the intervening sequence of numbers.

I should be delighted to see readers' diagrams that explore the effects of iterative squaring on finite realms of varying size. The diagrams can be done on a computer or by hand. Discrete iteration is a newly developing mathematical field with applications in biology, physics, and sociology. Theorists might wish to consult a book on the subject by François Robert of the University of Grenoble (*see* Further Readings).

ADDENDUM

Since the previous discussion first appeared in the "Computer Recreations" column of SCIENTIFIC AMERICAN magazine in August, 1985, the MANDELZOOM program has been incarnated in hundreds of homes, schools, and workplaces. Although the program has apparently awed adults, intrigued teenagers, and frightened a few small children, to my surprise the mail on iteration diagrams, the secondary topic, nearly equaled that on the Mandelbrot set.

Many readers have lost themselves in the colored intricacies of the Mandelbrot set by zooming ever deeper. Other readers, whose equipment is limited to black and white, may quite effectively develop shades of gray. Such pictures can be nearly as inspiring as their colored counterparts. The best gray images were produced by David W. Brooks, who works with equipment at Prime Computer, Inc., in Framingham, Mass., to compute and plot his pictures. In his fabulous and delicate riots of halftones each shade of gray is rendered by tiny black squares of a certain size; the squares are made by a laser printer. Brooks has been searching for the tiny filaments that are thought to connect miniature Mandelbrots to the main set. So far they have not appeared at any magnification used by Brooks. Mandelbrot has advised him that they are probably infinitesimal.

Those with less sophisticated equipment can still work with shades of gray on a black-and-white monitor. John B. Halleck of Salt Lake City varies the density of points per pixel to indicate different shades.

Another approach depends on black and white contours. Yekta Gursel of Cambridge, Mass., has generated views of the Mandelbrot set that rival the ones Brooks generates. Gursel replaces a discrete spectrum of colors with alternating bands of black and white. Gary J. Shannon of Grants Pass, Ore., suggested the same technique and Victor Andersen of Santa Clara, Calif., took it to an extreme. He suggested changing from black to white (or the converse) whenever the *count* variable changes from one pixel to its neighbor.

Two other explorations are worth mentioning. James A. Thigpenn IV of Pearland, Tex., uses height instead of color. The Mandelbrot set becomes an immense plateau seen from an angle, with a complicated arrangement of spiky hills approaching the plateau in various places. Richard J. Palmaccio of Fort Lauderdale dispenses with the set altogether. His interest is in tracking individual complex numbers in the course of iteration. Their choreography near the boundary can result in spiral ballets or circular jigs.

The function $z^2 + c$ gives rise to the Mandelbrot set. Naturally other functions are possible, but they produce other sets. For example, Bruce Ikenaga of Case Western Reserve University has been exploring what appears to be a cubic cactus. The function $z^3 + (c - 1)z - c$ produces a prickly and uncomfortable-looking set (at least in stark black and white) surrounded by mysterious miniature spiral galaxies.

Readers interested in pursuing the Mandelbrot set further may wish to subscribe to a newsletter devoted to the stunning fractal and related objects: *Amygdala* (*see* List of Suppliers).

There are mysteries in iteration diagrams as well: when the integers modulo n are squared, each number migrates to another, in effect. The iteration diagram appears when each number is replaced by a point and each migration is replaced by an arrow. I raised several questions about such diagrams. How many components do they have? Readers sent diagrams documenting their explorations for various values of n.

The largest diagrams were completed by Rosalind B. Marimont of Silver Spring, Md. She examined the integers modulo 1000 and reported four pairs of components in the resulting iteration diagram. Each component sported a single attractor, as usual, and the largest attractors had 20 numbers. As a mathematician, Marimont is allowed to conjecture that the integers modulo 10^k will produce $k + 1$ pairs of components and that the largest attractors will have $4 \times 5^{k-2}$ numbers.

Stephen Eberhart of Reseda, Calif., investigated the case where n is a Fermat prime (a prime number of the form $2^{2^k} + 1$). Here the number 0 forms an attractor by itself and the remaining numbers all lie in one single, grand tree. A number-theorist friend affirms that this will always be the case for Fermat primes and that the tree is binary: Each internal point has two incoming arrows.

Iteration diagrams, like numbers, can be multiplied. If n is the product of two relatively prime numbers, say p and q, the iteration diagram for the integers modulo n is the product respectively of the diagrams for p and q. This interesting observation was made by Stephen C. Locke of Florida Atlantic University. Locke has also described a fascinating relation between the nth iteration diagram and a diagram of a seemingly different kind, one in which the numbers, instead of being squared, are merely doubled. When n is a prime, the latter diagram for the integers modulo $n - 1$ is the same as our nth iteration diagram, except for a single isolated number forming an attractor by itself. Much the same observation was made in number-theory terms by Noam Elkies of New York City.

A powerful tool for analyzing the (squared) iteration diagrams was developed by Frank Palmer of Chicago. Apparently all the trees attached to a given attractor are isomorphic. This means essentially that they have precisely the same form.

Finally, Bruce R. Gilson of Silver Spring, Md., and Molly W. Williams of Kalamazoo, Mich., examined a quite different generalization of the numbers from 0 through 99. These may be regarded as numbers to different bases. As numbers to the base 3, for example, one would count 00, 01, 02, 10, 11, 12, 20, 21, 22 before arriving once more at 00. Such numbers also produce iteration diagrams that look like those arising for integers modulo n. Gilson proved the diagrams always have paired components when n is even but not a multiple of 4.

Readers who, for lack of time or programming expertise, insist on buying a program that displays the Mandelbrot set, may order one as indicated in the List of Suppliers.

○ 2 ○

Visions of Julia

The Mandelbrot set has emerged as the newest and brightest star in the firmament of popular mathematics. It is both beautiful and profound. Indeed, the beauty of the Mandelbrot set is only a veil over its significance: The casual observer sees a miniature riot of filaments and curlicues near the set's boundary without suspecting that such patterns encode the various forms of chaos and order (*see* illustration on page 18).

The Mandelbrot set has an important connection with stability and chaos in dynamical systems. The connection is made by way of closely related sets that are called Julia sets, after the French mathematician Gaston Julia. One Julia set corresponds to each point inside (or outside) the Mandelbrot set. Julia sets have an intrinsic fractal beauty of their own (*see* illustration on page 19). Before turning to them I had better review the set itself.

The Mandelbrot set inhabits the complex plane, an ordinary plane with some numbers attached to it. To be more precise, each point on the complex plane is represented by a number of the form $a + bi$. It does no harm to imagine that a and b are coordinates of the point. The a coordinate is called the real part of the number $a + bi$ and the b coordinate is called the imaginary part. The i acts partly as a marker to remind

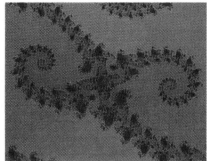

The Mandelbrot set (*left*), a section of which (*square*) is magnified (*right*)

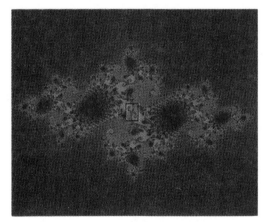

Julia set (*left*) corresponding to center of picture at top right; magnified section (*right*)

the reader which part is which. Complex numbers can be added and multiplied just as ordinary numbers are. They can be added by summing the coordinates separately. On page 5 in the previous chapter, the process of multiplication has already been described. The formulas for addition and multiplication open the door to the Mandelbrot set, draw forth the Julia sets and, in a peculiar way, bring order to chaos:

$$z \leftarrow z^2 + c$$

Here z and c are complex numbers, each composed of a real and an imaginary part. The z is squared and the c is added by means of complex

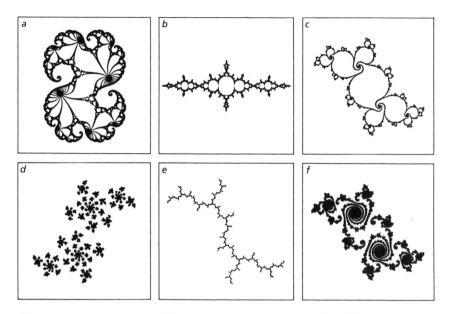

Six Julia sets, some connected (*a, b, c* and *e*) and some not (*d* and *f*)

multiplication and addition respectively. The formula springs to life when it is iterated: computed repeatedly, with the previous value of z being used to get the next one. The resulting succession of complex numbers amounts to a strange little jig on the complex plane. At each iteration of the formula the newest complex number z lies at some distance from its predecessor. Distance is critical in computing the Mandelbrot set.

I like to think of the succession of complex numbers (points on the complex plane) produced by the formula as the wanderings of the initial point. Does it long for infinity, long to dance ever outward on the complex plane? Some complex numbers enjoy that fate. Others are for-ever confined within a certain area having a complicated shape. They might be called prisoners. Their prison, the area of confinement, has fractal walls.

In the foregoing description I have implied that the iterative process is repeated over and over again. But how is one to select c and the initial value of z? One answer is to make z always zero and to select different values of c. Will the prisoner escape? The experiment is repeated again and again, with c varying systematically over a portion of the complex plane. If the prisoner escapes, color c white; otherwise color c black. The prison walls take on the shape of the Mandelbrot set. If instead of coloring the escapees white one gives them a color that varies with the speed of escape, even more beautiful images emerge.

Under the rule just described, z started with the complex value 0, namely $0 + 0i$. What would happen if some other fixed starting value were adopted, say $z = 3.5 + 6i$? Would one get a different shape for the resulting set? Actually the result is always a deformed version of the Mandelbrot set. One prefers the canonical object.

Under the opposite rule, when c is fixed and z plays the role of initial point, the resulting set looks rather different from the Mandelbrot set. It — or rather its boundary — is called a Julia set. I would have liked to say "the" Julia set, but the sets are legion: For each fixed value of c one uses in the iteration formula, a new and different Julia set appears, filled in with prisoners.

My inspiration for this visit to the Mandelbrot set lies in *The Beauty of Fractals*, a large-format book by Heinz-Otto Peitgen and Peter H. Richter of the University of Bremen (*see* Further Readings). With its stunning images in black and white and in color, it is both a mathematics textbook and a coffee-table adornment. The lore of the Mandelbrot set, its associated Julia sets, and other complex systems is crystallized in theorems and occasionally spelled out in readable paragraphs.

Let me describe the effect of one theorem. A reader who writes a program to display Julia sets might notice that for some values of c the sets are obviously connected, or of a piece, but that for other values of c the sets are not connected. What makes the difference? The answer is both simple and charming: If the point c is chosen from inside the Mandelbrot set, the corresponding Julia set is connected. If, on the other hand, c is selected from outside the Mandelbrot set, the Julia set for c is not connected.

One could make a fascinating motion picture illustrating the applicable theorem. Draw a straight line L from an arbitrary point inside the Mandelbrot set to another point outside it and imagine that a point c moves slowly and steadily along L, inside the Mandelbrot set and toward its boundary. The associated Julia set becomes increasingly pinched and crinkled in appearance until, when c reaches the boundary of the Mandelbrot set, the Julia set shrinks to a fragile dendritic skeleton enclosing no area whatever. As c passes beyond the boundary, the corresponding Julia set explodes into fractal dust.

Readers willing and able to write a program can explore the Mandelbrot set and the Julia sets by embedding certain basic algorithms in the language of their choice. The algorithms share the core iterative process, which depends heavily on a certain theorem: If the size of the so-called iterate z ever reaches 2, it is destined to leak into infinity, never to return. This distinguishes escapees from prisoners, for the most part. The algorithm allows 100 iterations for z to reach 2. Because a relatively small number of would-be escapees will not reach magnitude 2 by 100 iterations, the discriminant is not 100 percent accurate. One could, of course, allow 1000 iterations for a slightly more accurate image, but this becomes time-consuming even on fast computers.

The magnitude of a complex number $a + bi$ is simply the square root of $a^2 + b^2$, in other words, its distance from complex 0. The core algorithm follows:

$$n \leftarrow 0$$
$$\text{while } n < 100 \text{ and } mag(z) < 2$$
$$z \leftarrow z^2 + c$$
$$n \leftarrow n + 1$$
$$\text{color the current point}$$

Here an index variable n starts life at 0. Within a while-loop that controls the iteration process, n increases by 1 at each iteration. The while-loop continues to turn the crank of the basic formula as long as n has not reached 100 and the magnitude of z has not reached 2. If either condition fails, the algorithm exits from the loop. How to color the current picture point is left up to the reader. The color assigned will of course depend in some simple way on n, the slowness with which z escaped or failed to escape. The reader must also bear in mind that the picture point is a pair of screen coordinates that will differ from the coordinates of the complex number being plotted there.

The reader's program must contain a separate computation of the magnitude of z, represented by $mag(z)$ above. Indeed, because most programming languages have no provision for complex numbers, z must be retained in two-part form, say x (the real part) and y (the imaginary part); c must receive the same treatment, perhaps as a and b. The following would therefore be closer to a working program:

$$n \leftarrow 0$$
$$\text{while } n < 100 \text{ and } x^2 + y^2 < 4$$

$$xx \leftarrow x^2 - y^2 + a$$
$$y \leftarrow 2xy + b$$
$$x \leftarrow xx$$
$$n \leftarrow n + 1$$
color the current point

Astute readers will have noticed the small trick introduced in this version of the basic process: Rather than comparing the square root of the quantity $x^2 + y^2$ with 2, the algorithm compares the quantity itself with 4. The result is the same, and one can avoid continually invoking the square-root function, which can be time-consuming. The variable xx temporarily holds the newly computed x value while a new y value is being computed. The old x value is thus saved for the later computation before it is replaced by xx.

The program I called MANDELZOOM in my first foray into the subject (Chapter 1) is now reintroduced in slightly more detailed form. It wraps the basic algorithm inside a loop that systematically varies the complex number c rather than its parts, a and b. If the picture is to be 100 by 100 pixels (grid points) in size, for example, there must be a double loop:

$$gap \leftarrow side/100$$
$$a \leftarrow acorner$$
for $j \leftarrow 1$ to 100
$$\quad a \leftarrow a + gap$$
$$\quad b \leftarrow bcorner$$
$$\quad \text{for } k \leftarrow 1 \text{ to } 100$$
$$\quad\quad b \leftarrow b + gap$$
$$\quad\quad x \leftarrow 0$$
$$\quad\quad y \leftarrow 0$$
$$\quad\quad \text{[basic algorithm]}$$

Before reaching these instructions MANDELZOOM allows the user of the program to input the complex number that sits in one corner of the square of interest. It has the coordinates *acorner* and *bcorner*, the smallest values that a and b will assume in the square. This square, specified by the user of MANDELZOOM, gives the algorithm its name. It is a window through which we can peep. It can be made very, very small, in effect zooming us into the part of the set over which the window is placed. MANDELZOOM must also request the user to input a value for *side*, the width of the picture on the complex plane. The algorithm then computes the gap between successive complex numbers c, thereby giving proper increments to a and b.

The values of the indices j and k do not enter any of the computations within the double loop, and so one is free to change the indices to some more useful form. For example, instead of j and k running from 1 to 100, they could run through 100 successive screen coordinates each. When the basic algorithm has decided what color to assign to the iterate z, the color is plotted at coordinates (j,k).

I cannot leave MANDELZOOM without mentioning a modification suggested by Peitgen. Instead of comparing the magnitude of the iterate z with 2, use 100 or even 1000. Once the magnitude reaches 2, after all, it increases very quickly; it attains such values in just a few iterations. Still, different iterates pass such a threshold value at different speeds. The speeds themselves can be colored — and colored continuously! Red may evolve into orange, provided one has a reasonably sophisticated palette. In any event, it was by means of this technique that the color images accompanying this article were produced. Peitgen likens the speeds to values of an electrostatic field surrounding the Mandelbrot set. The "field" values are represented in the imaginary Mandelbrot landscape (see Color Plate 3) as slopes of a mountain range surrounding what can only be called Lake Mandelbrot.

Although I am not enamored of the name, I feel compelled to follow earlier usage and call the program that generates images of Julia sets JULIAZOOM. Here also we can zoom in on a set to examine it at great magnifications. JULIAZOOM uses the same core algorithm as MANDELZOOM but wraps it in a somewhat different rind.

JULIAZOOM first asks the user for *xcorner*, *ycorner*, and *side*. It also asks for a value of c given in terms of the variables a and b. It then employs the same double loop with some important differences:

$$gap \leftarrow side/100$$
$$x \leftarrow xcorner$$
$$\text{for } j \leftarrow 1 \text{ to } 100$$
$$\quad x \leftarrow x + gap$$
$$\quad y \leftarrow ycorner$$
$$\quad \text{for } k \leftarrow 1 \text{ to } 100$$
$$\quad\quad y \leftarrow y + gap$$
$$\quad\quad [basic\ algorithm]$$

The basic algorithm colors screen points according to the slowness with which iterates reach (or fail to reach) the magic threshold of magnitude 2. Some of the most effective graphics result from the simplest assignments. For color monitors even three colors assigned according to the following kind of scheme can be striking: Assign the first color to points with a slowness value (n) of from 0 to 10, the second color to points with a slowness of from 11 to 20, the third color to a slowness of from 21 to 30 — and then go back to the first color for the next decade, and so on. Monochrome monitors can get black-and-white (or green-and-yellow) effects by using the two colors and alternating by decades.

Equipped with a working version of MANDELZOOM or JULIAZOOM (perhaps both), readers will be able to explore these magnificent and meaningful fractal sets on their own. One can roam the complex plane in the vicinity of the sets or zoom in on specific parts with the computer microscope provided above. Up to the limits of resolution set by the arithmetic precision of one's machine, either set reveals amazing detail. For the guidance of voyagers into the infinitesimal world of fractals, the following coordinate ranges enclose both kinds of sets on all four sides:

Julia sets: x and y from -1.8 to $+1.8$;
Mandelbrot set: x from -2.25 to $+.75$,
y from -1.8 to $+1.5$

In the coming Chapter 4, "The Strange Attractions of Chaos," we will explore the subject of chaos in dynamical systems such as pendulums and electronic circuits. The simplest of such systems has a formula that involves real numbers, not complex ones:

$$x \leftarrow rx(1 - x)$$

The formula is evidently quadratic: Multiplied out, it contains a squared term. Depending on how the parameter value r is chosen, the formula behaves simply or strangely when it is iterated. For each r value, the iterates settle down into an orbit, a set of values that x systematically visits. At a critical value in the neighborhood of 3.5699 the iterates oscillate wildly and more or less unpredictably among a host of values. This corresponds to the situation where an underlying system, whether double pendulum or electronic circuit, becomes completely stymied in its search for stability. It wanders wildly in a manner that cannot be predicted in advance. Chaos.

A similar phenomenon occurs with the complex iteration formula described here, $z \leftarrow z^2 + c$. For a given value of c, however, there is more than one attractive orbit, depending on how the initial value of z is chosen. If z has a relatively small initial magnitude, it will gravitate to a specific point. If the value is large, it will get larger without limit: Infinity is the attractor. The specific point and infinity itself constitute two separate one-point attractive orbits for points on the complex plane. The boundary between their domains of attraction, the Julia set itself, is unbelievably crinkled and crumpled. It is also an orbit, but it is not attractive in the technical sense. Points already in the boundary hop about chaotically within it. The Julia set is not easy to compute directly, however, because a computer's numerical precision may not allow one to specify points that are exactly on the boundary in the first place; under iteration the precision degrades and the iterate wanders off into the night.

Each possible value of c results, as I have indicated above, in a new and different Julia set. In a sense the Mandelbrot set summarizes, in one fell swoop, all possible Julia sets. It describes the fate of iterates of complex 0 for all possible values of c. For some Julia sets the chaotic region is a mere treelike figure or even a symmetrical sprinkling of pepper. Readers will remember that such Julia sets correspond to c values on or beyond the boundary of the Mandelbrot set.

I met Peitgen once at a conference in Asilomar, Calif. As we strolled along the beach between talks he described the Mandelbrot set as a kind of vast book in which each Julia set is a mere page. From the position of c in the Mandelbrot set one can predict the generic behavior of iterates in terms of the overall shape and size of the associated Julia set. There is more to it all than mere connectedness. For example, if c is chosen from the neck between the main body of the Mandelbrot set and one of its buds, the corresponding Julia set turns out to be pinched into necks and buds of its own. The analogy of the Mandelbrot set as a kind of dictionary for the Julia sets implies a fundamental distinction between the two. The Julia set is self-similar but the Mandelbrot set (even its boundary) is not. If it were self-similar, Peitgen argues, it would not have the capacity to encode its uncountable infinity of relatives called Julia.

There is much more of all this in *The Beauty of Fractals* (*see* Further Readings). I am most grateful to Peitgen for providing the images illustrating this chapter. Not all were colored in the way I have described here but Peitgen's book describes the method.

I close with a glance at the higher-dimensional cousin of the Mandelbrot set. The iteration formula that produces the extraordinary image sent to me by Peitgen and appearing in Color Plate 4 uses z^3, not z^2. It has *two* complex parameters, which means that the object can only be properly "seen" in four-dimensional space. The object has many possible three-dimensional cross sections, so to speak, one of which is shown in the illustration.

ADDENDUM

Programs that generate Julia sets are as simple as those that produce the Mandelbrot set. Consequently, hundreds of readers, perhaps even thousands, who saw my article on Julia sets in SCIENTIFIC AMERICAN wrote programs — and many more may like to now. Those who would wish to pursue the subject further may want to subscribe to the fractal newsletter (in subject, not appearance) called *Amygdala*, which is filled with numerous programming hints. The newsletter also contains addresses of programmers willing to share or sell software (*see* List of Suppliers).

At the end of my account of Julia sets I displayed a three-dimensional monster that was actually a cross section of a four-dimensional Mandelbrot set. Heinz-Otto Peitgen, the West German mathematician and artist, has revealed the prescription for the four dimensional set. Iterate the equation $z \leftarrow x^3 - 3a^2z + b$, where a and b are both complex parameters. What points play the special role of $z = 0$ in the four-dimensional set? Actually two candidates appear, namely $z = +a$ and $z = -a$. There are consequently not one but two four-dimensional Mandelbrot sets.

Gary Teachout of Everett, Wash., wrote to me that he views the Mandelbrot and the Julia sets as cross sections of a four-dimensional set, although his four-dimensional set did not correspond to either of Peitgen's. The basic iteration formula, $z \leftarrow z^2 + c$, produces a Mandelbrot set if z remains fixed and c is varied. It produces a Julia set if c is fixed and z is varied. But z and c together define four dimensions, two for each number. By "stacking" together all the Julia sets, not in a one-dimensional pile but in a two-dimensional pile, the superset emerges. M. G. Harman of Camberley, England, speculated on the existence of the same object.

The four-dimensional prize for initiative goes to Winston D. Jenks of Stamford, Conn. Not content with ordinary complex numbers, Jenks invented his own, four-part numbers. His numbers are similar to quaternions, a sophisticated set of numbers invented by mathematicians in the nineteenth century but used today by physicists. Jenks sent me a three-

James E. Loyless' addition to the Mandelbrot gallery

dimensional representation of his solid as a sequence of 29 slices through it.

Of course, readers who want to generate images of the Mandelbrot set also want to save time in doing so; besides images, the iteration process has produced many chewed fingernails. Dick Holt of Silver Spring, Md., found that he could increase speed 8 percent by avoiding the squaring routine of his programming system. Multiplication (x times x) works faster than squaring (x squared).

Finally, the illustration above is another addition to the ongoing Mandelbrot gallery. The image was sent by James E. Loyless of Lilburn, Ga. His equipment sounds like an Indianapolis 500 car: an "XT turbo clone with an 8087 math coprocessor and a Toshiba 321 24-dot printer."

○ 3 ○

Mandelbrew and Mandelbus

Not Art and Science serve, alone;
Patience must in the work be shown.
A quiet spirit plods and plods at length;
Nothing but time can give the brew its strength.
—JOHANN WOLFGANG VON GOETHE, *Faust*

Art and science seem to blend in the Mandelbrot set. Its astonishing complexity symbolizes the growing field of chaos and nonlinear dynamics, and yet even people who have no idea of the set's real physical significance find a strange beauty in its murky interior and bejeweled halo. And, as Goethe's insightful passage reminds us, patience is indeed required when one sets out to "brew" an image of the Mandelbrot set. Although a personal computer can carry out the necessary calculations thousands of times a second, it may take up to several hours for the computer to deliver a finished image.

The Mandelbrot set actually consists of an uncountable infinity of points. The images are constructed by determining which points in a smallish collection of points (a mere few thousand or so) are members of the set. Each pixel, or picture element, in an image corresponds to a point in the collection. Each image therefore represents one part or another of the set magnified to some degree and colored according to the taste of the Mandelbrot mappers featured here. Looking at the pictures, readers may well wonder: What restless beauty stirs within the Mandelbrot set? What process creates these extraordinary forms, this complexity that plumbs the very depths of infinity? The simplicity of the answer stands in stark contrast to the complexity of the set.

In the two previous chapters I have already described in some detail how to generate the Mandelbrot set by computer. Now I want to ensure that even readers who suffer from acute math anxiety gain some insight into the set. Explaining to certain people that the Mandlebrot set has something to do with "complex numbers" causes them to blanch and mumble excuses about having to be somewhere soon. Fortunately it is possible to avoid the subject of complex numbers altogether. I invite those readers (and all the rest, of course) to accompany me to an imaginary flat surface where the Mandelbus will take us on a special tour of the Mandelbrot set.

Like points on the earth's surface, which can be specified in terms of a latitude and a longitude, the points on the plane also have coordinates. The point (0,0), called the origin, lies at the center of the plane. With a stroke of a magic wand I convert the reader into an unimaginably tiny being sitting on a point whose coordinates are (a,b). Where exactly is that? Why, anywhere the reader wants to be. But once the decision is made, we shall agree that a and b will have specific values, such as 2.78 and $-.43$, in which case the reader would be 2.78 units north and .43 unit west of the origin. What is a unit? It makes no difference whether one thinks of it as a mile or a meter. After all, any distance seems enormous when one is as small as a point.

Now that the cooperative reader — tiny and alone — sits on a point on the plane, he or she is ready to catch the Mandelbus. Before the bus arrives I must explain its route. It begins its journey at (0,0) and then goes directly to (a,b) pick up the reader. The ride will be solitary, for no more readers will be picked up as the Mandelbus careens from point to point, making an infinite succession of stops. To be specific, the Mandelbus route is given by a relatively simple formula that tells the driver what point to visit next after stopping at (x,y). It is

$$(x,y)^2 + (a,b).$$

What does the formula mean? The term $(x,y)^2$ is merely shorthand for the point having coordinates $x^2 - y^2$ and $2xy$. Adding (a,b) to $(x,y)^2$ means one has to add a to the first coordinate and b to the second. At the risk of becoming tedious, the coordinates that result from all this arithmetic are therefore $(x^2 - y^2 + a, 2xy + b)$. Where is this? To find out, substitute into the formula the coordinates x and y of the previous stop as well as the coordinates a and b of the first stop.

The Mandelbus always starts at the origin, and from there it zips to (a,b). To see this the reader has only to substitute 0 for both x and y in the formula above. All the squares and products of x and y vanish, leaving only a and b as the new coordinate positions. To see where the Mandelbus goes next, one merely substitutes the coordinates a and b for x and y. When that is done, one sees that the second stop is always $(a^2 - b^2 + a, 2ab + b)$.

It is a jerky, bone-jarring ride on the Mandelbus. To give the reader some idea of what it is like, an aerial view of part of two possible rides is shown in the illustration below. In one case the bus leaves the origin, stops to pick up the reader, and then visits a strange series of points that seem to spiral back to the starting point. In the other case the reader visits a sequence of stops that are at first close together but gradually become spaced farther apart before they head for infinity. It might be a good idea to get off at the next stop if you happen to be on that particular trip.

Although the two trips are markedly different in character, each was determined entirely by the first stop (a,b) according to the formula. In the first case, for example, the reader gets on the Mandelbus at $(.300, .100)$.

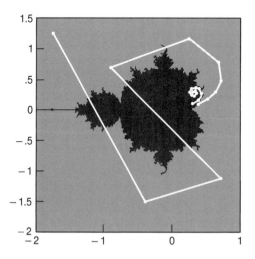

Two possible Mandelbus routes

When those coordinates are substituted into the formula, the coordinates (.380, .160) of the second stop are derived. To gain some confidence in Mandelbrot mechanics it would not be a bad idea to take a calculator and actually work out the coordinates of the third stop by substituting .380 for x, .160 for y, .300 for a and .100 for b in the formula. The answer is (.419, .222). This simple, repetitive arithmetic powers the Mandelbus indefinitely.

Although the journey can last for as long as one is willing to repeat the calculation, the route the Mandelbus actually follows will be either bounded or unbound. By this I mean that the succession of stops either will be confined forever within a zone around the origin (as in the first case) or will eventually escape the zone and head out to infinity (as in the second case).

The Mandelbrot set is the set of all points (a,b) that result in bounded Mandelbus routes. As seen in previous chapters, the set is a solid continuum in the middle of the plane, but it sends out filaments into its surroundings in highly complicated and subtle ways. Computer programs that generate images based on the Mandelbrot set decide the color of a pixel on the screen by determining whether the Mandelbus roars off to infinity from the point (a,b) represented by that pixel and, if so, how quickly.

Some readers may be most comfortable riding the bounded routes that start within the Mandelbrot set; they shudder at the thought of the trip to infinity. The prospect of taking only bounded trips, however, seems to depress mathematicians. That is probably why they color the set black.

It is proved theorem (and therefore undeniably true) that if the Mandelbus ever reaches a point two or more units from the origin, it is destined for infinity. In such a case its first stop (a,b) lies outside the Mandelbrot set. But how many stops does an infinity-bound Mandelbus need to make before it is at least two units away from the origin? That number is called the dwell of (a,b).

When one attempts to compute the dwell of (a,b), one never quite knows when to stop. The point might result in 100 or 1,000 stops before the Mandelbus leaves the scene for good. On the other hand, the point might be inside the set, in which case no amount of waiting justifies any color but black for its corresponding pixel. Near the set's boundary are points that have very high dwell values. For such points it may take a million iterations before the Mandelbus equals or exceeds the critical distance of two units from the origin. A program must therefore make a more or less arbitrary decision about when to stop iterating the formula for a given point (a,b). Limits as low as 100 or even 50 iterations produce beautiful and reasonably accurate images of the set, in spite of the fact that some pixels will be colored black erroneously.

The assignment of other colors to a pixel is also based on the dwell of the point corresponding to the pixel. The programmer might decide, for example, to color pixels either black, violet or chartreuse depending on whether their corresponding points have respectively a dwell value of 100 or more, between 50 and 99 or between 49 and 1. The colors and the ranges of dwell to which they apply are arbitrary, yet they are choices that can result in breathtaking beauty (as is evident in the collection of images in the illustrations at the right or aesthetic disaster (as I suspect my color-assignment example would be). Indeed, half of the programmer's task lies in assigning colors to points outside the set; the other half lies in finding interesting areas of the plane to map. Actually one is affected by the other, since it is the assignment of color that makes visible the regions that have been given names such as Sea Horse Valley and the Uttermost West (which is populated by topknots, midgets, and other odd creatures).

To fill an entire computer screen with colored members and non-members of the Mandelbrot set, one must systematically assign a value of a and b to each pixel on the screen from a given range of values for a and b. This can be done by means of two loops. One loop varies a from one end of its range to the other in, say, 200 equal steps. The second loop, which contains the first, varies b in as many steps from one end of its range to the other. The number of steps for each loop reflects the number of pixels one's display screen has in the horizontal dimension (for the values of a) and in the vertical dimension (for the values of b).

Because each image contains only a finite sampling of points in a particular area of the Mandelbrot set, it can never show all the detail that is actually there. But by making the ranges of a and b narrower, one can increase the level of "magnification." Indeed, the Mandlebrot set has detail at all levels of magnification. For this reason one of the most popular games Mandelbrot enthusiasts play is magnifying areas of the set until they exhaust the capability of their hardware, software, or patience.

The magnification of a particular image can be calculated as follows. Suppose one computes an image of a square region of the plane that has a length s on a side. The magnification of the displayed image will then be $1/s$. A square image that is .02 unit wide, for example, will have a magnification of 50 when it is displayed on the screen.

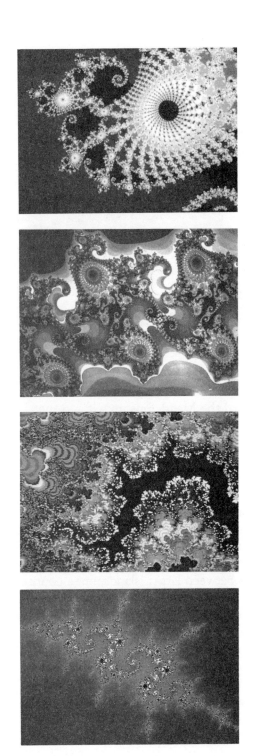

A collection of Mandelbrot images

Ornate spirals (*left*) and a "mini-Mandelbrot" (*right*) (These are Images 5 and 6 discussed on page 35.)

I am often tempted to climb aboard the Mandelbus myself and switch its control from automatic to manual. It would be high adventure indeed to drive up one of the Mandelbrot set's filaments on a sightseeing tour. Far from the Mandelbrot set, for example, one can find miniature copies of the set, apparently floating on the plane. According to mathematicians, the entire Mandelbrot set actually is connected, so that one might think it possible to drive the Mandelbus out to one of the "mini Mandelbrot" copies. But the road is like no road on the earth. If one enlarges repeatedly almost any of the filaments that surround the Mandelbrot set, one finds only a series of tiny black islands that are seemingly disconnected. To be sure, there are smaller islands between larger islands, but a continuous road rarely if ever shows up.

Now I shall turn the tour over to some readers who, after long hours of exploration and aesthetic fine-tuning, have created exemplary renderings of the set. Walter S. Strickler of Boulder, Colo., provides Image 1 on page 33. The image, which he calls Peacock, was created by a program he wrote for his Amiga computer. The *a* values in the image range from −.750 to −.746, and the *b* values range from .0986 to .1014. The magnification of Strickler's image can be calculated according to the simple formula I mentioned above. The smaller of the two sides of the rectangular area covered by the image has a length of .0028. Its inverse (1/.0028) yields an approximate magnification of 357.

Images 2 through 4 are actually slide benefits of my subscription to *Amygdala*, the newsletter published by Rollo Silver. One can order the full set of images on transparencies (*see* List of Suppliers).

Image 2, generated by John Dewey Jones of Burnaby, British Columbia, shows a magnified portion of a "sea horse" tail. Sea horses accompany the mini-Mandelbrots that line the deep cleft dividing the eastern body from the western head of the Mandelbrot set. Virtually any sea horse will yield such images if one picks the right magnification and colors.

Image 3 is called Love Canal by its programmer, Andrew LaMance of Wartburg, Tenn. I presume the name refers to a certain infamous polluted site near Niagara Falls, N.Y. Indeed, the black of the Mandelbrot set suggests a drainage ditch filled with toxic chemicals where strange vegetation struggles to survive. This image is centered at $(-.235125, .82722)$ and the magnification happens to be a whopping 24,800.

Ken Philip of Fairbanks, Alaska, another *Amygdala* contributor, achieved a remarkable magnification of 54,000 in Image 4, which displays one of the small "scepters" that are found near sea horses. Readers who want to probe this regal region must be prepared for heavy computing: this particular image is centered at the point $(-1.26446153, .04396696)$.

Michael Adler used a network of computers at the Apolla R&D facility in Chelmsford, Mass., to compute the ornate spirals in Image 5. Readers who would like to reproduce this part of the Mandelbrot set must plot colors, for a and b values that range respectively between .31186 and .31458 and between .75322 and .75594. One does not need a network of computers to produce such an image (which has a magnification of 368) unless one wants the image within a second.

Image 6 was generated by R. Terry Sproat and photographed by Rick McCauley of San Francisco, Calif. The image shows one of the mini-Mandelbrots that bud from the parent set along its sides. The magnification here is approximately 20.

Plotting parts of the Mandelbrot set on paper can result in as eye-catching an image as can be achieved on the screen. James L. Crum, a gemologist from Louisville, Ohio, has plotted an eye-catching arrangement of rubies, emeralds, amethysts, and other jewels that hint at the riches of the Mandlebrot set in an area not far from that covered by Sproat's image.

There are ways amateurs can produce such images much more quickly than was once possible on home computers. For example, one can use Mariani's algorithm, developed by Rico Mariani while working as a programmer at the Ontario Science Centre in Toronto. The algorithm's basic idea is simple: If the pixels bordering a square region are determined to be black (that is, if their corresponding points are determined to be members of the Mandelbrot set), then all the pixels in the enclosed region will also be black. Another fast algorithm is described by Uval Fisher in a wonderful book, *The Science of Fractal Images*, edited by Heinz-Otto Peitgen and his colleague Dietmar Saupe of the University of Bremen. The algorithm's speed results from the fact that it does not compute points in the Mandelbrot set. Instead it divides the region outside the set into thousands of disks of varying size and confines its computations strictly to these circular regions.

For those who lack either the time or the inclination to explore the Mandelbrot set with their own machine, I must mention a videotape called *Nothing but Zooms* produced by ART MATRIX (*see* List of Suppliers). It contains stunning fractal imagery that was produced by more than $40,000 worth of computer time at the Cornell National Supercomputer Center.

ADDENDUM

Students in Italy, stockbrokers in Singapore and physicians in the United States joined the growing crowd of Mandelbrot-set devotees — all thanks to a ride on the Mandelbus, which I described in the February, 1989, issue of SCIENTIFIC AMERICAN. The effort to make the set's basic-iteration algorithm understandable paid off in ridership and perhaps even readership. Yet, as a number of letters showed, some confusion remained. It is only the Mandelbus' *first* stop that is being tested for membership in the Mandelbrot set. Subsequent stops may be either inside or outside the set, but if any of them turns out to be more than two units away from the origin, the first stop can be automatically excluded from the Mandelbrot set.

I may have been overly impressed by the magnification of 54,000 that Ken Philip of Fairbanks, Alaska, achieved in generating an image of a sea-horse scepter. Such magnification hardly marks the limit of a computer's acuity. Indeed, magnifications of that order are nearly routine both for A. G. Davis Philip of Schenectady, N.Y., and his brother Ken. The Schenectady Philip writes, "While I was in Fairbanks in November, my brother's Mac II produced a picture of a [Mandelbrot] midget at a magnification of 2×10^{31}. I consider that remarkable.

Peter Garrison of Los Angeles coincidentally explains that the double-precision mode available in most personal computers — in which the number of bits in the computer's "words" are doubled — actually more than doubles the computer's resolving power. In fact, the power is doubled for each one-bit increase in effective word size. Extremely high magnifications can therefore be achieved by means of the even greater precision made possible by special hardware and software.

In this chapter I mentioned a fast new algorithm for computing the Mandelbrot set that was described by Uval Fisher in the book *The Science of Fractal Images.* William S. Cleveland of the AT&T Bell Laboratories wrote to explain that the algorithm was actually developed by William P. Thurston and Allan R. Wilks. According to Cleveland, the new algorithm not only is faster but also produces more accurate pictures of the set than the standard algorithm does. As Cleveland says: "If you get on board the bus with the Thurston-Wilks algorithm painting the scene (in black and white), a wholly new and more realistic world will open up to you."

A new way to render beautiful Mandelbrot images using the traditional method was communicated to me by Carl G. Nugent of Seattle. It is now possible to see the set in delicate bas-relief, looking like the compressed fossil of an alien life-form. Although shaded in a single color, the images are just as beautiful as the full-color treatments because of their incredibly tactile nature: One can "feel" those delicate tendrils. The appearance is based on a trick that makes the tiny, intricate details of the set look from afar as though they were illuminated from one side.

The underlying idea is to divide the display screen into diagonal rows of pixels that run from the top left to the bottom right of the screen. If the iteration count generated for each pixel is taken to represent the pixel's "height," then an imaginary light source in the top left corner of the screen will cause a black "shadow" to be cast on certain pixels, depending on the height of the neighboring pixel (above and to the left) in its diagonal row. In even diagonal rows a pixel is not to be colored black unless its neighbor's height is strictly greater than that of the pixel; in odd diagonal rows, however, a pixel is colored black even if its neighbor has an equal height. Hence, in Mandelbrot "plateaus" (areas where all pixels have an equal iteration count), the diagonal pixel rows will alternate in color. Up close the displayed plateaus have a checkerboard appearance. "To make it look gray," says Nugent, "just throw away your microscope!"

$\circ 4 \circ$

The Strange Attractions of Chaos

Chaos has strange attractions for the mind that can see patterns therein. Some physical systems that exhibit chaotic behavior do so because they are in a sense attracted to such patterns. As a bonus, the patterns themselves are strangely attractive. Some readers may already be aware that the geometric forms underlying chaos are called strange, or chaotic, attractors. Strange attractors can be generated with a home computer (*see* the SCIENTIFIC AMERICAN article on chaos referred to in Further Readings).

Before setting off with me, readers must be equipped with a protective coating of physical intuition. In particular, what is an attractor? Roughly speaking, an attractor is a generalization of the notion of equilibrium; an attractor is what the behavior of a system settles down to, or is attracted to. The pendulum is a simple physical system that illustrates the concept of an attractor. Suppose an ordinary pendulum moves under frictional forces that slow it eventually to a standstill. One can describe the pendulum's motion by means of a so-called phase, or state, diagram in which the angle the pendulum makes with the vertical is graphed against the rate at which the angle changes. The swinging motion of the pendulum is represented by a point circling the origin in the phase diagram; as the pendulum loses energy, the point spirals into the origin, where it ultimately comes to rest. In this case the origin is called an attractor because it seems to attract the moving point in the phase diagram. Readers would be correct in thinking there is nothing strange about an attractor consisting of a single point.

A slightly more complicated attractor underlies the motion of a grandfather clock. Here an escapement mechanism feeds energy to a pendulum to keep it from slowing down. If one starts the clock with an overly energetic push of the pendulum, it slows down to the tempo prescribed by the escapement but thereafter slows no further. If the clock is started with a push that is too gentle, however, the pendulum behaves like an ordinary one: it slows to a standstill as before. In the case of the overly energetic push, the pendulum's motion in a phase diagram is a spiral that winds ever more tightly about a circular orbit. Here the attractor is a circular loop. In this context a circle is no stranger than a point.

An ordinary pendulum can be made to show chaotic behavior by introducing a vertical, vibratory motion: If the point of support is moved up and down in a sinusoidal manner by an electric motor, the pendulum may begin to swing crazily, exhibiting no evidence of periodic behavior whatever.

To introduce chaos, however, I have selected a different physical system. Imagine an arrangement of three amplifiers in which the first amplifier outputs a signal x that is fed to the other two. The second amplifier outputs the signal $1 - x$ in response to x. The third amplifier takes the two signals, x and $1 - x$, as input. It generates the product, $x(1 - x)$, of the two signals and feeds it back to the first amplifier, which also receives a control voltage, r, as input. One additional component, a device that samples its input and delivers the same voltage as output for a short time, completes the circuit; it is inserted in the output line from the first amplifier. The three-amplifier circuit does a voltage dance that becomes more hectic as the control voltage r is gradually increased.

When r is less than 3 and x initially has some nonzero setting, the circuit oscillates briefly before it settles down to a specific value of x that remains the same thereafter. This value constitutes a single point attractor. If the control voltage, r, is now raised to a level just above 3, the circuit flutters between two values of x. At this level of r the circuit is said to be bistable and the attractor consists of two points. As r is increased further, the circuit oscillates among four points; yet another increase yields an eight-point attractor. The pattern of doubling and redoubling goes on as the knob controlling r is turned to higher values, until at a setting roughly midway between 3 and 4 the circuit suddenly goes crazy. It hunts endlessly at electronic speed for the simple recurring patterns that marked its earlier existence. Its behavior is now governed by a strange attractor that has a potential infinity of values. The result is chaos.

Electronically literate readers may be tempted to build such a circuit. Others may simulate it on a computer of any size, viewing the dance with great clarity on the display screen. To do so, they merely need to write a simple program that computes the iterated equation $x \leftarrow rx(1 - x)$. The program, which I call CHAOS1, has a core that consists of six instructions:

$$x \leftarrow .3$$
$$\text{for } i \leftarrow 1 \text{ to } 200$$
$$x \leftarrow rx(1 - x)$$
$$\text{for } i \leftarrow 1 \text{ to } 300$$
$$x \leftarrow rx(1 - x)$$
$$\text{plot } (200x, 100)$$

The variable x starts at the value .3. CHAOS1 then enters a loop that iterates the basic equation 200 times to allow transients to die away. The transients are inherent in the equation itself, not in imprecise arithmetic. The reasons for this will be made clear in geometric terms below. The program then enters a new loop that iterates the equation 300 more times, plotting the value of x on each occasion.

The number 100 used in the plot instruction above is more generic than specific; here the screen has dimensions 200 by 200. The horizontal coordinate, $200x$, spreads the various values computed for x (always between 0 and 1) across one row of the screen, which is set at a height of 100 — halfway up the hypothetical screen.

Depending on the setting for the control variable r, the core program will either plot a single point 300 times or several points fewer than 300 times each. It may even try to capture chaos by plotting 300 different points of a strange attractor. If the iteration limit is increased, more of the strange attractor will be seen. In all cases, once the iteration process has settled down, the x values jump in a systematic way from one point of the attractor to another. The attractors are also called orbits, regardless of whether they have a finite or an infinite number of points.

A complete picture of the behavior of the simple amplifier circuit emerges if the program computes a raft of plots, each plot below the last one (*see* illustration at the right). The plots result from a succession of r

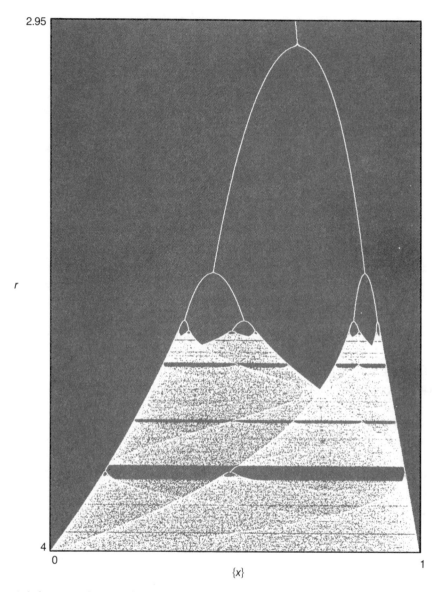

A bifurcation diagram shows the transition to chaos

values that run from 2.9 to 4.0 in, say, 200 steps from the top of the screen to the bottom. A more elegant picture emerges if more steps are used, say 4,000, but in this case the diagram will not fit on the screen and it must be plotted to be seen as a whole.

For values of r less than 3.56 (the more precise value is 3.56994571869) the attractors of the simple dynamical system embodied in the iterated equation $x \leftarrow rx(1 - x)$ consist of a few points. These points, which represent nonchaotic behavior, are arranged in three large bands and an infinity of smaller ones. The attractors become strange as r approaches 3.56. Here chaos sets in as the hitherto smoothly bifurcating lines suddenly fall into a pepper-and-salt madness. Strangely enough, the chaotic regime vanishes from time to time as r continues its inexorable march to 4.

The entire plot is called a bifurcation diagram. When it is viewed sideways, it resembles the spectrum of chaos from a star named x. The plot is embellished by curves and attractively shaded folds. The reasons for the ornamental details are mysteries that can be explained only by the theory of chaos. I shall delve more into that topic below. For the present there is a mystery closer to home in the minds of most readers: Why does the innocent-looking equation behave so strangely?

The equation's behavior for nonchaotic values of r can be simulated geometrically by drawing a parabola described by the equation $y = rx(1 - x)$, where x is the horizontal variable and y is the vertical variable. Now superpose on the parabola the diagonal line $y = x$. Such a procedure has been followed in the illustration at the right where r has been set at 3.3, a value at which the system's attractor consists of two points. To show how the system behaves, an initial value of x is chosen. I have picked .3, although almost any other value will do as well.

The first iteration of the equation is simulated by drawing a vertical line beginning at the point $x = .3$ at the bottom of the graph and continuing it upward until it hits the parabola. I have labeled the point where the line hits the parabola as A. The height of the intersection determines the corresponding value of y. In the second iteration that value of y is fed back into the equation as the x variable. Graphically the procedure corresponds to measuring the height of the intersection, marking it on the horizontal axis and drawing another vertical line from that mark until it hits the parabola. Here a short cut is employed by drawing a horizontal line from point A to the diagonal line $y = x$; I call the new point of intersection B. Note that point B and the origin lie at

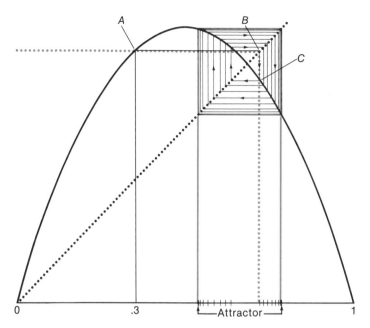

A two-point attractor appears in a geometric simulation of a simple system

diagonally opposite corners of a square whose sides have a length equal to the value of y determined in the first iteration. As a consequence the y value can be fed back into the system by drawing a vertical line from B until it hits the parabola (point C). By continuously repeating the procedure of moving vertically until the parabola is hit and moving horizontally until the diagonal line is hit, one produces a rectangular path that spirals into a square.

The geometric recipe mimics the core procedure within CHAOS1. The two places where the resultant square intersects the parabola correspond to the two-point attractor. Enterprising programmers might undertake the interesting project of generating such figures by computer. In doing so armchair investigators could gain insights into the "simple" iterative equation under study. Specifically, what do the figures look like when chaos sets in? Are the random-looking numbers generated by values of r that produce chaos truly random?

I owe the idea for an excursion into chaos to a number of readers who wrote in. Among them was James P. Crutchfield, one of the authors of the article "Chaos" referred to in Further Readings. Crutchfield and his coauthors explain that "the key to understanding chaotic behavior lies in understanding a simple stretching and folding operation, which takes place in the state space." In the case of the simple amplifier system the state space is a line segment that contains the attractor points and the point representing the current value of x. Where do the stretching and folding come in?

Iterating the equation $x \leftarrow rx(1 - x)$ amounts to mapping the points between 0 and 1 into a parabolic curve. Points that are close together on the unit interval, particularly those close to 0, end up farther apart when they are mapped into the parabolic curve. This happens, of course, when the number $rx(1 - x)$ replaces x. The folding operation comes about because of the bilateral symmetry of the parabola; except at the apex of the curve, there are always two points on the unit interval that map into the same value $rx(1 - x)$. Those points are of course x and $1 - x$.

Much of the structure of the bifurcation diagram has been analyzed by chaos theorists. The boundaries of the chaotic regions are set by the minimum and maximum values of the iterates of $x = .5$. The curves followed by the minima and maxima, as well as those followed by the "veils" that hang so strangely down in the chaotic regions, are all simple polynomials in r. At the places where the shading is densest one finds the highest concentration of points in the strange attractors that cross them. In the empty bands mentioned above chaos gives way to order. Theory tells us that for every whole number there is a band (however narrow) with orbits of precisely that size. Finally, it will come as no surprise to readers familiar with chaos that strange attractors, even in the humble system just explored, have a fractal nature; an infinite number of points show interesting detail at all levels of magnification, like the Mandelbrot set described in Chapter 1.

More complicated dynamical systems are embodied in the equations named after Michel Hénon, a French mathematician. The so-called Hénon mappings not only describe physical systems such as moving asteroids and dripping faucets but also generate beautiful images in the process. An Hénon mapping consists of not one equation but two. Here is an example:

$$x \leftarrow x\cos(a) - (y - x^2)\sin(a)$$
$$y \leftarrow x\sin(a) + (y - x^2)\cos(a)$$

Current values of two variables x and y are used in the right-hand sides of both equations to produce new values (also symbolized by x and y) in the left-hand sides.

A program called CHAOS2 exploits the two equations to produce images of the order and chaos inherent in a wide class of dynamical systems. CHAOS2 has a core program that is similar to the core program of CHAOS1

> input x and y
> for $i \leftarrow 1$ to 1,000
> $\quad xx \leftarrow x\cos(a) - (y - x^2)\sin(a)$
> $\quad y \leftarrow x\sin(a) + (y - x^2)\cos(a)$
> $\quad x \leftarrow xx$
> $\quad plot\ (100x,\ 100y)$

The differences between the two core programs stem from two sources: CHAOS2 has two iterated variables instead of one, and the system described by the Hénon mapping is conservative rather than dissipative. The presence of two variables forces one to employ a temporary variable xx for the new value of x while the current value of x is still being used in the second equation. The fact that the underlying dynamical system is conservative means the primary iteration loop for eliminating transient values can be removed. There are no losses of energy due to friction or other dissipative leaks. Consequently there are no attractors as such. One might say, however, that every orbit computed by the system is its own attractor. In any event, strangeness (and chaos) is certainly present in the Hénon mapping. Finally, for each setting of the parameter a the resulting system has a multitude of orbits and, owing to conservatism, any initial pair of values for x and y will represent a point that is already on one of the orbits; the attraction is instant, so to speak. For these reasons the core of CHAOS2 does not use standard initial values for its iteration variables. They must be input by the computer programmer.

CHAOS2 is complete when its core is preceded by an imput statement that allows the programmer to select the value of a. As in CHAOS1, each new value of a leads to a new system. But because the system is two-dimensional, a sampling of orbital plots takes up all available room; one cannot systematically vary the control parameter a without invoking chaos of an unwanted kind.

The user of CHAOS2 therefore specifies an initial orbit by typing in the coordinates of a point on it. Sitting back, he or she watches in fascination as the orbit is plotted. It might turn out to be a curve (traced not continuously but intermittently) or it might turn out to be something a little stranger. For example, the illustration below displays a succession of 38 orbits in an Hénon mapping with the value of *a* set at 1.111. From the center of the plot outward the orbits form a nest of closed curves until the sudden appearance of small "islands": individual orbits wedged between the larger nested ones. Farther out the nested orbits continue until the onset of chaos. In the outer reaches of the phase plot more islands appear, along with a random sprinkling of points that denotes the onset of chaos. One of the chaotic areas (outlined by a rectangle in the right side of the illustration) is shown in magnified form. Readers who want to magnify Hénon diagrams are warned to use the most precise arithmetic available on their machines.

As I have mentioned, Hénon mappings represent a great variety of conservative systems, such as asteroids orbiting the sun. Unfortunately the orbits in the diagrams are not the orbits of the asteroids but phase plots of those orbits. In the diagram just described the horizontal axis may represent the position of an asteroid in terms of its distance from the sun. The vertical axis may represent the radial velocity, or the rate of change, in this distance. Each point on the orbit computed by the Hénon mapping represents the radial distance and velocity of an asteroid at a specific

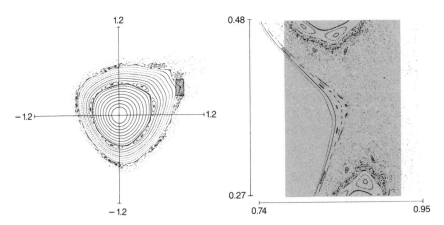

Successive orbits of a Hénon mapping (*left*) degenerate into chaos (*right*)

angular position with respect to the sun, that is, when the asteroid passes through a vertical plane making that angle with the sun. Successive points computed by the mapping represent the asteroid's successive reappearances on the plane. The islands mentioned above are resonance bands due to perturbations in the asteroid's orbit by larger bodies in the solar system such as Jupiter. In the chaotic regions the radial position and velocity of an asteroid will vary in an essentially random way every time an asteroid revisits the specified plane. Its motion is unpredictable. Almost anything can happen.

On the aesthetic side it is worth looking at some other plots generated by Hénon mappings; quite apart from physical interpretations, there is a whimsical quality present, as is seen in the illustration below. They resemble strange, aquatic creatures.

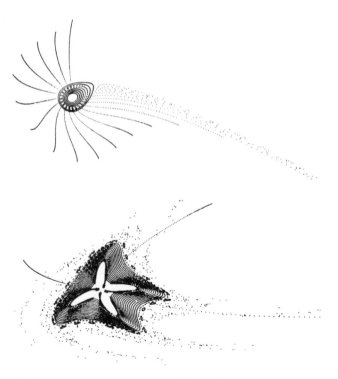

The Hénon mapping generates different figures for $a = .264$ (*above*) and $a = 1.5732$ (*below*)

Readers wanting to learn more about Hénon mappings should get a copy of the December 1986 issue of *Byte* magazine. There Gordon Hughes, a professor of mathematics at California State University, has engagingly described some of the relevant physics and mathematics underlying Hénon mappings. PASCAL programs are also listed.

A reader in Holland, Peter de Jong of Leiden, has already suggested some other iteration formulas that produce bizarre shapes and images. He recommends the four-parameter iterations $x \leftarrow \sin(ay) - \cos(bx)$ and $y \leftarrow \sin(cx) - \cos(dy)$. Begin with x and y both set equal to 0. Then, to get the figure de Jong calls "chicken legs," try $a = 2.01$, $b = -2.53$, $c = 1.61$ and $d = -.33$. The respective values -2.7, $-.09$, $-.86$ and -2.2 yield a "dot launcher," and the values -2.24, $.43$, $-.65$ and -2.43 produce a "self-decorating Easter egg." Readers are free, like de Jong, to invent their own iteration formulas and to experiment with them.

ADDENDUM

Chaos was probed by numerous people ready and willing to program the iteration formula which I supplied in SCIENTIFIC AMERICAN in the August, 1987, column. In fact, a number of people, including Howard Mark of Suffern, N.Y., followed my suggestion of tracking the iterative process itself by weaving a mirrored web about a parabola. Here convergence of the process could be seen as the web wove itself into a stable shape. But in the chaotic regime it filled a portion of the screen with solid white, a confusion of squares that settled to no discernible pattern. Charles A. Plantz of West Brownsville, Pa., used his microcomputer as a microscope, zeroing in on the stirrup-shaped arc of the bifurcation diagram just above one of the chaotic regions. He found not the pepper and salt I would have expected but folds and strata invading the texture of chaos.

Peter de Jong notes that he has created strange music through chaos. Readers can create similar sounds by converting the numbers generated by CHAOS1 into musical notes. Outside chaotic zones there will be simple, repetitive musical phrases; inside the zones will be the very sounds of chaos.

○ 5 ○

Catching Biomorphs

Sometimes I consider myself a fisherman. Computer programs and ideas are my hooks, rods and reels. Computer pictures are the trophies and delicious meals.
—CLIFFORD A. PICKOVER, *Computers, Pattern, Chaos and Beauty*

On a number of occasions in recent years I have been sorely tempted to metnion one or more of the strange and beautiful graphic concoctions of Clifford A. Pickover, a well-known investigator at the IBM Thomas J. Watson Research Center. In addition to his more serious research endeavors, he has a box full of fun programs — his "fishing tackle" — that generate chaotic but oddly aesthetic forms. I cannot resist Pickover's delectable catches any longer and have decided to describe in this column how readers can go angling for three simple but savory recreations of his: biomorphs, Truchet tilings, and fractal popcorn. Readers will also get just a taste of the three-dimensional logarithmic snails captured by this soulful but sober man.

Pickover's biomorphs look distinctly microbial, which has prompted *Omni* magazine to characterize Pickover as "van Leeuwenhoek's twentieth-century equivalent." (Anton van Leeuwenhoek, a seventeenth-century Dutch draper and lens grinder, was one of the first microscopists.)

Biomorphs inhabit the complex plane home of the famed Mandelbrot set. They are produced by an abbreviated version of the process that traces the delicate fractal geometry of Julia sets, close relatives of the Mandelbrot set. Each biomorph is generated by multiple iterations, or repetitions, of a particular function, or sequence of mathematical operations. Each iteration takes the output of the previous operations as the input value for the next iteration.

For example, the 12-spiked radiolarian biomorph in the bottom left part of the whimsical microscopic view below was generated by the iterated function

$$z_{n+1} \leftarrow z_n^{\,3} + c.$$

An initial value for a complex-number variable (designated Z_0) is raised to the third power, and a fixed complex number, c, is added to it. The same arithmetic operations are then performed on the resulting sum, Z_1, to yield Z_2 and so on.

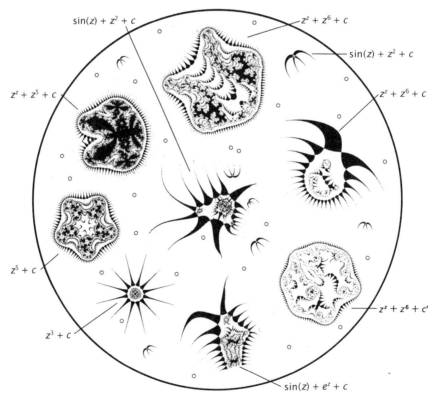

A microscopic view of some biomorphs and their respective generating functions

As I have explained in previous chapters, a complex number consists of two numbers of the ordinary kind; one is called the real part, and the other is called the imaginary part. The two numbers are best regarded as Cartesian coordinates on a two-dimensional plane. Traditionally a complex number is written as a sum of its two parts. For example, the complex number $3 + 5i$ has 3 as its real part and 5 as its imaginary part. (The i acts as a kind of marker to remind nonmathematicians which part is which.) To avoid any further digression, I show in a box in Chapter 1 (page 5) how to add, multiply, and cube complex numbers.

To generate a biomorph, one first needs to lay out a grid of points on a rectangle in the complex plane. The coordinates of each point constitute the real and imaginary parts of an initial value, z_0, for the iterative process outlined above. Each point is also assigned a pixel, or picture element, on the computer screen. Depending on the outcome of a simple test on the "size" of the real and imaginary parts of the final z value, the pixel is colored either black or white.

All the biomorphs pictured in the illustration at the left were found in a 20-by-20 square centered on the origin of the complex plane. How many others can intrepid readers find? I shall provide the necessary viewing apparatus: a program I call BIOMORPH that follows Pickover's basic algorithm. The version I list below generates the radiolarian.

$c \leftarrow .5 + .0i$
for $j \leftarrow 1$ to 100
    for $k \leftarrow 1$ to 100
        compute z_0
        $z \leftarrow z_0$
        for $n \leftarrow 1$ to 10
            $z \leftarrow z^3 + c$
            if $|\text{real}(z)|$ or $|\text{imag}(z)|$
            or $|z| > 10$
                then jump out of loop
        if $|\text{real}(z)|$ or $|\text{imag}(z)| < 10$
            then plot (j,k) black
            else plot (j,k) white

The seemingly simple instruction "compute z_0" is actually not so trivial. It requires the conversion of each pair of pixel coordinates (j,k) into a complex number. This is done by dividing the length and the breadth of an area on the complex plane by the number of j values and the number of k values, respectively. The quotients then serve as the increments by which the real and imaginary parts of z_0 are systematically increased in each of the algorithm's cycles.

For example, the radiolarian is actually found in a square "window" of the complex plane delineated by the following ranges for the real and imaginary parts of z_0.

$$-10 < \text{real } (z_0) < 10$$
$$-10 < \text{imag}(z_0) < 10$$

Because j and k both run from 1 to 100, both the real and imaginary parts of z_0 are systematically increased in steps of .03. The version of BIOMORPH given above must therefore rely on statements of the type

$$\text{real}(z_0) \leftarrow -1.5 + .03j$$
$$\text{imag}(z_0) \leftarrow -1.5 + .03k$$

to compute 10,000 values of z_0, each of which is iterated and tested.

Within the innermost loop of 10 iterations, the size of z ($|z|$) as well as the size of its real and imaginary parts ($|\text{real}(z)|$ and $|\text{imag}(z)|$) is continually monitored. The size of a complex number is simply the square root of the sum of the squares of the number's real and imaginary parts, and the size of its component parts is given by their respective absolute values. (The absolute value of a number is its numerical value irrespective of sign.)

If the size of z or of its component parts ever exceeds 10, the program must promptly leave the loop — even if it is before the 10th iteration — and proceed to retest the size of z's real and imaginary parts. (When comparing the size of z with 10, it is actually simpler to compare the sum of the squares of z's real and imaginary parts with 100 than to compare the square root of the sum with 10; the result would be the same in either case.) Regardless of the number of iterations, if the size of either the real or imaginary part of the final z value is less than 10, the pixel having coordinates (j,k) is colored black. Otherwise it is colored white.

In most personal computers the pixels whose coordinates range between 1 and 100 will lie in one corner of the screen. To center the image, the initial and final values of j and k may have to be altered. For example, j and k may have to run from 50 to 150 instead of from 1 to 100.

All other details about BIOMORPH will have to be worked out by the adventuresome. I shall only remind readers that z, z_0, and c are all complex numbers and must be added and multiplied as such. For that same reason every assignment statement in the algorithm involving z, z_0, and c represents two assignment statements in ordinary computer languages — one for the numbers' real parts and one for their imaginary parts.

How are the other creatures made visible through Pickover's imaginary microscope produced? Actually, BIOMORPH can produce them as well. One only has to substitute a different iterative function at the heart of the algorithm. In other words, one merely replaces $z^3 + c$ in the above program by another function.

Those who write the BIOMORPH program may well want to fish for other creatures that inhabit the central 20-by-20 area of the complex plane. The simplest search would entail scanning the entire area; one can then zoom in to inspect the graphic details of whatever creatures the preliminary search turns up. Any small value of c will normally serve as bait.

Some alternative biomorph-generating functions make use of a strange power of z, z^z; others rely on trigonometric operations. Pickover has kindly agreed to send those who ask a short primer on the mysteries of complex-number trigonometry and self-powered complex numbers (*see* List of Suppliers). Armed with that knowledge, one can write versions of BIOMORPH that yield the protozoan morphologies shown.

Biomorphs began for Pickover as a bug in a program intended to probe the fractal properties of various formulas. He accidentally used an OR instead of an AND in the conditional test for the size of z's real and imaginary parts. Thus, it would be possible for one component to be large in a number otherwise regarded as "small." That unintentional change colors a great many more pixels black than otherwise be the case. The cilia that project from the biomorphs consist solidly of such pixels.

Although they were serendipitously created, the biomorphs seem to have taken on a life of their own. As Pickover puts it: "In some sense the mathematical creatures exist. These objects inhabit the complex plane, though they resemble microscopic organisms that we could easily imagine flourishing in a drop of pond water." In what sea might we fish for more advanced forms of life? Pickover also finds it meaningful that the complexity of both natural and artificial organisms results from the repeated application of simple dynamic rules.

Pickover's current work at the research center revolves around new ways of rendering complex data meaningful at a glance. For example, ordinarily it is quite difficult to detect regularity or randomness in a page full of 0's and 1's, which is a fundamental way to depict bits of data. Yet

Pickover can make the data's degree of randomness clear by means of a simple graphic device based on Truchet tiles, which get their name from the eighteenth-century French monk and polymath P. Sébastien Truchet. Pickover has modified Truchet's original tiles to consist of two quarter-circles in a square, each centered at opposite corners and intersecting two of the square's sides at their midpoints. The resulting tile (*see* illustration below) exhibits only two distinct orientations.

If one paves a flat area with Pickover's Truchet tiles, strange sinuous curves appear. There are no loose ends, except at the edges of the area. Each curve is guaranteed to be continuous because the midpoints of the sides of adjacent squares (which is where the quarter-circles begin and end) abut.

Any array of 0's and 1's can be converted into a Truchet tiling merely by arranging the individual tiles in the same order as the binary digits, orienting a tile one way wherever there is a 0 and the other way wherever there is a 1. If the data bits are random, Pickover maintains, one discerns no particular pattern in the tiling: the curves loop and meander in a perfectly confusing (albeit fascinating) way.

Introduce a slight element of regularity in the data, however, and definite patterns of curves are perceived. For example, if one generates an array of bits in each row of which a 0 is slightly more likely to be followed by another 0 than a 1 and a 1 is slightly more likely to be followed by another 1 than a 0, the curves in the corresponding tiling would show a

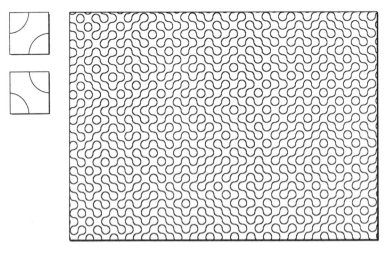

A Truchet tile's two orientations (*left*) and a random Truchet tiling (*above*)

distinct diagonal trend. Readers may enjoy discovering for themselves why this is so.

Actually, I prefer the tiling patterns created by random bits, such as the one shown in the illustration. They suggest a host of recreational pastimes. Are they mazes, for instance? Try to find a channel that leads from the top of the tiling all the way to the bottom or from one side to the other. In the course of tracing channels, one often comes across "islands" — curves that rejoin themselves. Any curve that does not strike the edge of the square must of course come back to itself sooner or later. Some of these curves are small circles; some are dumbbell-shaped, and some are more complicated still. Readers are encouraged to classify the other types of closed curves. What are their average numbers per tile?

Writing a program that turns bits into Truchet tilings is easy. Assuming that one has an array of binary digits to begin with, one merely sets up a double loop that scans each element of the array and draws the corresponding Truchet tile at the appropriate place on the computer screen. This much explanation will have to suffice so that I can turn to another Pickover graphic recreation: fractal popcorn.

Pickover's popcorn stands out, curiously tactile, in the illustration below. It is actually a tracery generated by the solution of a pair of iterated

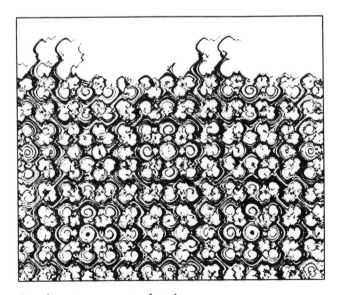

A cyclic system generates fractal popcorn

differential equations in discrete form. The x coordinate of a solution point is computed by subtracting the value of a function of y from the x coordinate of the previously calculated solution. Likewise the y coordinate of a solution point is computed by subtracting the value of a function of x from the y coordinate of the previously calculated solution. Such a set of equations is called a cyclic system. Cyclic systems based on trigonometric functions seem to be a particularly rich source of spectacular graphics.

The crossed-variable iteration process in the program POPCORN is described by the pair of equations:

$$x_{n+1} = x_n - h\sin(y_n + \tan(3y_n))$$
$$y_{n+1} = y_n - h\sin(x_n + \tan(3x_n))$$

A small constant, h, multiplies the trigonometric functions so that a new value of x or y is never far from the previous one, regardless of how long the iteration continues. Pickover gives h a value of .05 in his program.

As the following algorithmic outline indicates, POPCORN iterates the formulas 50 times for each of 2500 initial pair values (x_0, y_0), each time plotting a pixel on the computer screen.

```
for j←1 to 50
    for k←1 to 50
        x₀←−6 + .24j
        y₀←−6 + .24k
        x←x₀
        y←Y₀
        for n←1 to 50
            xx←x − hsin(y + tan(3y))
            yy←y − hsin(x + tan(3x))
            x←xx
            y←yy
            compute jp and kp
            plot (jp,kp)
```

(The variables xx and yy are temporary variables that serve to keep track of the current values of x and y within an iteration cycle.)

The initial values for both coordinates are chosen from points within a square area of 12-by-12 units centered on the origin of the x-y plane. In other words, initial values of x are between −6 and +6, as are the initial values of y. Like BIOMORPH, POPCORN relies on a nested loop structure to compute a set of initial values. In POPCORN, however, both loops run from 1 to 50.

Finally, the points specified by the 50 (x,y) pairs generated for each initial pair $(x_0 y_0)$ must be plotted as pixels on the screen. That is done by a simple formula that scales and shifts x and y to jp and kp.

$$jp \leftarrow 4.166x + 25$$
$$kp \leftarrow 4.166y + 25$$

Pickover's fractal popcorn therefore consists entirely of pixels whose coordinates are given by the iterations. Readers are free to zoom in on individual pieces of popcorn to discover quite beautiful and completely unexpected detail. They can also "dye" the popcorn, as Pickover does, by plotting the pixels in a different color each time the inner loop begins anew.

Pickover's graphics have caught the public eye on more than one occasion. His work has been discussed not only in various magazine articles but also in television shows; it has even been shown at exhibitions in Switzerland, Japan, and at the Computer Museum in Boston.

I shall end this column by drawing the reader's attention to one of Pickover's latest creations: a beautiful snail shell, complete with stunningly realistic coloring and highlights. The image, shown in Color Plate 5, is constructed from a sequence of spheres whose centers track a gentle, logarithmic spiral. The highlights are generated by a ray-tracing technique that mimics various kinds of light reflections.

To obtain the guidelines on complex arithmetic or to receive a special bibliography of Pickover's papers, consult the List of Suppliers.

ADDENDUM

The banquet of biomorphs, snails, and fractal popcorn offered in this chapter in SCIENTIFIC AMERICAN in July, 1989, was eagerly devoured by a great variety of readers, especially connoisseurs of the Mandelbrot set and fans of fractals. Clifford Pickover, the fisherman and chef whose research inspired the repast, creates a biomorph by inserting extra conditions into the iterative process to produce images that resemble microscopic views of living organisms.

David J. Hoffman of Greenville, Tex., has found numerous new biomorphs. He notes that biomorphs, which use higher powers of z in their formulas than Julia sets do, generate more quickly. He sees biomorphs as Julia sets with "a little bit more" added to them. The extra pixels include not only the spikes and cilia but the cell body itself: "The central portion of the biomorph is either a connected Julia set or the fractal dust of an exploded Julia set."

Delmer D. Hinrichs of Washougal, Wash., turned the higher-powered formulas on the Mandelbrot set itself. Using cubic instead of quadratic powers, Hinrichs obtained a two-headed monster. Or was it two-tailed? Readers having their own Mandelbrot program ready to hand can make the requisite changes and judge for themselves.

David Fichman of San Diego, Calif., developed a general method for raising complex numbers to the nth power. He converts the complex number z to polar coordinates, that is, he replaces the real and imaginary coordinates, x and y, of z by the distance r that z lies from the origin and by the angle θ that z makes with the real line. To raise z to the nth power, Fichman converts it to polar coordinates, raises r to the nth power, multiplies θ by n, then converts back to x and y.

Strange that the serving vessel should excite more admiration than the food! Truchet tiles, our fanciful serving platters, turned out to interest nearly as many readers as the biomorphs and other delicacies. These tiles are squares decorated with a circular arc that cuts two opposite corners. An array of 0's and 1's may be converted into a crazy quilt of meandering curves by replacing each 0 by a tile in one orientation and each 1 by a tile in the other orientation. Pickover notes that even slight biases in the randomness of the bits can result in easily discernable patterns, a fact with implications for those who search data for patterns.

Rich Durrett of the mathematics department of Cornell University in Ithaca, N.Y., and Robert M. Ziff of the chemical engineering department at the University of Michigan in Ann Arbor, Mich., note a connection to percolation of chemical bonds in a square lattice, among other things. Joseph V. Saverino of Trexlertown, Pa., is a chemical engineer of more aesthetic bent. By varying the design on the tile, Saverino obtains a variety of designs that range from random Moorish and Byzantine patterns to strange urban plans. By flooding some of the connected areas with color, Saverino can instantly pick out the connected areas in his patterns.

Daniel C. Spencer of Valencia, Calif., has proposed an animated film program. Once the random bits have all been made into tiles, switch randomly located bits one at a time and change the corresponding tile accordingly. Such a program, according to Spencer, should make "the entire screen squirm and undulate."

Weird Machines

Computers, whatever the magic they produce, are not always the mysterious gray boxes on our desks. The computational process, after all, may dwell in a great variety of mechanisms. For example, complete general-purpose machines could, in principle, be constructed of materials as diverse as ropes and pulleys, Tinker Toys, or even individual molecules! These weird machines materialize here, as well as two special-purpose machines. One, when implanted in a simple vehicle, produces "behavior" that is bizarre or charming, depending on how one looks at it. The other produces gold—lots of it. Some would say that such a machine is simply too magical to be true. The mathematics behind it, however, is real enough.

Imagine hundreds of toy cars wandering a darkened plain. Here and there are light bulbs set on pedestals. Some of the cars gather worshipfully like moths before the bulbs, while others flee the light and run deeper into the night. These are the "vehicles" by which Valentino Braitenberg, the German cybernetician, would study behavior by the route of synthesis: Each vehicle is equipped with a simple neural machine which we can alter at will. If the simplest circuits can produce complicated behavior, what might we expect of a human brain? Readers may pause here and, like the good rabbi of Prague, design a wheeled golem or two.

What can one find in the name of a certain island—Apraphulia? It is there, I allege, that a certain now-vanished race once constructed a computer entirely out of ropes and pulleys. The principles are sound. After a piece on the subject appeared one April, a distinguished scholar called in despair from the map-room of a certain well-known university. Where on earth was Apraphulia? Perhaps, some day, a keen-eyed reader will spot it on a map of the seas around New Guinea.

Most magicians trick their audiences, but some hope for true magic. If the Apraphulian computer is fakery, the nanomachines of K. Eric Drexler seem chillingly imminent. Can we really build mechanical computers out of atomic parts? If so, we can watch for a transformation of our technology. Tiny machines may repair our bodies while a gray film (billions of tiny machines) builds us new homes from a pile of sand.

The Banach-Tarski paradox is not fakery either. Starting with an ideal solid, say a sphere, one may cut the solid into a finite number of parts, then reassemble them into a new solid with twice the volume! This smacks of the deepest sorcery, but the conclusions are as solid as a brick of gold. Speaking of the yellow stuff, if only one could program a computer that somehow uses the Banach-Tarski paradox to direct the cutting and assembly operation! There was a chap by the name of Arlo Lipof who actually tried this.

·6·

Vehicles of Thought

A vast plain hums with the activity of hundreds of toy vehicles. Some cluster worshipfully at the base of giant light bulbs. Others seek darker places or hover uncertainly between light and shade. What land is this? What madness?

It could be called the land of synthetic psychology, a gedanken ground invented by Valentino Braitenberg of the Max Planck Institute for Biological Cybernetics in Tübingen. Braitenberg's thesis that biological behavior is easier to synthesize than to analyze is aptly illustrated by the vehicles that inhabit the great plain. Employing only elementary mechanical and electrical devices, even the simplest control circuits give rise to behavior that Braitenberg calls love, aggression, fear, and foresight. A complete description of Braitenberg's thought experiment can be found in his handy little book titled *Vehicles: Experiments in Synthetic Psychology*.

Before exploring the world of Braitenberg's vehicles, there is a story of my own that illustrates his thesis. A certain professor of computer science once brought a curious object into his artificial-intelligence classroom. He displayed a golden sphere that he claimed (tongue in cheek) had fallen from a UFO that very morning as he was on his way to the campus.

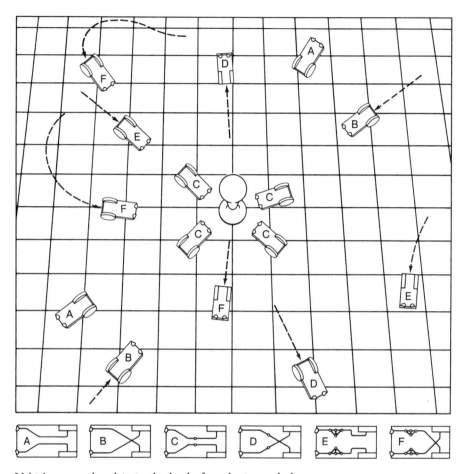

Vehicles roam the plain in the land of synthetic psychology

Turning his back to the class, he made a few adjustments and the sphere began to buzz. When he placed the sphere on the smooth classroom floor, it abruptly began to roll by itself. Whenever it bumped into an obstacle such as a chair leg, it would pause for a moment and then roll around it. At one point the sphere even rolled behind the door that stood open against one wall. The sphere buzzed and bumped mysteriously for a minute and suddenly reemerged from the cul-de-sac as though satisfied with its explorations. Readers might enjoy pondering what secret force controls the sphere. How does the sphere avoid obstacles in the way I have described?

Braitenberg's vehicles share with the golden ball the characteristic that only the initiated know how they work; others can only shake their heads in puzzlement. In what follows I have taken some liberties in simplifying and formalizing Braitenberg's game so that readers can join the initiated and engage in the adventure.

A vehicle can be visualized as a toy-size schematic automobile with two independent driving wheels at the back and two slave wheels (like casters) at the front (*see* illustration below). The difference in turning rates of the back wheels determines where the vehicle will go.

The wheels are attached to the simplest body possible, namely a rectangular slab of material. The vehicle designer can fasten various sensors around the edge of the slab. A circuit that connects the sensors to the rear wheels completes the vehicle. The wiring is mounted on the top of the slab somewhat in the manner of a printed circuit. Only one piece of optional equipment is available for the vehicles, a rectangular cover that can be placed over the circuit. The cover is not meant to protect the

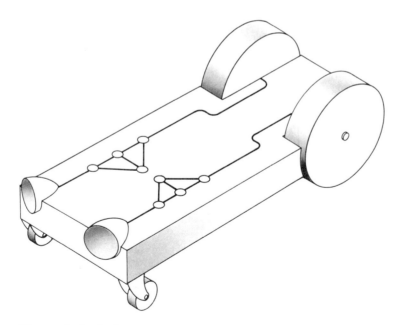

The standard vehicle

vehicular brain from the rain (the land of synthetic psychology has no weather) but to shield it from the prying eyes of outsiders; we have no wish to reveal how simple the little circuits actually are. Outsiders are therefore free to draw the most fantastic conclusions about what the vehicles are up to and just how they work. We do not want to spoil their fun.

The standard vehicle has two wide-angle "eyes," or photoreceptors, attached to the front of the slab. Each receptor is aimed slightly to the outside of the medial line. A light source ahead and to the left of the vehicle will therefore register more strongly in the left receptor than in the right receptor.

The two receptors are connected by wires to motors that operate the rear wheels. Signals in the wires consist of trains of discrete electric pulses: The more light a given receptor receives, the more pulses it sends along its output wire. At low levels of illumination only a few pulses are sent per second. At high levels many are sent. In both cases we imagine the pulses to be evenly spaced in time. At the other end of the wires the pulse trains are translated into motor commands. The more pulses that arrive per second at a given wheel, the faster its motor will drive it.

In the simplest vehicles two wires connect the eyes directly to the wheels. Two possibilities arise: The wires may be crossed or uncrossed. In the latter case each wire connects directly to the motor behind it. What happens when such a vehicle is placed in the middle of an infinite, darkling plain punctuated here and there by brightly shining light bulbs? If the vehicle is near one of the bulbs, more or less facing it, the vehicle will rush forward but immediately begin to turn away from the light as though frightened by its brightness. The fearful vehicle will run out into the night, slowing as it goes. In general it will creep slowly about the plain, avoiding bright places. Occasionally it may be forced to run through a gap between two relatively close bulbs. It will speed up like a frightened rabbit, hoping to get over the uncomfortable experience as quickly as possible.

An outside observer might be baffled by the vehicle's behavior, but the explanation is quite simple (*see* illustration at the right). If there is a light source ahead of the vehicle and to its left, for example, the left eye will receive more illumination than the right one (top). Consequently the left motor will run at a higher speed than the one on the right; the vehicle will therefore turn to the right, away from the source of light. The mirror image of this behavior is exhibited when the light source is to the right.

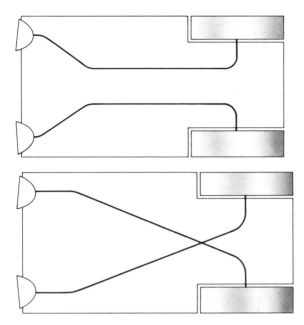

Direct (*top*) or crossed (*bottom*) connections make for different behaviors

The vehicle turns to the left, away from the source. Once the light is out of sight the vehicle immediately slows down, its speed governed only by the average illumination of distant sources in its visual field.

What about the vehicle with crossed connections (bottom)? Its behavior could hardly be more different. Placed on the plain at a great distance from any light bulb, it swings slowly in the direction of the one dominating its visual field. As it draws near, it goes faster and faster. Finally, at top speed, it runs straight into the bulb, smashing it. Would an outside observer not conclude that the vehicle with crossed connections behaves aggressively?

In the absence of any electronic intermediaries between receptors and motors, the two vehicles I have described virtually exhaust the available behavioral repertory. To produce more complicated behavior one can introduce a kind of abstract neuron. I call it a neurode to distinguish it from the real thing.

A neurode is actually a formal computing element that receives pulses from other neurodes or from receptors. The pulses are conducted by wires. A neurode will generate pulses of its own under certain conditions. Somewhere a clock ticks at the arbitrary rate of 100 cycles per second. A neurode will fire at the end of a cycle—and only at the end of the cycle—if the number of pulses it receives from other neurodes during the cycle equals or exceeds a preset number. (A pulse takes somewhat less than a complete cycle to travel between any two neurodes that are directly connected.) The preset number is called the neurode's threshold.

In the most general form of vehicle, pulses are delivered to neurodes by means of two kinds of wire, excitatory wire and inhibitory wire. A neurode will fire if it receives enough pulses along its excitatory wires so that its threshold is met. The neurode will be stopped from firing during a cycle if it receives a pulse along an inhibitory wire during the cycle.

The clock also governs receptors and motors. A receptor may send a pulse only at the end of a cycle. If it fires every cycle, it will send 100 pulses per second, the maximum level of activity a receptor is capable of sustaining. The motors may also receive a maximum of 100 pulses per second from the neurodes that control them. We assume, moreover, that each pulse delivered to a motor turns its wheel by a small angle. Such devices actually exist. They are called, appropriately enough, stepping motors.

By incorporating two neurodes into the hitherto ultrasimple circuits, the behavior of the two vehicles is radically altered: The fearful vehicle becomes a light-bulb lover and the formerly aggressive vehicle becomes shy. Their behavior is not simply reversed, however; the change is subtler. In both cases a single neurode of threshold 0 is inserted in the middle of each wire connecting a receptor to a motor. The section of ordinary wire between the receptors and the neurodes is then replaced with inhibitory wire. As a consequence, when the neurode receives a pulse from the receptor, it will send nothing to the motor attached to it. Conversely, when the neurode receives nothing from the receptor, it will fire a pulse to the motor. In other words, the higher the pulse rate from the eye is, the slower the motor runs; the lower the pulse rate from the eye is, the faster the motor runs.

Now form a mental image of the first vehicle, the one with uncrossed connections. As it approaches a light source, it steers directly toward it, slowing as it goes. Finally it comes to a stop, facing the light bulb in quiet adoration. The second vehicle's crossed connections, on the other hand, now cause it to turn slowly away from a nearby source, then to speed off into the darkest area it can see.

The reasons for the two behaviors should be clear to anyone who knows the circuits. In both cases the greater the illumination of the eye receptors is, the slower the motors run. But in the first case the more fully illumined eye drives a slower motor on the same side. This tends to correct deviations from dead center. In the second case, however, the more fully illumined eye drives a slower motor on the opposite side. This tends to increase deviations.

So far the response of the motors to receptor signals has been either directly proportional or inversely proportional to the pulse rate. By means of a simple little circuit of four neurodes, a nonlinear response can be arranged. The behavior of the four-neurode circuit is quite ordinary as long as the receptor sends fewer than 50 pulses every second to its motor: the more pulses per second from the receptor there are, the faster the motor goes. Beyond 50 pulses per second, however, matters become interesting. The motor begins to slow down: the more pulses per second from the receptor there are, the slower the motor goes.

To explain how the four-neurode circuit works, I must introduce a term called a pulse rate, which is the average number of pulses per cycle. A receptor that fire 50 pulses per second, for instance, has a pulse rate of ½, because 50 pulses per second divided by 100 cycles per second equals ½ pulse per cycle. (Remember that the clock ticks at 100 cycles per second.) Because a receptor or a neurode can fire a pulse only at the end of a cycle, the pulse rate can never exceed 1. In brief, the four-neurode circuit is constructed so that if an eye sends pulses at a rate less than ½, all the pulses get through to the motor. If the pulse rate is greater than ½, however, the circuit acts as a filter: the more pulses that are sent, the fewer that get through to the motor.

The four-neurode circuit consists of a chain of three neurodes of threshold 1 and an additional neurode of threshold 2 (*see* illustration on page 68). The first two threshold-1 neurodes send pulses to the threshold-2 neurode, which in turn sends an inhibitory pulse to the third threshold-1 neurode in the chain. The net effect, so to speak, is to kill off all but the first pulse in any train of consecutive pulses that travel through the miniature plexus. Readers are encouraged to confirm this operation for themselves. The assumption is that for pulse rates less than ½ no two pulses are consecutive. At rates greater than ½, however, clusters of pulses appear.

Outside observers are invited to ponder the behavior of the vehicles when each inhibitory receptor wire is replaced by an excitatory wire and

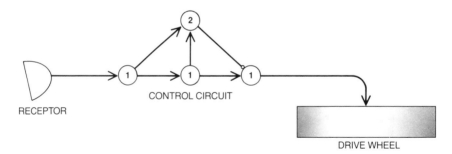

A nonlinear motor control circuit

each threshold-0 neurode is replaced by a four-neurode nonlinear network. Near the light source, where receptor pulse rates are greater than ½, the vehicle with uncrossed eye-to-motor connections behaves like the light-bulb lover. Away from the light source it becomes fearful, shrinking from light of any kind. The vehicle with crossed connections, on the other hand, vacillates. Outside the pulse-rate boundary of ½ it is aggressive, heading toward the nearest visible bulb with increased velocity. Within the boundary it becomes hesitant and turns shyly away.

One can readily imagine the great plain populated by all six types of vehicles (*see* illustration at the beginning of this chapter). Each light bulb would have a handful of quiet worshipers. Farther away vacillating vehicles would follow complicated orbits of indecision. In the outer darkness, meanwhile, the shy and fearful vehicles would creep quietly or whiz anxiously in complicated patterns. Occasionally the devotions of the quiet vehicles would be shattered by the arrival of a violent vehicle. If the process destroyed a bulb, all the vehicles would race off in search of another light source. The instigator of the destruction (assuming it survived the crash in perfect shape) would move off more slowly than the worshipful cars.

For vehicles equipped with neurodes the sky is the limit, behaviorally speaking. Indeed, one can build a perfectly good computer from interconnecting neurodes. But what good is a powerful brain with such limited sensory inputs? To add spice, vehicles could be equipped with enhanced vision, hearing and touch. The actual senses added are largely irrelevant; one would only like to construct a reasonably interesting and varied environment. Enhanced vision involves not only the wide-angle receptors already used but also narrow ones that can be assembled into compound arrays. Visual receptors could also have filters placed over them so that the vehicles could distinguish colors and detect heat (which is infrared radiation). Sound receptors might include primitive ears tuned to various frequency ranges. For touch I visualize long, whiplash antennas extending well out in front of the vehicles.

One could then add buzzers and heat sources to the plain. Vehicles themselves might give off heat. Some light bulbs might buzz.

While I was reading Braitenberg's book an arresting passage caught my eye. In reference to the superior abilities of neurode-equipped vehicles, he writes: "You can already guess some of the things that a vehicle fitted with this sort of brain can do, but you will still be surprised when you see it in action. The vehicle may sit there for hours and then suddenly stir when it sights an olive green vehicle that buzzes at a certain frequency and never moves faster than 5 cm/sec."

The description set me to imagining a species of predatory vehicle that would attack any and all vehicles that happened to cross its visual field (*see* illustration below). I have designed only the portion of the predator's brain responsible for pursuit; I offer my design as a sample exercise. Readers might enjoy designing a brain for a behavior that intrigues them.

The predatory brain is made up of two levels of interconnected neurodes. The neurodes in the first layer might be called decision neurodes

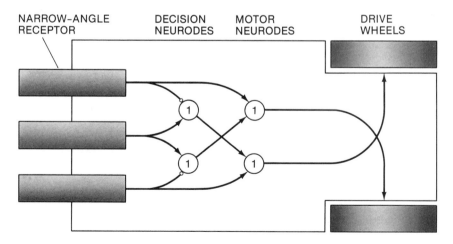

A predatory vehicle

while those in the second layer might be called decision/motor neurodes since they not only decide what the vehicle is looking at, but send drive commands to the motors as well. It is easier to understand the predatory brain by analyzing one of the latter neurodes, say the lower one in the diagram on page 69. When it fires, it sends a drive signal to the right wheel motor. This causes the vehicle to veer to the left (if the left wheel motor happens not to be on). But what causes this neurode to fire? Since it has threshold 1, it will fire if it gets a signal either directly from the left retinal cell or from the upper neurode in the first layer. The latter will fire if the central layer cell is seeing something *and* the right retinal cell is seeing nothing. In other words, the neurode in question will fire if either the left retinal cell sees something *or* the middle cell sees something and the right cell sees nothing. With these operating rules in mind, readers may easily work out the behavior of the predatory vehicle, remembering that the other decision/motor neurode functions in mirror-image fashion compared with the one just analyzed: The vehicle will stop if it sees nothing, drive straight ahead (both motors running) if the retinal cells detect any dark pattern that is symmetric, and veer toward a dark pattern that occupies one side of the retina or the other.

Admittedly it is much easier to synthesize one of Braitenberg's vehicles than it is to analyze the inner workings of a living nervous system, even the primitive one found in the large marine snail *Aplysia* (*see* "Small Systems of Neurons," by Eric R. Kandel, SCIENTIFIC AMERICAN, September, 1979). Undoubtedly observers familiar with the rules of the synthetic-psychology game could understand many of Braitenberg's vehicles simply by synthesizing ones of their own. At the same time Braitenberg's vehicles teach us that even the most primitive nervous systems may be capable of behavior that seems complicated or surprising. In any event, neurophysiologists have their hands full with creatures whose complexity is several orders of magnitude greater than that of the vehicles described here.

Michael A. Arbib is a computer scientist and brain theorist who recently moved to the University of Southern California to help develop a program of studies in neural, informational and behavioral science. Arbib's "vehicle" for brain research is a computer-simulated frog called *Rana computatrix*. The frog brain is at present only partially implemented: There is a crude retina, an advanced tectum, and as yet little else. Already, however, the frog hops around barriers and distinguishes prey from inanimate objects. It displays simple learning.

According to Arbib, there is something of a resurgence of interest in neural models both as simulations of living creatures and as potential computers. In the case of the former a number of workers have constructed computer simulations of isolated neural systems in simple animals such as locusts, frogs, and sea slugs. The simulations are already leading to testable predictions. In the case of the latter, a small number of engineers are investigating formal neurons as elements in parallel computers.

The gulf between synthesis and analysis does not imply that Braitenberg's vehicles should be viewed merely as frivolous playthings. Perhaps more germane than the current gulf between the two is the tendency of some observers to describe the actions of the vehicles in terms of human behavior, to say the vehicles love or hate based on behavior that appears complicated but really is not to those who understand it. Braitenberg seems to imply that the phenomena of love and hate are manifested by human systems as definite in principle as vehicular systems are; as one ascends a scale of complexity, passing from abstract to real creatures in the process, one might be forced to conclude that love and hate were present almost from the beginning.

Braitenberg illuminates the topic in his *Vehicles* by carefully constructing a sequence of machines ranging from simple to complex. At the end of the book he explains how each assumption, behavioral or mechanical, is grounded in real observations. The ability of an array of narrow-angle visual receptors to distinguish among objects might ultimately account for how a fly can choose one's nose to land on in a crowded room.

ADDENDUM

Reactions to my description of Valentino Braitenberg's vehicles in "Vehicles of Thought" were enthusiastic and ranged from practical suggestions to philosophical reflections. The vehicles are conceptual: A slab supports a printed circuit, a battery of sensors (usually two eyes) in front and two motors that drive rear wheels. With only the simplest circuits, Braitenberg's vehicles are amazingly varied, from lightbulb-loving machines that gaze at luminescent globes in silent adoration to aggressive vehicles that come zooming in from the outer darkness.

Joseph A. Coppola of Sherrill, N.Y., contends that an actual vehicle can be built for roughly $30 with parts such as a slab of plywood and off-the-shelf motors and electronic components. The Coppola vehicle

can be conveniently rewired to test different behaviors. Readers interested in the project may consult the List of Suppliers. Would it be
reasonable to suggest that in one year's time those who have built successful vehicles might send them to the big city for a lark under the
streetlights?

Tom Napier of Dresher, Pa., has reminded me of a sophisticated
vehicle constructed in the 1950's by W. Grey Walter of the University of
Bristol (see "An Imitation of Life," by W. Grey Walter, SCIENTIFIC
AMERICAN, May, 1950, and "A Machine That Learns," by W. Grey
Walter, SCIENTIFIC AMERICAN, August, 1951). The vehicle was called a
tortoise. According to Napier, it

> "had a single drive wheel and used two freely rotating fixed-axis support
> wheels. A steering motor rotated the drive wheel and drive motor about a
> vertical axis. Both the drive motor and the steering motor turned contin-
> uously but were switched to half or full speed by two relays. The relays
> were operated by two vacuum tubes whose input came from a vacuum
> photocell that rotated with the steering direction. Since the drive and
> steering motors had two states but neither ever turned off, the tortoises
> moved toward light sources in a cycloidal path."

To produce vacillating behavior in a Braitenberg vehicle, I proposed
employing a circuit consisting of four neurodes: simple, formal computing elements that are the vehicular equivalent of neurons. Frank Palmer
of Chicago points out that two neurodes will do just as well as four. In his
scheme the wire carrying the input signal is split in two, and each half is
connected to a threshold-1 neurode. One of the neurodes inhibits the
other. The inhibited neurode transmits what is left of the signal as
output.

The mysterious golden sphere mentioned at the beginning of the
chapter was a toy called Moonwalker that I purchased during the early
1970s. It consisted of a small windup car with rubber tires enclosed in a
transparent plastic sphere that would come apart into two hemispheres.
The trick? As the car tried to climb up one side of the sphere, the sphere
would roll in that direction. If the sphere struck an obstacle, the car
would climb higher until the slippage built into its right rear wheel took
effect. Veering to the right, the car would cause the sphere to begin
rolling in a new direction. The sphere could "solve" any maze because
the behavior of the car inside it amounted to a right-hand rule. Finally,
spray-painting the sphere gold obscured its simple internal workings.

∘ 7 ∘

The Apraphulian Wonder

On the island of Apraphul off the northwest coast of New Guinea, archaeologists have discovered the rotting remnants of an ingenious arrangement of ropes and pulleys thought to be the first working digital computer ever constructed. Chief investigator Robert L. Ripley of Charles Fort College in New York dates the construction to approximately A.D. 850.

The Apraphulians were excellent sailors. Their ships were wonderfully built and equipped with the most elaborate rigging imaginable. Were the Apraphulians led to the digital computer by their mastery of rope or was it the other way around? Experts continue to debate the topic hotly.

The ancient rope-and-pulley computer has recently been partially reconstructed by Ripley and his team at the Tropical Museum of Marine Antiquities in nearby Sumatra. Scouring a site that extends through several kilometers of dense jungle east of the Pulleg Mountains, the group found faint traces of buried jute fibers and noted the exact position of badly corroded brass pulleys and associated hardware. The reconstruction has given me an ideal opportunity to introduce readers to the principles of digital computing without resorting to tiny and mysterious electronic components. Here are gates, flip-flops, and circuits made entirely of rope and pulleys. It is all visible and perfectly easy to understand.

The Apraphulians used a binary system just as we do, but the numbers 0 and 1 were represented by the positions of ropes instead of by electric voltages. Imagine a black blox with a hole drilled in one side. The reader holds a taut rope that passes through the hole. This position of the rope represents the digit 0. If the reader now pulls on the rope, a creak and squeal inside the box is heard as a foot or so of rope comes out. The new position of the rope represents the digit 1.

One can represent numbers with such boxes. Any number from 0 through 7, for instance, can be represented by three boxes (*see* table below). By employing more boxes, larger numbers can be represented. Ten boxes suffice to represent all numbers from 0 through 1023.

My example of the black box is not arbitrary. The Apraphulians apparently loved to enclose their mechanisms in black wood boxes, small and large. It may be that the construction of computers was the prerogative of a special technological priesthood. The sight of great assemblages of black boxes may have kept the masses trembling in awe.

One of the key devices used by the Apraphulians converted a 0 into a 1 and a 1 into a 0. (It is occasionally convenient to speak of 0 and 1 instead of "in" and "out.") Akin to what modern computer engineers call an inverter, this interesting mechanism consisted of a box with a hole drilled in its front and another in its back (*see* illustration at the right). When

How Apraphulians Represented Numbers

BOX 1	BOX 2	BOX 3	NUMBER
IN	IN	IN	0
IN	IN	OUT	1
IN	OUT	IN	2
IN	OUT	OUT	3
OUT	IN	IN	4
OUT	IN	OUT	5
OUT	OUT	IN	6
OUT	OUT	OUT	7

t
t

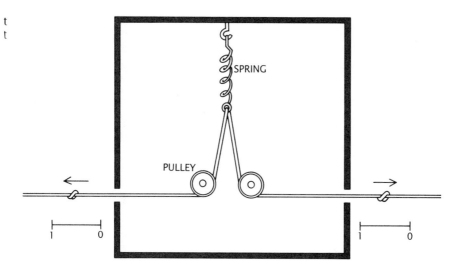

The Apraphulian inverter

someone (or something) pulled the input rope at the front of the box, an equal amount of output rope would be played out of the hole in the back. On peering into the box, the reason is obvious: The ropes entering the box from front and back pass over two fixed pulleys toward one side of the box, where they attach to a single spring.

As some readers may have surmised already, the digits 0 and 1 were not encoded so much by "out" and "in" as they were by the direction in which the rope moved. The point is best illustrated by a box that has no mechanism in it whatever. A piece of rope enters a single hole in the front of the box and leaves by a single hole in the back. If one pulls the rope from the 0 position to the 1 position at the front of the box, the rope moves from "in" to "out." The direction of movement is toward the puller. The rope simultaneously moves from "out" to "in" at the back of the box, but since the direction of movement is still toward the puller, the rope at the back of the box also moves from 0 to 1.

Two additional mechanisms almost complete the ancient Apraphulian repertoire of computing components. The first mechanism had two input ropes entering a box. If either rope was in the 1 position, the single output rope would also be in the 1 position. The Apraphulians managed this trick by absurdly simple means (*see* top illustration on page 76). Each rope entering the front of the box passed over a pair of pulleys that

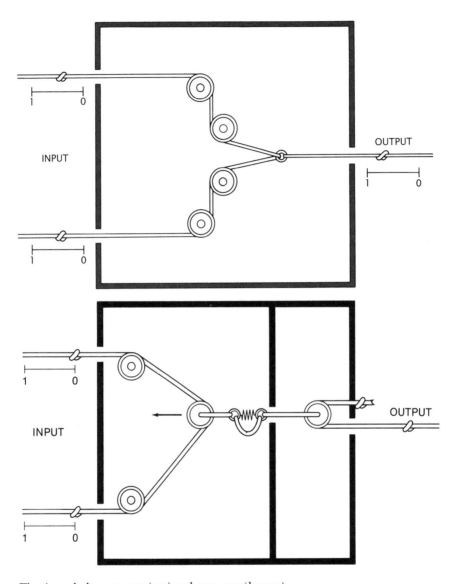

The Apraphulian OR gate (*top*) and AND gate (*bottom*)

brought it close to the other rope. The two ropes, passing toward the rear of the box, were then tied to a single ring linked to the output rope. If either or both of the input ropes were pulled, the ring would be pulled directly. Because the output of the box was 1 if one input *or* the other was 1, today's engineers would call this an OR gate.

The ancient Apraphulians fabricated what we would call an AND gate from four pulleys and a spring (*see* bottom illustration on the left). The two input ropes, in reality the same rope, passed over three of the pulleys, two of which acted as guides. The third pulley acted as a numerical divider; if one pulled one input rope by the amount x, the third pulley would move toward the front of the box by the amount $\frac{1}{2} x$. If x should happen to be one unit, indicating an input of 1, nothing would happen at the output end owing to a curious linkage between the third pulley and a fourth one situated in the back of the box. The third pulley was attached to the fourth by means of two rods (ropes would do equally well) joined by a weak spring. When the third pulley moved $\frac{1}{2}$ unit toward the front of the box, the spring would extend and a parallel rope of $\frac{1}{2}$ unit length would tighten to take up the slack. If the other input rope were now pulled into the 1 position, the third and fourth pulleys would move in unison $\frac{1}{2}$ unit toward the front of the box. Since the fourth pulley acted as a two-multiplier, multiplying any forward motion by 2 in terms of its associated output rope, the ensemble would convert the second 1 input into an output of 1.

The name AND gate is derived from the fact that the output of this device is 1 if and only if one input rope *and* the other are in position 1.

With these components one can build all the control circuits of a digital computer. These include circuits that compute arithmetic functions, interpret program code, and direct the flow of information among the parts of the computer.

Did the Apraphulians construct their computer along such lines? The evidence is too fragmentary to reach a definitive conclusion, but archaeo-computologists working with Ripley maintain they have discovered a simple multiplexer within the half-buried complex. In electronic computers a multiplexer is essentially an electrical switch that directs the passage of many signals through a single wire. For example, the simplest multiplexer would have two input wires we might label a and b. At any given moment each wire could carry a 0 or 1 signal. Which of the two signals, a or b, will be allowed to pass through the device and out a single output wire d? The answer to that question is the business of a control wire, c; if it carries a 1 signal, the signal from wire a will be transmitted along the output wire. If the control wire carries a 0, on the other hand, the signal in wire b will be transmitted (*see* illustration on page 78).

This reconstructed double-input Apraphulian multiplexer consists of two AND gates, an OR gate and an inverter. The whole thing is so simple that one dares to believe computer recreationists might build their own

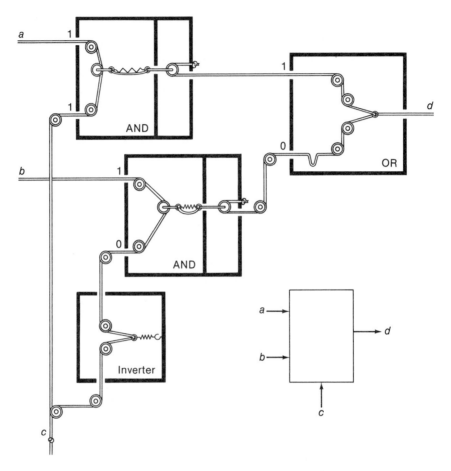

An Apraphulian multiplexer: rope c determines whether signals from *a* or *b* reach *d*

Apraphulian multiplexer at home. Hardware stores might suffer a puzzling run on rope and pulleys. In any event, one can follow operations of the multiplexer by referring to the illustration. Ropes *a* and *b* enter the multiplexer from the top left, each going to its own AND gate. Rope *c* is split. One branch runs directly to the other input port of the AND gate to which rope *a* goes. The second branch of rope *c* passes through an inverter and then runs to the AND gate to which rope *b* goes. If rope *c* is pulled to a value of 1 and held, any sequence of 0's and 1's sent along rope *a* will be faithfully transmitted through the upper AND gate and on to the

OR gate. At the same time any signal sent along rope *b* will be stopped at the lower AND gate. If rope *c* is relaxed to its 0 position, the inverter creates a 1 at the lower AND gate. In this case any signal sent along rope *b* will now be transmitted through the lower AND gate and signals on rope *a* will be ignored.

The OR gate merely ties the two output signals together, so to speak. If the signal from rope *a* is currently being transmitted, one can easily visualize exactly what happens directly from the diagram: If rope *a* is relaxed to the 0 position, the rear pulley in the AND box moves toward the rear of the box. A 0 is thus transmitted along the output rope and into the OR box. The other input rope to this box is already in the 0 position (slack). The natural tension on the output rope *d* immediately pulls it into the new position, namely 0. If one pulls on rope *a* again, the pull is transmitted along the path that has just been described, with the result that rope *d* is retracted.

The matter of slack ropes compels me to take up the question of tension in the Apraphulian computer. Sometimes, as in the OR gate of the example, a rope will become slack. There is naturally a danger that such ropes will slip right off their pulleys. Ripley tells me that in such cases the Apraphulians used a specially modified inverter with an extremely weak spring to remedy the problem. Wherever a rope was likely to develop slack, a "weak inverter" was installed to maintain the minimum tension associated with the signal 0.

No general-purpose computer is complete without a memory. The memory of the Apraphulian computer consisted of hundreds of special storage elements we would call flip-flops. Here again the remarkable simplicity of the Apraphulian mind is immediately evident. In line with modern terminology, the two ropes entering the mechanical flip-flop are labeled set and reset (*see* illustration on page 80). The two ropes were connected over a series of three pulleys in such a way that when the set rope was pulled away from the box into the 1 position, the reset rope would be pulled toward the box into the 0 position. The common rope was connected to a sliding bar at the back of the flip-flop box. The output rope, physically a continuation of the set rope, had a large bead attached to it that engaged a slot in the sliding bar. As the set rope was pulled, the bead rode over the end of the bar, popping into the slot when the set rope reached the end of its travel. In this position, 1 was "remembered."

As a consequence the output rope was held in position until the enormous rope computer changed things by pulling on the reset rope.

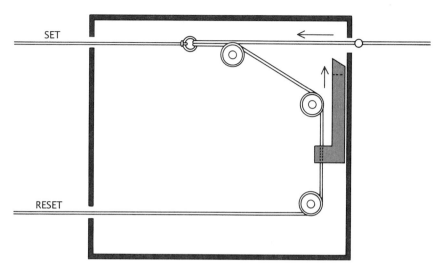

The Apraphulian flip-flop served as a memory element

That had the effect of pulling the sliding bar away from the bead, releasing it and playing the output rope into the 0 position. In this case the flip-flop would henceforth "remember" 0. How were such memory elements used in the Apraphulian computer?

Ripley and his team were puzzled to discover in the midst of the vast Apraphulian computer complex a large overgrown field nearly a kilometer wide. Buried just below the surface of the field were several thousand rotting flip-flop boxes arranged in rows of eight. Ripley, with the aid of the archaeocomputologists, eventually surmised that the field represented the Apraphulian computer's main memory. Each row of eight boxes would have constituted a single, eight-bit "word" in the same sense that the three boxes of my earlier example would have constituted a three-bit word. In that vein, imagine a row of three flip-flops that had been set to the values 1, 0 and 1. They would have stored the number 5.

The content of this particular memory word would have been accessed by the rope-and-pulley computer as follows. Each flip-flop in the row would send an output rope to an associated AND box. The other input to each AND box would come from a special rope used to retrieve the contents of the word in question. When the ropes were pulled, the outputs of the AND boxes would be identical with the outputs of the flip-flops. The AND box ropes would lead to a large assemblage of OR boxes and thence into a special array of flip-flops we would call a register. A single tug on the rope associated with the word under examination would place the same binary pattern of rope positions in the register.

The computer's main logic unit undoubtedly would have directed the flow of information not just from memory to registers but between registers as well. In particular, by the use of multiplexers and demultiplexers (which perform the opposite function of multiplexers), the computer would have sent patterns from register to register. At a specific register that we would call the arithmetic register, patterns would have been combined according to the rules of addition and multiplication.

The Apraphulian computer is believed to have been programmable. If it was, part of its vast memory would have been used to store the program. Program instructions would also have been merely patterns of 0's and 1's retrieved by the same mechanism outlined above. Those patterns would in due course have been sent to an instruction register for interpretation by the computer's logic unit.

It is a pity I can do little more in these pages than to hint at the marvelous complexity of the Apraphulian machine. It must have been an amazing sight when in operation. Because of the enormous lengths of rope involved, no human being would have had the strength to pull the input levers into the appropriate positions. The presence of elephant bones in the Apraphulian complex makes the source of input power immediately clear. At the output end large springs maintained appropriate tensions in the system. Perhaps flags on the ultimate output ropes enabled members of the technological priesthood to read the outcome of whatever computation was in progress.

The Apraphulian rope-and-pulley computer makes for an interesting contrast with the nanocomputer introduced in the next chapter. The rope machine, of course, inhabits a distant past, whereas the nanometer-scale machine dwells in a hazy future. The Apraphulian computer is relatively massive in scale, covering thousands of acres; the nanocomputer is incredibly tiny, occupying an area one-thousandth the size of a human cell nucleus. The mere concept of either machine serves as a springboard into a speculative realm where recreation blends with science. Think, for example, of the ongoing dream of artificially intelligent machines. We find it easier to accept the possibility of an electronic computer that thinks since our own thoughts are to a great extent electronically mediated. Because any modern computer (and its program) is conceptually translatable into Apraphulian form, any artificially intelli-

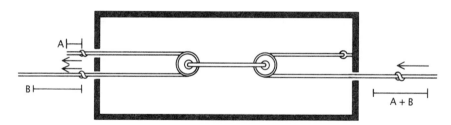

An Apraphulian adding machine

gent device ever realized now or in the future will have its rope-and-pulley counterpart. Can we imagine HAL 9000, the paranoid computer in the movie *2001: A Space Odyssey*, being so constructed? Are we willing to admit that an enormous building full of ropes and pulleys could be just as smart as we are?

We leave the island of Apraphul with just one backward glance at its misty past: How might the vast digital computer have evolved? From analog ones, of course. The illustration above shows an analog adding machine made from two ropes and two pulleys. The two ends of one rope enter the front of a box through two holes. The rope passes over a single pulley that is linked with another pulley by an axial connector. One end of the second rope is attached to the back of the box. The rope passes over the second pulley and then through a hole in the back of the box. Readers might find some diversion in discovering for themselves how the machine adds two numbers; if the two input ropes are pulled a distance a and b respectively, the output rope travels a distance $a + b$.

So much is clear. But how did the Apraphulians manage analog multiplication?

ADDENDUM

The Apraphulian excursion fooled few people when it first appeared in SCIENTIFIC AMERICAN in April, 1988. Those who nonetheless entered into the spirit of the account were challenged by the reconstruction of the Apraphulian analog multiplying machine: a device that multiplies two numbers entirely by means of ropes and pulleys. Some entered into the spirit of the enterprise so fully that they asserted they had firsthand knowledge of the ancient Apraphulian culture. The champion letter in this vein was sent in by Clive J. Grant of Chichester, N.H. A long document describes Grant's correspondence with a mysterious Dr. Ebur Grebdlog, renowned scholar of Apraphulian lore:

"After reading your 'Computer Recreations' column on the state of Apraphulian mathematics, I contacted Dr. Grebdlog to ask him if his work had ever covered . . . an Apraphulian Analog Multiplier. . . . Indeed, he replied, he had investigated that matter, and he sent along a copy of his work."

The "work" was beautifully written in Grebdlog's spidery hand, accompanied by technical drawings of pulleys and cams connected by bridges. Grebdlog notes that the drawings "appear to have guided the Apraphulians in constructing a device truly remarkable for the unstinting technological effort applied to its development but more remarkable for its total lack of utility."

The multiplier most often suggested by readers made use of a rod, one end of which is attached to a fixed hinge. An input rope tied partway along the rod pulls it forward so that an output rope tied to the free end is also pulled in the same direction. Since the rod is in essence a lever with the fulcrum at its hinged end, the output rope moves a greater distance than the input rope. The problem with this design arises from a loss of proportionality: As the input rope is pulled farther, the rod follows a circular arc and the amplifying effect on the output rope eventually fades. Variations on this theme sometimes corrected for the rod's circular motion by means of guides or fancy systems of parallel jointed rods. All of this struck me as too complicated. Perhaps I should have explicitly forbidden the use of rods.

Robert Norton of Madison, Wis., used spiral pulleys to compute logarithms and antilogarithms. The input ropes A and B are unwound from two drums (which are not against the rules, since they are just wide pulleys). Each drum is attached to a spiral drum that winds up an output rope. The two outputs are then added in the way outlined at the end of "The Apraphulian Wonder." The antilog of the sum is computed by winding the addition rope onto a spiral drum that is connected to a straight drum on which the final output rope is wound. A similar machine was "discovered" by Robert A. Eddius of New York City. The Apraphulians, he contends, used the shells of certain mollusks whose spiral shape enabled them to compute logarithms exactly! On the other hand, David A. Fox of Lima, Ohio, writes us that a similar culture inhabited a small island off the Marshall group known as Hardy Atoll. Here were found not only the same log-antilog devices but also a contraption rather like a yo-yo that was capable of squaring numbers. Readers might want to ponder whether Fox's assertion is possible.

Caxton C. Foster of East Orleans, Mass., is of the opinion that the Apraphulian civilization was destroyed by logical gain: the problem encountered by a computer in which the "1" output of each gate is not quite 1. To prevent such inaccuracies from creeping into the sacred computations, the high priests stationed an Apraphulian at each gate to pull a little harder on any output ropes lacking the necessary tautness. Thus absorbed, the people were unable to procure food and eventually starved to death.

The final word belongs to modern-day computer architect Michael Pagan of Mount Laurel, N.J. Concerned about the cultural gap between the analog branch and the digital branch of Apraphulian society, Pagan developed a marvelous analog-to-digital converter. A single rope carrying the analog signal enters the device and a number of rope bearing the digital equivalent of the input number leave it. Such a machine may have been introduced on Apraphul, but the priests would certainly have banned the pagan device.

·8·

Atomic Computers

Will machines the size of a mitochondrion someday be injected into the human body? If the thought of tiny machines creeping within one's flesh makes one's flesh creep, consider the possible advantages. Microscopic machines might be made to act as tiny vascular submarines that destroy unwanted organisms and fat in the human circulatory system. With such machines a person might be destined for a longer life span (*see* Color Plate 6).

The minuscule healing machines are in part the brainchild of K. Eric Drexler, a visiting scholar at the department of computer science of Stanford University. For more than a decade Drexler has been laying the blueprints for nanotechnology, a revolutionary concept of machinery in the nanometer (a billionth of a meter) size range. He has designed gears and bearings of atomic dimensions and described molecular manipulators. He has even laid out the logic for a nanocomputer, the centerpiece of this chapter's excursion. Although nanotechnology is currently hardly more than a gleam in the eye of Drexler and a handful of other scientists, it has a curious ring of inevitability. The future it implies seems an order of magnitude more wonderful than anything in science fiction.

Drexler is not the first to explore the territory of nanotechnology. In 1959 Richard P. Feynman envisioned a succession of machines built to progressively smaller dimensions; machines at one scale of magnitude would construct those at the next level of size downward. According to Drexler, the ultimate products would have moving parts no larger than a few atoms across. Such products, depending on design and purpose, might roam through the human body, invading cancerous cells and rearranging their DNA. Other machines might swarm as a barely visible metallic film over an outdoor construction site. In the course of a few days an elegant building would take shape.

Drexler believes a key step in developing nanotechnology is the creation of assemblers, small machines that would guide chemical bonding operations by manipulating reactive molecules. Programmed to carry out certain construction tasks, assemblers would turn out specific machines by means of miniature assembly lines. Every hour entire factories no larger than a grain of sand might generate billions of machines that would look like a mass of dust streaming steadily from the factory doors — or like a cloudy solution suspended in water.

There are already aqueous nanomachines (of a kind) in nature. Consider the well-known T4 bacteriophage, which replicates itself by invading the body of a bacterial host. The phage attaches itself to the outer cell wall of the bacterium and then, like a tiny hypodermic syringe, injects its own DNA into the host. The phage DNA redirects protein synthesis inside the bacterium so that hundreds of minuscule phage parts are manufactured. Through random encounters the parts proceed to assemble themselves into new DNA-loaded syringes that, once the bacterial wall disintegrates, are free to search for new victims.

Another example of nanomachinery is already a part of some bacteria possessing a flagellum, a long, helical structure protruding from one or both ends of the bacterium. The organisms swim by rotating the flagellum, which whips about in a circular, corkscrew fashion. A secret motor just inside the bacterium's cell wall drives the flagellum. The motor consists essentially of a protein rotor powered by ionic forces.

A key device in any conceivable nanotechnology is the bearing. Bearings normally require lubrication of some kind. In 1959 Feynman noted that

> lubrication involves some interesting points. The effective viscosity of oil would be higher and higher as we went down. . . . But actually we may not have to lubricate at all! We have a lot of extra force. Let the bearings

run dry; they won't run hot because the heat escapes away from such a small device very, very rapidly.

Would a lighter lubricant work? Even if kerosene were substituted for oil, viscosity would increase. As Drexler has pointed out, however, "from the perspective of a typical nanomachine, a kerosene molecule is an object, not a lubricant." In a paper devoted to gears and bearings, he addresses the problem of friction in roller bearings. Owing to what could be called atomic bumpiness, one might expect nanometer-size roller bearings to experience considerable static and sliding friction. Such bumpiness is described in part by a formula known as the van der Waals interaction potential. The formula contains a repulsive exponential term that generates most of the bumps.

Drexler suggests that the friction problem can be handled by employing roller bearings in which surface atoms arranged in rows are meshed with similar rows in the race, the track in which a bearing moves. An assembler that can arrange single atoms of elements such as carbon and fluorine might construct the bearing and race from carbon atoms arranged in the single-bond structure characteristic of diamond. The bearing would thus be a sheet bent back on itself to form a hollow cylinder. The surface of both bearing and race would be studded with fluorine atoms arranged in angled rows (*see* illustration below). The same strategy could be followed to construct gears that mesh.

Drexler also addresses the problem of sliding friction between atomic surfaces. Given the ability to arrange atoms in positions that do not violate physical laws, one can exploit patterns that smooth out the van der Waals repulsive forces. For example, an atom that moves close to a

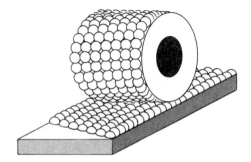

A roller bearing of fluorinated diamond

surface consisting of rows of other atoms suitably staggered would experience a relatively smooth ride. But it must proceed along a straight path just above the groove between two rows. Drexler bubbles over with additional plans. Some are available only in technical papers, which Drexler has kindly agreed to make available to readers who want to know more about the speculative nuts and bolts of nanotechnology. The papers can be ordered by writing Drexler after consulting the List of Suppliers. A more general overview of the field will be found in Drexler's book, *Engines of Creation* (*see* Further Readings).

Suppose for the moment that something like the miniature vascular submarine I mentioned above is actually possible. How will it be controlled? By a nanocomputer, of course, but of what kind? Electronic computers may be possible, Drexler says, but he has concentrated on mechanical computers based on what he calls "rod logic." Although their logical operations are mediated entirely by molecular rods that slide through a miniature matrix, they are not at all slow. At the atomic scale such rods take only about 50 picoseconds (trillionths of a second) to slide.

The principal element of a computer is the logic gate. One or more signal paths enter a logic gate and one path (which may later split off into other paths) leaves it. Signals are of two types, denoted by 0 and 1. Because the signal in a given path varies with time between two values, a variable such as x can be used to label the path. A formula describes the logic function of the gate. For example, the formula "x AND y" describes the so-called AND gate; the gate's output signal is a 1 if and only if the input signals, x and y, are both 1. Similarly, the formula "x OR y" describes the OR gate. In this case the gate's output is a 1 if either of the input signals, x or y, is a 1. From these two types of gate, along with a third called a NOT gate, or inverter, one can build any logic function whatever. The NOT gate changes a 1 into a 0 and a 0 into a 1.

In current computers, logic gates are made out of micron-scale transistors implanted in the surface of a chip. A layer of specially treated silicon infused with impurities that carry an excess or a shortage of electrons is covered with a layer of polycrystalline silicon. A third, metallic layer, usually aluminum, overlies the first two. It acts as a conductor between transistors. Of course, not all points on the surface of a chip contain all three layers. The precise pattern in which the layers are deposited actually defines the transistors and their interconnections. The metal layer, for example, consists of ultranarrow aluminum strips running helter-skelter all over the surface.

In a microchip, signals that travel the tiny aluminum paths vary between two distinct levels of voltage that encode the logic values 0 and 1. The gates in general are NAND gates, which, in terms of the simple logic functions described above, can be represented by the expression "not (*x* and *y*)." In other words, the NAND gate has an output of 1 when it is not the case that both inputs *x* and *y* are 1. Thus if either input is 0, the output is 1. One can build any logic function, no matter how complicated, from NAND gates alone.

Microchips are small. Their components are scaled in the micron (millionth of a meter) range. Drexler now asks us to consider a computer that would fit inside a single silicon transistor!

The logic in Drexler's hypothetical nanocomputer is mediated by infinitely small rods instead of wires holding particular voltage levels that encode 0 and 1. A rod of atomic dimensions is free to slide into one of two positions. The positions of the rod encode the values 0 and 1 by convention. The rod is made of carbyne, a chain of carbon atoms that are linked by alternating single and triple bonds. Carbyne turns out to be strong and stiff enough for the job, yet it can be bent around gentle corners and still slide. Along their lengths the carbyne rods sport knobs. The knobs come in two varieties (*see* the illustration below). Some of the knobs simply project outward, and they are called probe knobs. Others look like panels or doors, and they are called blocking knobs.

The base of both kinds of knob is formed by a hexagonal pyridazine ring, linked on either side to the carbyne chain. A probe knob consists of a second carbon ring above the pyridazine ring. The superior ring holds a

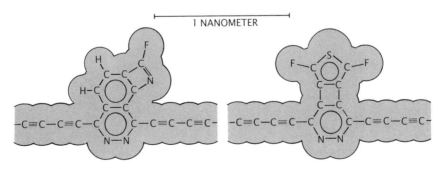

A probe knob (*left*) and a gate knob (*right*) on a carbyne logic rod

single fluorine atom in a forward position, ready to act as a logic probe. A blocking knob differs slightly from a probe knob in that it is surmounted by a fluorinated thiophene ring. But names are not important. We assume in what follows that such structures can handle the jobs of probing and blocking. Suffice it to say that Drexler has calculated much more than I have room to discuss here, particularly the amount of tension the rods must have to endure amid thermal jostling.

Besides its rods, the logical heart of the mechanical nanocomputer consists of a three-dimensional matrix made of atoms near carbon in the periodic table. It is a framework penetrated by channels that run in two orthogonal directions on a great many levels. How do the rods compute logic functions within the matrix?

Imagine a single, horizontal rod resting in its channel in one of the two allowed positions. It is called a logic rod, and it will, for the sake of simplicity, have two probe knobs and one blocking knob (*see* illustration below). The rod therefore passes through three locks, hollow parts of the matrix in which two rods (and their knobs) meet at right angles. For a given lock the question is whether the probe knob will slide easily past the blocking knob or be held by it. Of the three locks the logic rod in our example passes through, the two leftmost ones contain blocking knobs that are attached to vertical rods labeled x and y. The lock at the right contains a probe knob, which is attached to a third vertical rod labeled f.

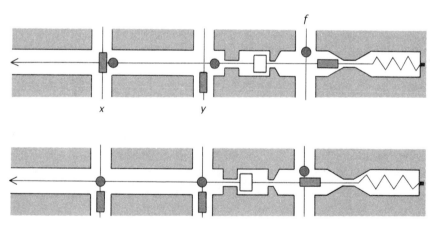

A logic rod defines the nand operation

The horizontal rod and its locks serve to compute the NAND operation. The two vertical rods at the left encode input variables x and y. The vertical rod at the right represents the output of the nand operation.

If one supposes that a vertical input rod encodes 0 in the up position and 1 in the down position, it may happen that x is 0 and y is 1. In other words, rod x is up and rod y is down. In such a case it is impossible to pull the logic rod leftward past both vertical rods because rod x is in the up position; its blocking knob gets in the way of the logic rod's probe knob. Only if rod x is also down will both probe knobs of the logic rod clear their respective blocking knobs so that the logic rod can slide to the left.

What about the output rod f? It may test whether the logic rod has found its new position by pushing into the lock containing the logic rod's blocking knob. It happens that when the horizontal rod is in its right-hand position, rod f will clear it, going from logic value 0 to 1. But if the logic rod is able to slip to the left, its blocking knob prevents rod f's probe knob from moving through the lock, and so f has a value of 0. Thus the value of f must be 1 if x and y are not both 1, in keeping with the rules of the nand function.

The computational cycle of Drexler's rod computer involves three distinct stages that follow one another with lightning speed repeatedly. In the first stage, the input locks are set by temporarily pulling on the ends of input rods. This allows all the logic rods to be withdrawn to their initial positions. In the second stage, the input rods take up their current positions. They might be connected to various sensors of the nanomachine or to outputs of the nanocomputer itself. Now a source of displacement tugs all the logic rods to the left, so to speak. In the final stage the values of output variables are decided when the output rods are all pulled. The rods that can move do so.

Investigators working in artificial intelligence are sure to raise objections at this point; granted even that adequate computing power can be built into such a small package, how does Drexler propose to incorporate the requisite intelligent behavior into his little autonomous vehicles?

Drexler replies that in spite of the fact that quite powerful central processing units might be embedded in quite minute spaces, some of his conceptual nanomachines do not have to be terrifically smart in any case. Take the nanosubmarine described earlier, one of the engines of healing. The submarine travels through the bloodstream, absorbing glucose and oxygen as it goes. Those chemicals supply it with power. Presumably someone hosting a fleet of billions might feel a bit peaked from time to time. In any event, each nanosub uses the energy from its glucose engines (which are currently being designed) to drive two helical propellers. It uses no guidance whatever. When it bumps into something, it is notified by the nano equivalent of a contact switch in its forward sensors. The same sensor then tries out a variety of molecular fits by matching templates against patterns built into the sensor.

If the submarine detects wall cells, red cells, leukocytes or a finite number of other benign entities, it reverses engines briefly and then continues on its way. But if it encounters a hostile bacterium or virus, it opens its mechanical jaws to engulf what it can of what it has found. This includes fat deposits and virtually anything else it is programmed for. Whatever is engulfed is broken down and released into the bloodstream for removal by the kidneys. The chances of unwanted bodies' surviving for more than a few hours in such a busy bloodstream would be small indeed.

Of course, it is all a dream—for now, at least. We are barely at the threshold of a possible plunge into the nanorealm. Can Drexler possibly be right in asserting that something close to the dream could actually take place? He is used to defending his ideas and on occasion altering them in the light of serious objections from fellow scientists. He remains, however, a technologist without a technology, an informed speculator whose greatest contribution might be to stimulate the dreams that guide our technological development. As such he is not among the gung ho. The dangers of abuse make atomic weapons and genetic runaways look tame.

I was recently told by a nano enthusiast that "thousands now living will never die!" Strange to relate, an evangelist once made the very same pronouncement to my father half a century ago.

ADDENDUM

Nanotechnology, the topic of "Atomic Computers," drew responses from skeptics and enthusiasts alike. An amusing version of skepticism arrived from the Humanist Association of Oklahoma, an organization represented by Clinton L. Wiles of Oklahoma City. Wiles puts little store in the promise of eternal life that some enthusiasts see in nanotechnology. In particular, the nanosubmarine I took some delight in describing may never be built, much less deliver eternal life, according to Wiles. He writes: "Being skeptical enough not to have bought any supernatural eternities, we'll suggest that anyone investing in nanotechnology expecta-

tions be prepared to wait awhile for a return on the investment. . . .
Even if submarines in the bloodstream is a godless idea, we'll file it as an
incredible claim requiring incredible proof, right next to the supernatural
eternal-life claims."

Eric Drexler is among the principal defenders of nanocomponents.
Responsibly enough, he carefully avoids any claim beyond the ultimate
prolongation of human life at the hands of his "engines of healing."
Science-fiction author Paul Preuss of San Francisco admires Drexler and
has studied some of the possibilities nanotechnology seems to offer.
Preuss's latest book, *Human Error*, describes a hypothetical, self-replicat-
ing nanomachine that is accidentally ingested by a brilliant but unlovable
investigator at a biotechnology company on the West Coast. The investigator changes in surprising ways and even learns about love.

° 9 °

Paradoxical Gold

Nil posse creari de nilo.
—LUCRETIUS, *De rerum natura*

I was not surprised to receive, nearly a year ago, a long missive from someone who claimed to have invented a matter fabricator. After all, among those who write to me suggesting interesting ideas there are a few whose assertions do stretch credulity. But since the essence of science is an open mind (if not a fully ventilated one), I try not to dismiss such letters until I have read them to the end.

I am glad I did just that with this particular letter, because the inventor based his assertion on a legitimate mathematical result known as the Banach-Tarski paradox. Named for the Polish mathematicians who discovered it in the 1920's, the paradox reveals how under certain conditions an ideal solid can be cut into pieces and then reassembled into a new solid twice as large as the original one.

Indeed, the inventor turned out to be a professional mathematician who has many published papers to his credit. For reasons that will soon become clear, he shuns any kind of publicity and has asked that I call him Arlo Lipof. It was Lipof's familiarity with the Banach-Tarski paradox that first led him to investigate the possibility of applying the paradox to real matter instead of ideal matter. His investigation has paid off handsomely: He has written a computer program that gives precise directions for cutting a solid into many odd-shaped pieces and then reassembling them into a solid twice the size, leaving absolutely no space between the pieces!

Needless to say, the implications of Lipof's program are profound. To explain the paradox and how the program exploits it, I can hardly do better than to quote from Lipof's letter:

> On its surface, the paradox resembles the well-known puzzle involving tangrams, little pieces of paper cut into simple geometric shapes. Four such shapes can be assembled into a square that has an area of 64 square inches. Yet the very same pieces can also be assembled into a rectangle that has a greater area — 65 square inches, to be precise. If you do not believe such a thing is possible, try cutting up the pieces as shown in my drawing [*see the* illustration below].
>
> If the little pieces of paper were instead pieces of gold, there would seem to be an automatic increase in wealth in going from the square to the rectangular configuration. Start with a square of gold, say, eight inches on a side and an inch thick. Then cut it according to the figure at the left. If the pieces are reassembled according to the figure at the right, an extra cubic inch of gold will have appeared. The extra cube would weigh approximately 4.3 ounces and at current prices would be worth about $1,800.

Lipof goes on to concede that the appearance of getting something for nothing in the above example is purely illusory. But he asserts that although the Banach-Tarski paradox has "the same effect on one's mind," there is no flaw in the theory on which it is based. The Banach-Tarski paradox is real — at least in a mathematical sense.

The paradox arises from a proved theorem that, even when stated in technical language, is almost comprehensible: If A and B are any two bounded subsets of R^3, each having a nonempty interior, then A and B

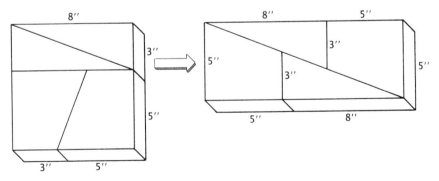

How to get a cubic inch of gold for nothing

are equidecomposable. The theorem can be stated in less technical language if one initially considers a pair of bodies, of virtually any shape and size, that meet two criteria. Each body must be "bounded," or capable of being enclosed in a hollow sphere of some definite size. And each must have a "nonempty interior": It must be possible to envision a sphere somewhere inside the body that is entirely filled with the material of which the body is made.

The two criteria are actually rather modest ones. Indeed, almost any object we might imagine that violates them is hardly the kind of object we would normally call a body. A straight, infinitely long line, for example, violates both criteria: It is not bounded, and its interior is empty in the sense that it has no interior to speak of. Also disallowed would be an imaginary cloud of points stretching to infinity in all directions — hardly a body in the usual sense of the word.

According to the theorem, then, any two such bounded bodies having non-empty interiors are "equidecomposable." This means that one can dissect both bodies into a finite number of pieces that are congruent in a geometric sense: A piece of one body can be made identical with a piece of the other body merely by rotating it, that is, swinging the piece by a rigid rotational motion about some invisible center until it coincides exactly with the congruent piece. Hence one can in theory dissect a body into pieces and label them A_1, A_2, A_3 . . . and dissect a different body into pieces and label them B_1, B_2, B_3 . . . , so that the pieces A_1 and B_1, A_2 and B_2 and so on are identical. That is the essence of the Banach-Tarski paradox.

"It is thus possible," Lipof writes, "to take two solid spheres, one twice as large as the other, and cut them into pieces that are pairwise congruent [see illustration at right]. Forget the larger sphere and consider only the smaller one. Imagine that it is made of gold. In principle it can be cut into a finite number of pieces that can then be reassembled into a sphere twice as large."

There is no trickery here, although one must realize that there are certain topological qualifications implied in the innocent word "pieces." For one thing, they are not necessarily simple in form, or even composed of connected parts. Some parts of the same piece may come arbitrarily close to one another without actually touching. Moreover, the pieces cannot be measured in any precise way. For example, one cannot even imagine a way of gauging their exact volume. What would be the actual appearance of such pieces? Lipof says they are "like nothing you have ever seen before. They make fractals look like tangrams."

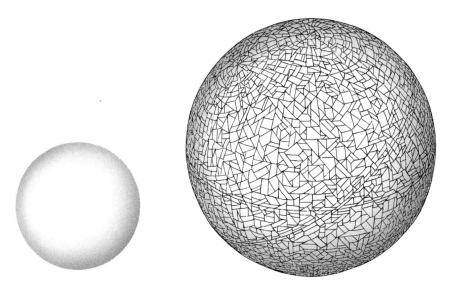

Original gold ball (*left*) and Arlo Lipof's reconstruction of it (*right*)

The Banach-Tarski paradox holds in its most general form only in spaces of three or more dimensions. There are, however, closely related theorems that illustrate the nature of the paradox in spaces of lower dimensions. A crude example of this phenomenon is given by the one-dimensional "space" consisting of all integers, since the subset of even integers represents simultaneously both half of and the whole of the set. The subset is half of the set of all integers in the sense that only every other integer is in the subset. Yet a simple transformation — dividing each element in the subset by 2 — turns the even integers into the entire set of all integers; the set and its subset are the same size.

Most people do not find this fact very remarkable, because the size of both set and subset happens to be infinite. After all, infinity divided by 2 is still infinity. It would be more exciting to find a finite space that can be decomposed into paradoxical pieces, but that is not possible according to theory, at least if one limits oneself to spaces of a single dimension. The same applies for Euclidean spaces of two dimensions, or "flat" planes. It can happen, however, in certain non-Euclidean two-dimensional spaces.

A full explanation of the phenomenon is beyond the scope of this column, but I can give at least a glimpse of its paradoxical nature by projecting the exotic world of two-dimensional hyperbolic space onto an ordinary Euclidean disk, as is shown in the illustration at the right. The hyperbolic space occupies a half plane, as is shown in the upper part of the illustration. Its geometry is not Euclidean, wherein the shortest distance between two points is a straight line. Instead shortest distances are found along semicircles. In this illustration the hyperbolic space has been dissected into "triangular" regions that get smaller toward the bottom edge of the space. The triangles form the basis of a paradoxical decomposition of the space into three pieces that are colored dark gray, medium gray, and light gray. To mathematicians, in this context a "piece" may not be all of a piece, so to speak. It may be composed of an infinite number of fragments, triangular and otherwise.

The strange nature of the three pieces becomes most apparent when one views the hyperbolic space through a special mathematical porthole, that is, by projecting the space in two different ways onto a disk. The point labeled P in the hyperbolic space lies at the center of the left-hand disk and the point labeled I lies at the center of the right-hand disk.

In each disk a simple rotational symmetry involving the three pieces becomes evident. Consider the dark gray piece in the upper disk. If one imagines rotating the disk about its center by 120 degrees, or a third of a revolution, one sees that it would end up—fragment for fragment—on top of the light gray piece. Another 120-degree rotation would similarly match the dark gray piece with the medium gray one. In other words, all three pieces are congruent, and together the three pieces make up the entire hyperbolic space.

The paradoxical nature of the space becomes evident when one's attention turns to the lower disk. In this view of the very same space the dark gray piece is congruent to the other two pieces combined! To see this, merely imagine rotating the dark gray piece by 180 degrees, or half a revolution, about the disk's center. The dark gray piece will overlie exactly both the medium gray and the light gray piece. There is therefore a piece of two-dimensional hyperbolic space (the dark gray piece) that amounts simultaneously to a half and a third of the entire space.

The significance of this demonstration may have been lost in the mathematical shuffle. "Why," asks the reader, "should I be impressed?" The reason is that the three sets represented by the colored pieces are absolutely true congruences in hyperbolic space. The fact that the dark gray piece does not appear congruent to a half and a third of hyperbolic space at the same time on a single disk is a consequence of the distortions of hyperbolic space associated with such projections.

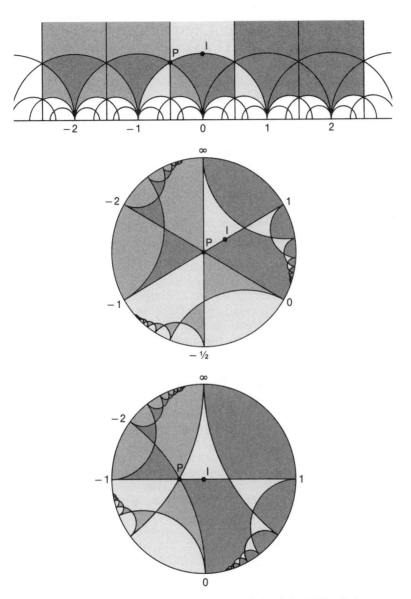

Two projections of hyperbolic space (*above*) on disks (*below*). The dark gray piece is both one-half and one-third of the hyperbolic space.

There is no need for hyperbole or hyperbolic spaces in proving the most general version of the Banach-Tarski paradox, however. The fact is that in Euclidean three-dimensional space (which approximates the world we live in) any two bodies that satisfy the most modest conditions imaginable are equidecomposable. Unfortunately the proof is nonconstructive: It gives almost no clue to precisely how one would go about demonstrating the equidecomposability of two unequal solid balls.

At this point I quote again from Lipof's letter:

> I spent many years studying the Banach-Tarski paradox and related results. What fascinated me most was the nonconstructive character of the proof in three dimensions. Although mathematicians know that in theory a solid ball can be taken apart into a finite number of pieces with which one can then construct another solid ball of twice the size, no one had any idea what the pieces might look like, because the cutting of the pieces is based on what set theorists call the axiom of choice.
>
> The axiom gets its name not because mathematicians prefer it to other axioms but because it postulates that for any collection of sets, no matter how big, there is a way of choosing an element from each set in the collection. Indeed, many mathematicians prefer not to invoke the axiom, because it does not stipulate just how the matching is done.
>
> No one, therefore, had any idea of what the pieces of a paradoxical decomposition might look like until I began to investigate the question. I mechanized the proof of the Banach-Tarski paradox. The proof specifies that the second (larger) ball can be assembled by rotating the pieces of the first ball in two ways about its center, somewhat like the situation in hyperbolic space. . . . These rotations carry each piece of the first ball to its corresponding place in the second ball. Knowing the points that make up each piece and the necessary rotations, it was easy to construct a backtracking routine to cut the different pieces from a solid ball. Whenever the proof invoked the axiom of choice, I merely relied on a random-number generator in my personal computer to choose which points of the ball were to be elements in which sets.
>
> To be honest, throughout this research I had no idea that I was headed in the direction of a matter fabricator. I am no fool: I know that normally one has to make a clear distinction between the ideal spaces of mathematics and the space we live in. But when I completed my first simulation of the Banach-Tarski theorem, I realized I had in hand something like a recipe for doubling the size of any solid.
>
> It occurred to me to try an experiment involving a real material, but I initially held back. The dimensions of the pieces produced by my program were all expressed in triple precision numbers, an accuracy that might well demand that I cut atoms in two in manufacturing the pieces! Besides, at this stage I was beginning to doubt my sanity: The idea of carrying out an

actual decomposition of a solid ball had given me a distinct feeling of unreality, as though I were living in a kind of dream.

Of course, I kept repeating to myself, it couldn't possibly work. But to no avail. I eventually reached a point where I couldn't put the experiment off any longer. I cashed in a good part of my life savings to buy 12 ounces of gold. I had the gold cast into a ball, bought a tiny jeweler's saw and began to cut the ball up according to my program's recipe. A second computer program was most useful in this process. It catalogued the size and shape of each piece. In particular, the second program told me where each piece was to go in the second sphere.

The entire experiment took seven months from start to finish. I worked nights and weekends. When at last I had finished cutting the pieces, I began assembling them into a second sphere of twice the diameter. It was delicate and demanding work. I nearly lost my eyesight and began to get headaches, but I persevered. Slowly the second ball took shape — but not as a smooth ball. The pieces did not fit as well as I had hoped. There were tiny spaces between the fragments I had so painfully and carefully put in place with tweezers.

After a few more weeks I finally completed the ball. I have sent you a drawing of the major joints on its surface (*see* illustration on page 97). Having your readers see the map gives nothing away: The surface of the ball is child's play compared with the intricate arrangement of its interior pieces. In any event, the actual ball was not as smooth and round as my picture implies. It was lumpy and irregular — downright ugly. But how I clutched the cloth bag that contained it on my way to the jeweler! The ultimate test of all my work, of course, would be to melt the ball down and find out whether I was indeed the owner of up to eight times as much pure elemental gold as I had started out with.

The next day the jeweler handed me a bar of pure gold weighing 49.58 ounces. It was less than I had expected; those interstitial spaces had taken their toll. Yet the thing was no longer in doubt. The world's first practical application of the Banach-Tarski paradox had been made. For days I staggered around like a drunk, reeling from my discovery. At this point I am not sure what to do next.

After the first letter I received no further correspondence from Lipof for several months. Then one day last November the mailman brought me a short missive from him, postmarked in a South American country:

You will no doubt be happy to learn that I have to some extent automated the procedure of producing large balls of gold from small ones. With the remainder of my life savings I have set up shop in the little town of _____. Here a few loyal employees assemble gold balls. There is a workroom lined with computers and with tables at which my people assemble the balls. The pieces are now not cut out but rather are cast directly and worked by my employees. There is always excess gold at the end of the process with which to begin anew. We produce approximately five pounds of gold a week from nothing. Is this not the philosopher's stone?

The time will soon come to move on. I do not think I will write again; To communicate with you is dangerous. Excuse me, my friend, but one becomes paranoid in the presence of such potential. There is much that I need to do!

I have not heard anything more from Lipof. But in December, 1988, out of curiosity, I began to track the price of gold from day to day. For nearly three months it has been in a slow but steady decline. Perhaps that is the ultimate proof for those who thought the Banach-Tarski paradox was merely a plaything of mathematicians.

I have, of course, been in touch with other mathematicians on the subject of the paradox. I owe a particular debt of gratitude to Bruno W. Augenstein of the Rand Corporation in Santa Monica, Calif. It was Augenstein who suggested that I use hyperbolic space as an example of the paradoxical properties of space.

Although he does not subscribe to Lipof's claims, Augenstein does concede that there may well be a relation between the Banach-Tarski paradox and the real world. One of Augenstein's papers, "Hadron Physics and Transfinite Set Theory," points out a relation between particle physics and paradoxical decompositions of objects in three-dimensional space. The paper suggests analogies that "give directly a large number of known physical results and suggest additional ones testable in principle. The quark color label and the phenomenon of quark confinement . . . have immediate explanations via analogies with the decomposition theorems." This much might interest the physicists, if not the alchemists, among the readers of this column.

ADDENDUM

My discussion of the subject of matter fabrication which appeared in SCIENTIFIC AMERICAN in April, 1989, brought a gratifying response from the great majority of readers who recognized that "Arlo Lipof" is an anagram of "April Fool." The column featured two methods of matter fabrication, both based on paradoxes, one fake and the other real. The first method involved cutting up an 8-by-8-inch square into four pieces and then reassembling them to obtain a 5-by-13-inch rectangle. If the operation is applied to a square gold bar, the excess gold amounts to an immediate increase in wealth.

Most readers solved the "paradox" by examining the diagram of cuts very closely. The reassembly shown in the illustration is faked (as Lipof clearly stated). If one cuts out the requisite pieces and attempts to reassemble the rectangle, a narrow gap shows up in the middle of the figure. Its area is exactly one square inch. Hence, the first paradox is no paradox at all but an old chestnut that I first discovered in the charming book *Tangrams — 330 Puzzles*, by Ronald C. Read (*see* Further Readings).

The second paradox is perfectly real even if, contrary to Lipof's claims, it cannot be applied to matter fabrication. The Banach-Tarski paradox states that it is possible to cut a solid sphere into a finite number of pieces in such a way that the pieces can be reassembled into an equally solid sphere of twice the volume! The exclamation mark may not seem fully deserved to those readers who realize that the "pieces" are not at all simple and are best described as mathematical sets.

The illustration accompanying my description of the paradox was adapted from the book *The Banach-Tarski Paradox*, by Stan Wagon of Smith College (*see* Further Readings). In the illustration, two-dimensional hyperbolic space is projected in two different ways onto a flat disk. It provides a visual demonstration of the paradoxical nature of the space. Three sets are shown, any one of which is simultaneoulsy equal to one half and one third of the space! The theorem underlying the illustration is the result of the joint work of Wagon and Jan Mycielski of the University of Colorado at Boulder.

The Banach-Tarski paradox actually made headlines recently in mathematical circles, since it is related to the work of Miklós Laczkovich of Loránd Eötvös University in Budapest (*see* "Science and the Citizen"; Scientific American, July, 1989). Laczkovich has proved that a circular disk can be decomposed into finitely many pieces (fewer than 10^{50}, in fact) that can then be reassembled into a square with no space left over.

Finally, a postscript on the April fool anagram-tangram gold scam. In "Paradoxical Gold" I quoted extensively from my correspondence with a shadowy character by the name of Arlo Lipof. Lipof maintained that he had driven down the price of gold by applying the Banach-Tarski theorem to make gold out of nothing. Recently I received an angry letter from the so-called International Gold Council in New York

City in which I am held accountable for the "turmoil" and the "collapse of civilization" that might now result from the divulgence of Lipof's secret.

"For years the I.G.C. has made the Banach-Tarski paradox inaccessible to the general public. . . . We have always known that the apocalyptic reality of making more gold from less gold would have dire consequences for the international balance of world monetary systems."

Deus Ex Machina

A s recently as the Renaissance, alchemists believed that the right mixture of ingredients (too disgusting to mention here) would produce living creatures. Some modern alchemy is afoot in the study called "Artificial Life." Some scientists now believe that lifelike phenomena spring more or less naturally from the right combination of independent, automatistic behaviors. Dozens, hundreds, or even thousands of individual units may interact in a very simple way, yet produce collectively quite complicated behavior. In fact, the interactions sum to a behavior that is greater than its parts. The magian imperative rules again!

The famous Lindenmayer systems, for example, produce plants that grow in a natural way by the application of simple interactions to their parts. Each cell, depending on its type, may replace itself by a few new cells in certain configurations. The plants, called graftals, spring forth in a landscape dominated by fractal mountains. All of this takes place in the magic machines at Pixar Computers. But some scenes can be coaxed out of personal computers.

If artificial life results from the interaction of parts, it is no surprise to find cellular automata playing a major role. The hodgepodge machine is a cellular automaton that was discovered by two West German magians. It simulates certain self-sustaining chemical reactions of a kind that are suspected to underlie the origin of life itself. Ripples of activity spread across the cellular space, forming bizarre curlicues and arcs. Even more astonishing are the goings on in a place called "cellular space." Here David Griffeath, a Wisconsin mathemagician, has discovered a four-stage scenario that begins with a disordered world and progresses to primordial droplets that give way, ultimately, to great spiral crystals that revolve as they grow. Are they in any sense alive?

What happens when we release a series of randomly walking particles from the edge of the computer screen? Nothing much unless we add one simple ingredient: a rule that if a wandering particle meets a fixed one, it too suddenly becomes fixed. Starting with but one fixed particle in the center of the screen, strange, riotous growths that look like fractal algae emerge before our very eyes.

As Mark Twain once remarked, college professors may evolve from amebae. The next *deus ex machina* is a computer party with human invitees. The humans are specified by the distances they prefer to keep from one another in social situations. We may watch from above as a roomful of wildly different simulated humans move restlessly between a snack table and various conversational knots in an endless (and in most cases, hopeless) search for social equilibrium. Lifelike? Sometimes!

Higher yet in the chain of being, we may coax protozoan forms to evolve as we look on. A California high-school teacher once mixed some strange, randomly moving pretend protozoa with purple bacteria that appeared randomly all over his screen. Given the simplest imaginable genetic apparatus, the protozoa evolved into efficient feeders. But even as the bacteria were eaten off the screen, strange genetic diseases, like the "twirlies," developed.

∘ 10 ∘

Fractal Mountains and Graftal Plants

I can readily imagine the first full-fledged, feature-length motion picture generated by computer. The year is 2001. I stumble down the aisle while carrying an oversize bucket of synthetic popcorn and a soft drink containing a few additives that make all the usual ingredients unnecessary. The house lights dim, the curtains part, and the silver screen comes alive with an adaptation of J. R. R. Tolkien's *The Lord of the Rings* trilogy. Frodo the Hobbit strolls through an open glen. In the distance jagged, snow-capped mountain peaks thrust into the sky. In the foreground exotic trees and plants of unknown species shimmer in the sunlight. The scene changes to a wizard gazing into a crystal ball. In the center of the sphere a fortress appears, flames leaping from its battlements.

Although it is hard to say just how convincingly Frodo will walk and talk in such a film, I am convinced that the mountains, the plants, the crystal ball, and the flames will all come off magnificently. The success will be due largely to the pioneering software and hardware of a company called Pixar, formerly the Lucasfilm Computer Graphics Laboratory. After visiting this fascinating hub of computer graphics in San Rafael, Calif., I am ready to share with readers the innermost secrets of mountains and trees. Anyone with a home computer can now generate images that closely resemble such objects. Space limitations preclude an extensive treatment of crystal balls and fire, but I shall lay bare the basic principles of generating them.

In the hypothetical film described the camera might zoom in on the snowy peaks behind Frodo. Never would a more forbidding land mass be seen. Each large peak consists of smaller peaks, which are composed of still smaller ones, and so on: an infinite regress of peaklets. Even an orc—that gargoylelike beast with leathery feet—would be uncomfortable standing on the rough slopes.

It is easy in principle to generate such a mountain range. For simplicity I assume that the terrain covers a triangular area. One then subdivides the triangle into four smaller triangles by finding the midpoint of each side and joining the new points by three line segments. Each triangle is then subdivided in the same way. The process is continued until the limits of resolution or of computation time are reached. The result—a rather boring lattice of triangles—can be enlivened by mixing in some vertical action: Each time a new midpoint is added to the scene one displaces it upward or downward by a random amount. The random displacements, which must in general be decreased as the triangles become smaller, transform the triangles into crumpled peaks and folds (*see* illustration at the right).

Why should such a technique produce natural-looking mountains? The answer may lie in part with the fact that the process yields a fractal: a type of object that reveals more detail as it is increasingly magnified. Fractals are seemingly seen throughout nature. One may use coastlines to illustrate the basic idea. Imagine being asked to measure the French coastline with a measuring stick one kilometer long. One swings the stick end over end in a ponderous march along the shore and counts the number of kilometers. Many small bays and points are missed, however, so that the final length as measured in this way is not strictly accurate. Repeating the exercise with a meter stick produces a more accurate, longer measurement. But even in this case a large number of miniature embayments and spits are missed. No doubt a centimeter stick would be more accurate.

As a general rule, the measured length of the coastline increases as the measuring stick becomes smaller. The relation between the measured length and the size of the stick is a special number. It is called a fractal dimension. A fractal dimension differs from an ordinary dimension in that it is usually expressed as a fraction, not as a whole number. The

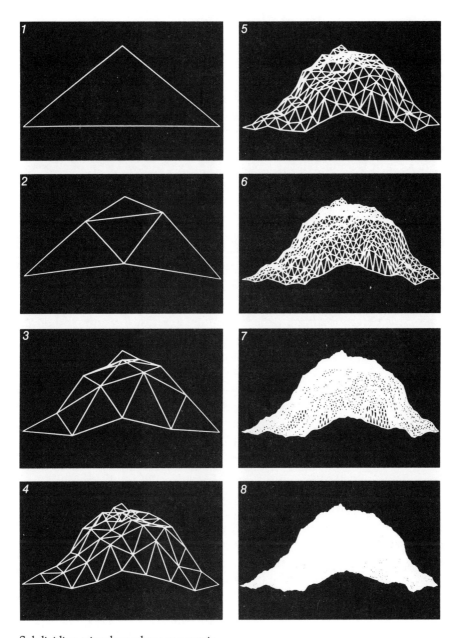

Subdividing triangles makes a mountain

coastline in question might, for instance, have a fractal dimension of 3/2. Such a shape can be thought of an intermediate between a shape that has one dimension (a straight line) and a shape that has two dimensions (a plane). If a coastline were relatively straight, its fractal dimension would be close to 1; if a coastline were very rough, its fractal dimension would approach 2 as it attempted to fill a two-dimensional plane.

The fractal model of nature implies an infinite regress of detail. From the perspective of computer graphics the question of infinite regress is a red herring; it is enough if the landscape appears to have detail at all levels of magnification. Up to the limits of screen resolution the mountains to be generated have features as fine as the final triangles used in the subdivision described above (*see* Color Plate 7). Although the complete mountain-drawing algorithm is too long and involved to describe here at a useful level of detail, there is a simple program called MOUNTAIN that draws Mount Mandelbrot in cross section. MOUNTAIN illustrates the essential idea of randomly displacing subdivision points along a vertical axis. The fractal artist begins with a single, horizontal line segment. The midpoint is determined and deflected up or down by a random amount. Each of the two resulting line segments is then subdivided and perturbed. The process can be continued in a manner analogous to the triangle-sub-division technique.

MOUNTAIN maintains two arrays called *points* and *lines* to keep track of the mountainous profile. Each array has two columns and enough rows (say 2,048) to accommodate handily one's screen resolution. The two columns of *points* contain coordinates and the two columns of *lines* contain indexes; each line is specified as the pair of positions in the array *points* that designate the coordinates of the line's endpoints. Because it is interesting to watch the successive subdivisions form a mountainous outline from an unpromising polygon, MOUNTAIN puts each generation under the user's control. At the end of a single, main loop the program asks the user if another iteration is wanted. If the answer is yes, execution branches back again to the head of the program.

The main loop converts the current sets of points and lines into new sets that are twice as large. To do this it scans *lines* one row at a time, looks up the indexes of the corresponding points and retrieves their coordinates from *points*. Armed with the coordinates of a given line's endpoints, the program computes the coordinates of the line's midpoint, altering the y coordinate randomly in the process. The following algorithmic listing provides an adequate basis for a program. In it the variables j and k point to the rows of *points* and *lines* that are currently being filled with the latest results of subdivision. The variables *pts* and *lns* record the numbers of points and lines making up the mountain before the main loop is entered. Initially *j* is equal to *pts* and *k* is equal to *lns*. The index *i* runs from 1 to *lns*.

$$j \leftarrow j + 1$$
$$k \leftarrow k + 1$$
$$a \leftarrow lines(i,1)$$
$$b \leftarrow lines(i,2)$$
$$x1 \leftarrow points(a,1)$$
$$y1 \leftarrow points(a,2)$$
$$x2 \leftarrow points(b,1)$$
$$y2 \leftarrow points(b,2)$$
$$points(j,1) \leftarrow (x1 + x2)/2$$
$$points(j,2) \leftarrow (y1 + y2)/2 + random(range)$$
$$lines(i,2) \leftarrow j$$
$$lines(k,1) \leftarrow j$$
$$lines(k,2) \leftarrow b$$

This part of MOUNTAIN is largely self-explanatory. When the coordinates of the *j*th point have been computed, the index *j* is stored as the second point of the *i*th line and the first point of the *k*th line. The first point of the *i*th line is the same as before and the second point of the *k*th line is identical with the original second point of the *i*th line, namely the one with index *b*. When the loop is finally computed, *pts* and *lns* must be reset to the latest values of *j* and *k* respectively. The variable *range* is initially set by the user as the maximum amount of vertical randomness that can be given to the subdivision point. Each time the loop is completed this variable must be divided by 2 in order to keep the random fluctuations in scale with the size of the features being varied. The function *random(range)* is intended to express the selection of a random number between 0 and the current value of *range*.

If the mountains behind Frodo seem impressive, the trees and plants that surround him are no less so. They are both realistic and eerie. They seem real because they have branching patterns similar to those of actual plants. They seem eerie because they are not familiar species; the graphic designer has so many parameters available that he or she cannot resist the temptation to create something new.

The new "species" are called graftal plants, because they are based on graphs and have an implicit fractal nature. By implicit fractal nature I mean that the rules for generating the plant's basic topology could be (but are not) applied to the limit of resolution of the screen. In short, a twig does not regress indefinitely into twiglets. Once the graph underlying a plant has been developed, it can be converted into a myriad of convincing species by interpreting the graph in terms of size, color, thickness, texture and so on.

The graphs that underlie a given plant are produced by *L* systems, a class of grammars introduced by the Danish biologist and mathematician Aristid Lindenmayer in 1968. An *L* system is essentially a set of rules for deriving new strings of symbols from old ones. The rules involve substituting sequences of symbols for single symbols. For example, using the numbers 0 and 1 and the symbols [and] one can generate a wide range of complex botanical forms with the following rules:

$$0 \rightarrow 1[0]1[0]0$$
$$1 \rightarrow 11$$
$$[\rightarrow [$$
$$] \rightarrow]$$

To see how the rules work, suppose one starts with the string consisting of a single 0. For each left-hand symbol from the list one substitutes its corresponding right-hand symbol to obtain the following strings in succession:

0

1[0]1[0]0

11[1[0]1[0]0]11[1[0]1[0]0]1[0]1[0]0

Such strings can be converted into treelike graphs by treating each number (0 or 1) as a line segment and each bracket as a branch point. Both 0 and 1 segments are equal in length; they are typically distinguished from each other by making all 1 segments bare and placing a leaf at the outer end of each 0 segment.

The stem (or trunk) of the 1[0]1[0]0 string, for instance, consists of the three symbols not in brackets; a 1 segment is surmounted by a second 1 segment and topped off with a 0 segment. Two branches, each consisting of a single 0 segment, sprout from this formula. The first branch is attached above the first segment and the second is attached above the second segment. Before studying the illustration at the right, readers might enjoy drawing the first few generations of the structure. For the sake of realism, additional interpretive features can be added to the

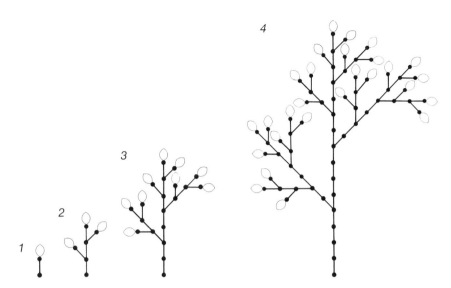

Four generations of a graftal plant

model. One might specify that for any given stem (irrespective of whether it is the main one or not) the branches should shoot off alternately to the left and right. Not wanting to impose anything more arduous on those readers who would like to program graftals, I am happy to suggest mere stick figures for plants. The professionals at Pixar convert the grammar just described into beautiful plants such as the ones in Color Plate 8.

A two-part program called PLANT generates the nth string in the sequence above and then renders it as a line drawing. In its first phase PLANT maintains the strings it generates in two symbol arrays known as *stringA* and *stringB*. Each generation of plants occupies one of the two arrays in an alternate manner: The generation in one array is derived from the previous generation in the other. It is not strictly necessary to store symbols in these arrays; the numbers 0, 1, 2, and 3 will do nicely as long as the program substitutes correctly.

The L-system rules are embodied in conditional statements. For example, the following bit of algorithmic code can be adapted to convert a 0 in the ith position of *stringA* into nine new symbols in *stringB*:

$$\text{IF } stringA(i) = 0, \text{ THEN}$$
$$string\ B(j) \leftarrow 1$$
$$string\ B(j+1) \leftarrow 2$$
$$string\ B(j+2) \leftarrow 0$$
$$string\ B(j+3) \leftarrow 3$$
$$string\ B(j+4) \leftarrow 1$$
$$string\ B(j+5) \leftarrow 2$$
$$string\ B(j+6) \leftarrow 0$$
$$string\ B(j+7) \leftarrow 3$$
$$string\ B(j+8) \leftarrow 0$$
$$j \leftarrow j + 9$$

Here 0 and 1 stand for themselves while 2 and 3 stand for [and] respectively. If the ith symbol of *stringA* is 0, then the program installs the sequence 1, 2, 0, 3, 1, 2, 0, 3, 0 in nine consecutive positions of the array *stringB* starting at index j (the first position of the latter array that has not yet been filled). A single loop in the first phase of PLANT contains four such conditional statements, one for each possible symbol encountered. The loop uses the index j as a reference to the symbol of the present generation currently being processed. The loop is executed for as many generations as the graftal artist wishes. At each stage PLANT may question the user whether or not another (longer) string of symbols is wanted.

The second, or graphic, phase of PLANT converts the string produced by the first phase into a drawing. It does this recursively. As long as no left bracket, or 2, is encountered, it draws a sequence of line segments in a given direction. When a left bracket of a given pair is scanned, the program draws the next line segments in a new direction, 45 degrees counterclockwise from the previous one. The end of the procedure is signaled by the appearance of the corresponding right bracket; here a leaf (whose shape and color I leave entirely to the reader's whim) can be drawn. The appearance of a second left bracket causes the process to repeat, except that now the new direction is 45 degrees clockwise. The rest is automatic.

PLANT uses a scaling factor that depends on the complexity of the plant being drawn. The nth generation, for example, is approximately 2^n segments high. If the screen is 200 pixels high, segments must be shorter than $200/2^n$. Ambitious readers will undoubtedly attempt variations in the generating grammar, branch angles, and leaf shapes. If such variations are run on the same screen, landscapes of plants and trees (not very realistic, admittedly) will appear.

The crystal ball in the hypothetical Tolkien film would be made by means of a technique called ray tracing; the flaming battlements would be simulated by tracking the motion of a large system of particles.

Ray tracing requires one to specify both the three-dimensional geometry of a scene and the position of a light source. When light leaves a source, it embarks on a complicated history of reflections and refractions. The eye of an observer standing in the scene will intercept some of the rays of light streaming from the source but will miss many—in fact most—of the others. To save computing time and power, the ray-tracing technique works in the opposite direction. Imagine for a moment that light leaves the eye instead. A wide bundle of rays fans out into the scene. If a ray strikes a reflecting or refracting surface, it zooms off in a new direction determined by the laws of optics. Ultimately the ray will strike an absorbing surface, and it takes on whatever color is assigned there. That color is recorded at the pixel corresponding to the direction of the original ray.

An example of an image generated by the ray-tracing technique is the surface of billiard balls. A relatively simple history is experienced by the rays traced in the billiard-ball scene. On the surface of the balls we might nonetheless see reflections of the interior of a poolroom and a man holding a cue as he stands and watches the shot.

The large system of particles that might be used to generate the flaming battlements is a logical outgrowth of the little clouds of dots that symbolize miniature explosions in video and computer games. A particle system at Pixar is much more sophisticated than such chicanery, however. Within a certain region a host of particles live, move, and have their being. Under computer control, each particle is a point that moves according to prescribed dynamics. Born at some time, it is allowed to move for a while, perhaps even giving birth to new particles. Then it may die.

Particle systems were spectacularly featured in a scene from the film *Star Trek II—The Wrath of Khan*. A Genesis bomb is dropped on a dead, cratered planet. The bomb creates a ring of strange, sparkling flames that eventually engulf the planet. When they finally die out, we see the surface transformed into a lush biosphere. The effect was produced by Pixar in its earlier incarnation as the Lucasfilm Computer Graphics Laboratory. The expanding ring of fire consisted of particle systems in which some particles gave birth to entire new systems. The new systems featured particles shooting upward from the planet's surface, changing color and even falling back again under the influence of gravity.

Alvy Ray Smith, who directs research and development at Pixar, took me on a tour of the company when I visited San Rafael. Smith is familiar to SCIENTIFIC AMERICAN readers for his work with cellular automata (*see* "Mathematical Games," February, 1971, and "Computer Recreations," August, 1985). In addition to Smith, who pioneered the graftal approach to computer plant life, I met Loren Carpenter, who specializes in fractal mountains, Robert L. Cook, an expert in ray tracing, and William Reeves, the originator of particle systems. In the middle of a discussion about graphics software, Smith surprised me by saying that the company's main business is not so much the production of special effects for Hollywood as it is the manufacture of a special-purpose graphics computer called, naturally enough, the Pixar Image Computer.

At the heart of the Pixar Image Computer is a 24-megabyte, 2,000-by-2,000 pixel memory. That is more than enough resolution for most applications. Each pixel, moreover, is represented by 48 bits of memory, enough to store copious information about color and transparency. The Pixar's massive memory is managed by four parallel, high-speed processors that are fully programmable. They can execute approximately 40 million instructions per second, a speed several orders of magnitude greater than that of ordinary computers. A video-display unit communicates with memory at a speed of 480 million bytes per second.

The first Pixars were shipped in May, 1986. They are employed in medical imaging, remote sensing, engineering design, and animation. Perhaps they will even be used to generate my hypothetical film.

ADDENDUM

I was charged with incompetence by William J. Slattery of Jamestown, R.I., after "Fractal Mountains and Graftal Plants" first appeared in SCIENTIFIC AMERICAN in December, 1986. What appears to be a fractal mountain drawn by the method of triangular subdivision is shown on page 109. According to Slattery, I did not have the wit to recognize Sherlock Holmes's hat when I saw it. For misleading readers I may even be apprehended by the great detective himself. There is, after all, no police like Holmes.

John McCarthy, an eminent computer scientist at Stanford University, has a more serious comment on the concept of fractal mountains. He notes that real mountains, which are formed by erosion, have many well-developed river valleys. Fractal mountains, on the other hand, do not share such features and would, in fact, be full of lakes. Is the resemblance of fractal mountains to real mountains merely an optical illusion? McCarthy warns against the acceptance of fractal objects as models for real ones without further investigation.

The cross-sectional object I called Mount Mandelbrot might not be a single mountain but an entire range of mountains. Graphic output sent to me by Ken Wright of Grayling, Mich., bears out this conclusion. One way back to singular orogeny is to take some care with the random deflection in the line segments that make up Mount Mandelbrot's profile; if the deflection is biased in the upward direction, rather than being allowed to range up or down with equal probability, one may see a more impressive peak develop.

The program outlined for Mount Mandelbrot wasted some memory by requiring two arrays to hold alternate generations of points constituting successive subdivisions of the mountain's profile. Richard E. Lang of Lincoln Center, Mass., finds a single array is sufficient. Essentially the same algorithm I suggested can be easily converted to make use of the single-profile array as the basis for its own subdivision, so to speak.

∘ 11 ∘

Hodgepodge Reactions

Cellular automata, computer models based on arrays of multivalued cells, have spread like a wave through physics, mathematics, and other sciences. Now a new cellular automaton has literally been making waves of its own. Called the hodgepodge machine by its designers, it imitates chemical reactions with a precision rarely seen in other models.

The reactions the hodgepodge machine simulates take place in excitable chemical mediums: two or more compounds that can dissociate and recombine in the presence of a catalyst. If the chemical states of the reactants have different colors, wavelike structures can be seen that propagate along simple or intricate frontiers in endless pursuit of an elusive equilibrium.

Does the automaton itself serve as an adequate physical explanation for the waves observed in actual reactions? This question now occupies the hodgepodge machine's creators, Martin Gerhardt and Heike Schuster of the University of Bielefeld in West Germany, along with an increasing number of colleagues at other universities.

A cellular automaton can be thought of as an infinite grid of square cells that advance through time in step with discrete ticks of an imaginary clock. At any given tick each cell is in one of a finite number of states.

The state of a cell at tick $t + 1$ depends in a fairly simple way on the states of the cells in its immediate neighborhood at the previous tick, t. The dependence is expressed in a set of rules that apply equally to all the cells in the grid. By applying the rules each time the clock ticks, an arbitrary initial configuration of states among the cells can be made to change and thus evolve with time. In some cases extraordinary patterns develop, prompting observers to believe that given the right initial configuration a cellular automaton could produce something capable of organizing itself, growing, and reproducing — in short, something "living."

The cellular automaton best known to readers is probably the famous game of Life invented in the 1960's by the mathematician John Horton Conway of the University of Cambridge. In Life each cell has only two possible states: alive and dead. The rules of Life are very simple. If a cell is dead at time t, it will come to life at time $t + 1$ if exactly three of its neighbors are alive at time t. If a cell is alive at time t, it will die at time $t + 1$ if fewer than two or more than three of its neighbors are alive at time t. These two rules are sufficient for the Life cellular automaton to display an amazing variety of behavior that depends entirely on the configuration of dead and alive cells with which one starts (*see* "Computer Recreations," SCIENTIFIC AMERICAN, May, 1985, and February, 1987).

The hodgepodge machine is not one cellular automaton but many. A particular version is chosen by specifying a number of parameters such as the number of states. If there are $n + 1$ states, each possible state of a cell can be represented by a number between 0 and n. Gerhardt and Schuster extend Conway's metaphor to describe the states of the cells in their machine. A cell in state 0 is said to be "healthy" and a cell in state n is said to be "ill." All states in between exhibit a degree of "infection" corresponding to their state number; the closer a cell's state number gets to n, the more infected the cell becomes. The hodgepodge machine selectively applies one of three rules to each cell, depending on whether it is healthy, ill, or infected.

If the cell is healthy (that is to say, in the 0 state), at the next tick of the clock it will have a new state that depends on the number of infected cells, A, and the number of ill cells, B, currently in its neighborhood and on two parameters labeled $k1$ and $k2$. To be specific, the state of the cell at time $t + 1$ is given by the following formula:

$$[A/k1] + [B/k2].$$

A pair of square brackets designates a rounding-down process applied to the fraction it contains. If, for example, $A/k1$ happens to equal 2.725, the square brackets reduce that number to 2. If the formula happens to yield a 0, the cell will of course remain healthy—at least for the time being.

If the cell is infected, its condition generally worsens with time. Its state at time $t + 1$ is the sum of two numbers: the degree of infection in the cell's neighborhood at time t and an unvarying quantity, g, that governs how quickly infection tends to spread among the cells. One may change g between runs. Try integer values between 1 and 20. The degree of infection is calculated by dividing S, the sum of the state numbers of the cell and of its neighbors, by A, the number of infected neighbors, including the cell itself. A cell in an infected state at time t therefore takes on at time $t + 1$ a state given by the formula

$$[S/A] + g.$$

The infected cell cannot get "sicker" than n, however. If it happens that the number given by the formula exceeds n, then n is taken to be the new state of the cell.

Finally, if the cell is ill (in state n) at time t, it miraculously becomes healthy (takes on a state of 0) at $t + 1$.

In addition to those three rules, a definition of what constitutes a cell's "neighborhood" is necessary. Two types of neighborhood have historically been used in cellular automatons: the von Neumann neighborhood and the Moore neighborhood. The von Neumann neighborhood of a particular cell consists of the four cells that share the cell's edges. The Moore neighborhood of a particular cell includes the cells in the von Neumann neighborhood and also the four cells that just touch the cell's corners—a total of eight cells. Given the three rules and the definition of a cell's neighborhood, the Gerhardt-Schuster cellular automaton is completely defined by specifying the values of four parameters: n, the number of states minus 1; $k1$ and $k2$, the "weighting" parameters for healthy cells; and g, the speed of infection.

A sample experiment done by Gerhardt and Schuster on a 20-by-20 grid using von Neumann neighborhoods reveals the typical behavior of hodgepodge machines. (Cells at the edge of the grid abide by the same rules that prevail elsewhere in the cellular automaton; they just have fewer cells in their neighborhood.) The parameters n, $k1$, and $k2$ were fixed respectively to the values of 100, 2, and 3. Four types of behavior emerged at different values of the parameter *g*. In a typical trial run Gerhardt and Schuster gave the 400 cells in the 20-by-20 grid a random initial configuration of states, specified a value of *g*, and let the hodge-podge machine loose for 10,000 computational cycles. Because one-dimensional data are easier to analyze than two-dimensional images, Gerhardt and Schuster recorded only the number of infected cells at each cycle in order to present their results in graphs like those below.

Not much happened to this hodgepodge machine at low *g* values. Apart from a few initial fluctuations, activity among the cells tended to die out; the cells became boringly and everlastingly healthy. But as *g* was increased, strange things began to happen. To begin with, most of the cells became infected and remained so, although there were irregular and random appearances of healthy cells. Gerhardt and Schuster labeled this type of behavior Type 1.

The next type of behavior they observed was labeled Type 2. It featured a generally regular series of infection "plateaus" roughly 30 cycles long, punctuated by the appearance of large numbers of healthy cells.

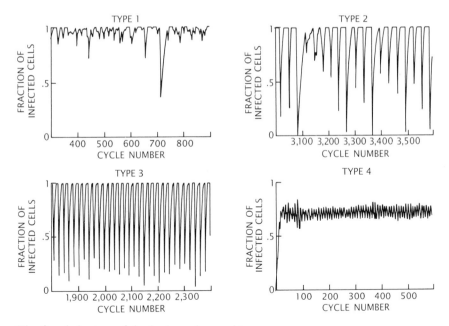

The four behaviors of the hodgepodge machine

(Sometimes nearly all 400 cells became healthy only to experience a new wave of infection.) As g was increased still further, Type 3 behavior appeared. It was heralded by the onset of a very regular alternation between saturation and virtual disappearance of infected cells every 20 cycles or so. Finally, Type 4 behavior emerged: Within a few cycles of start-up the number of infected cells would fluctuate with some regularity about a saturation value of approximately 75 percent.

The four types of behavior appeared in order as g was progressively increased, but with some overlap: Runs with transition values of g sometimes resulted in one type of behavior and sometimes in another type. In certain cases Gerhardt and Schuster even witnessed transitions between behaviors in a single run.

The four behaviors represent the appearance of specific types of wave patterns that are shown in the illustration at the right. In those color images the grid sizes vary from 100-by-100 cells to 500-by-500 cells. Waves associated with Type 1 behavior traveled only a short distance before dying out. Type 2 waves traveled outward in circular bands that varied greatly in width. Type 3 waves displayed the same circular shape but were more regular, in keeping with the regular ups and downs of infected cells displayed in its graph. Finally, Type 4 waves followed a spiral pattern that spread out from the center of the grid. As always, readers with computers are urged to repeat the experiment in some form. Waves of thought are sure to accompany the waves on one's screen.

Some of the wave patterns generated by the hodgepodge machine are similar to those displayed by a variety of chemical systems; certain ones in particular are dead ringers for the chemical waves found in the well-known Belousov-Zhabotinsky reaction. Compare, for example, the complex pattern of curlicues in the computer-generated image with the photograph of the Belousov-Zhabotinsky reaction in the illustration on page 124.

To what do we owe this similarity? Gerhardt and Schuster were not exactly surprised by it; they had deliberately designed the hodgepodge machine to mimic the features of a particular kind of "heterogeneous catalytic reaction" in which carbon monoxide and oxygen combine to form carbon dioxide while adsorbed at the surface of thousands of tiny palladium crystallites dispersed throughout a porous medium. Heat given off as the oxidation reaction proceeds changes the state of the catalyst. An abrupt phase transition by the crystallite liberates the carbon monoxide

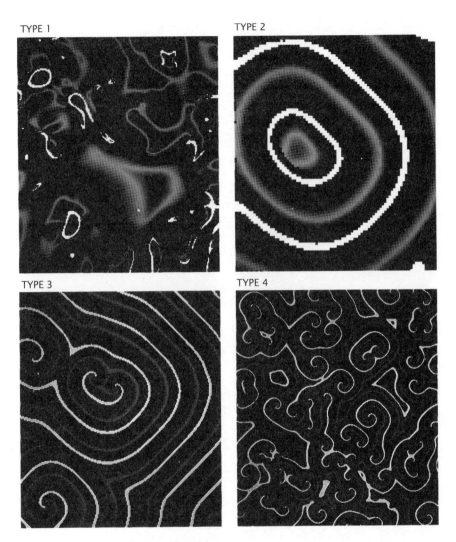

TYPE 1

TYPE 2

TYPE 3

TYPE 4

The hodgepodge machine produces distinctive wave patterns

adsorbed at its surface; the catalyst then abruptly cools and the reaction begins anew.

The hodgepodge machine proved capable of mimicking not only this reaction but also the Belousov-Zhabotinsky reaction quite well. In the Belousov-Zhabotinsky reaction malonic acid is oxidized by potassium

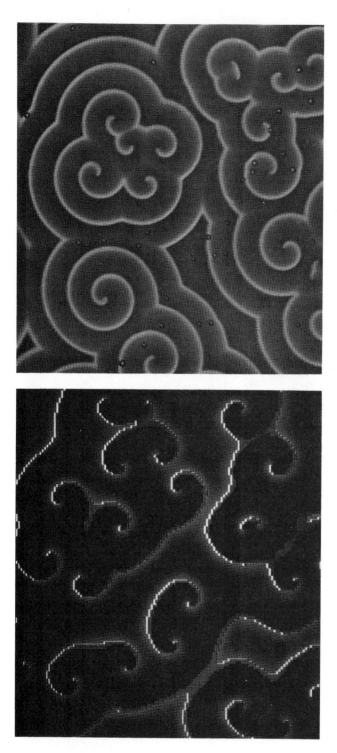

Wave phenomena in a Belousov-Zhabotinsky chemical reaction
(*top*) and their hodgepodge counterparts (*bottom*)

bromate in the presence of a catalyst such as cerium or iron. The grid cells of the hodgepodge machine in essence represent the catalyst particles, and the infection metaphor expresses the gradual saturation of the particles' surfaces.

But the analogy is not quite so simple; there are some subtleties here. For one thing, in the hodgepodge machine adjacent cells interact by exchanging infection, so to speak. How do the catalyst particles exchange reactivity? Gerhardt and Schuster reasoned that, at least in the case of the carbon monoxide oxidation, the participating catalyst units influence their neighbors by means of two basic mechanisms. A given unit could be made more reactive by the transfer of heat from a more active neighboring unit or by the diffusion of carbon monoxide from a less active neighbor.

The interaction between neighboring cells in the hodgepodge machine makes it possible for them to synchronize their activities. After a period of initial random disorganization (the hodgepodge phase), the patterns that appear reflect this synchronization. The same is presumably true of the actual chemical reactions as well. Does the hodgepodge machine thus explain the appearance of waves of excitation in the reactions it simulates?

There will be those who are ready to exclaim "Of course!" and to point to the pictures as evidence. But then, there are people who see a cellular automaton in everything. In April, 1988, *The Atlantic* carried an article about the cosmic ramblings of Edward Fredkin. A computer businessman and sometime academic, Fredkin supposes our universe to be composed of cells that tick from state to state like a vast cellular automaton. To be kind, the evidence for such an arrangement is not overwhelming. The hodgepodge machine is doubtless significant, but the attitude of its discoverers is more so. In spite of the fact that the hodgepodge machine simulates the Belousov-Zhabotinsky reaction remarkably well, Gerhardt and Schuster do not claim that chemistry is cellular. Instead they see their automaton as an approximation tool, the discrete version of a partial differential equation.

Originally inspired by the work of chemists Nils Jaeger and Peter Plath of the University of Bremen, Gerhardt and Schuster along with their mentor at Bielefeld, Andreas W. M. Dress, have enlisted the help of two chemists in studying the hodgepodge machine: S. C. Müller of the Max Planck Institute for Nutritional Physiology in Dortmund and John J. Tyson of the Virginia Polytechnic Institute and State University. The creators of the machine want to show that an array of chemical oscillators that interact locally according to certain simple rules will inevitably generate waves. Presumably there are only a small number of possible wave patterns, although they become far more complicated in three dimensions, according to Tyson. Because three-dimensional wavefronts are much harder to see in laboratory glassware, computer simulations may tell chemists what to look for. In science the trick is to use models well, not to be used by them.

Readers who would like to build their own hodgepodge machine have already received ample hints on how to proceed. One must declare an array of appropriate size and incorporate it into a grand loop that updates the array according to the three rules and then displays it for the edification of local hodgepodgers. Each element of the array must contain the state number for a particular cell. In computing the updated array, however, it is necessary to store the results temporarily in another array until the computation is complete. Then a simple double loop allows wholesale replacement of the original array by the updated one.

The updating is also carried out by a double loop. Two index variables, say *i* and *j*, count off the cells of the grid. For each cell given by the coordinates (*i,j*), the program (can we call it anything but HODGEPODGE?) decides by means of a pair of "if" statements whether the cell is healthy or infected. If it is healthy, the first formula is evaluated. If it is infected, the second formula is evaluated. In either case the states of the cells in its neighborhood must be checked. If the cell is neither healthy nor infected, it is obviously ill and will recover at the next cycle.

Readers who require a more complex algorithmic outline before building their own hodgepodge machine should refer to the large box that begins on the opposite page.

ADDENDUM

In "Hodgepodge Reactions" I described the hodgepodge machine, a cellular automaton constructed by two West Germans, Martin Gerhardt and Heike Schuster of the University of Bielefeld. The hodgepodge machine imitates beautifully the waves of color that ripple across certain excitable chemical mixtures. The waves sometimes develop edges that curl into spirals, producing a riot of Paisley forms. This does not necessarily mean, as several readers seemed to think, that chaos lurks in the coiling waves of excitation; one should not confuse chaos with hodgepodge.

There is not enough space to mention all the creative approaches taken by some readers to the hodgepodge challenge. I must, however, mention Donovan Smith of El Cerrito, Calif., who squeezed the hodgepodge rule into one dimension. Smith sets up initial states in a strip of cells across the top of his display screen. When his linear automaton is let loose, successive strips reveal intriguing patterns of healthy pasts giving way to infected futures. After one overnight run Smith discovered a configuration that repeated over and over again like an endless succession of rebounding one-dimensional waves.

A HODGEPODGE ALGORITHM

This algorithm uses standard algorithmic conventions for assignment statements, loops, and so on. Key words in the pretend language are given in capital letters so that readers can tell which statements will translate more or less directly into statements in the programming language they are using.

First, we list the data structures and variables used in the program and their meanings, limitations, or typical values to be tried. Next, we list the algorithm itself. Three parts of the algorithm require further expansion, and these are shown in expanded form near the end.

hodge: a 20-by-20 array that holds the current generation of hodgepodge cells

podge: a 20-by-20 array used as a temporary residence for cell values while *hodge* is being computed

To program a larger cellular space, declare hodge and podge to be larger arrays: 100-by-100, for example. As presented here, the arrays have the "wraparound" property: the cell "below" *hodge*(13,20), for example, is *hodge*(13,0).

n: the state-parameter that (partially) determines what version of the hodgepodge machine one will have. State values will run from 0 to

(continued)

(continued from previous page)

n. Unless one has a lot of colors at one's disposal, the full effect of high *n*-values will not be seen.

g: infection constant. The entire range of hodgepodge behavior, from *type one* to *type four*, will be observed as different integer values for *g*, from 1 to 20, are tried.

k1: weighting parameter 1. You may start with the value 2 as described in "Hodgepodge Reactions."

k2: weighting parameter 2. A value of 3 is suggested.

HODGEPODGE

INPUT *k1, k2, g, n*
[array computation section]
WHILE NOT key
    FOR *i* ← 1 to 20
        FOR *j* ← 1 to 20
          a ← 1
          b ← 0
          s ← *hodge(i,j)*
          for each neighbor *(k,l) of hodge(i,j)*

> IF *hodge(k,l)* < *n*
>   THEN *a* ← *a* + 1
>   ELSE *b* ← *b* + 1

               s ← *s* + *hodge(k,l)*
        IF *hodge(i,j)* = 0
           THEN *podge(i,j)* ← INT(*a*/*k1*) + INT(*b*/*k2*)
        IF *hodge(i,j)* > 0 AND *hodge(i,j)* < *n*
           THEN *podge(i,j)* ← INT(*s*/*a*) + *g*
        IF *hodge(i,j)* = *n*
           THEN *podge(i,j)* ← 0

Readers may wish to try the alternate test shown below if they do not obtain satisfactory results.

> IF *hodge(k,l)* < *n*
> THEN IF *hodge(k,l)* > 0
>   *a* ← *a* + 1
> ELSE *b* ← *b* + 1

[display section]
    FOR *i* ← 1 to 20
        FOR *j* ← 1 to 20

(continued)

(continued from previous page)

$hodge(i,j) \leftarrow podge(i,j)$
compute screen coordinates (x,y) for (i,j)
compute color as a function of $hodge(i,j)$
display color at (x,y)

The instruction "WHILE NOT KEY" sets up a loop that goes on and on until the user strikes a key. Such a loop can be set up in many other ways. Those who are not accustomed to using key interrupts may simply use a loop here like

FOR $d \leftarrow 1$ to 1000

Readers may allow for reentry by adding a few extra instructions to the end of the program: Input a value for a variable called, say, *restart*. The next instruction tests the value input. If it is non-zero, the program branches back to the beginning of the main loop again.

A few other "instructions" that appear in the algorithm above were not explicitly spelled out. These include

"for each neighbor, (k,l), of $hodge(i,j)$",

"compute screen coordinates (x,y) for (i,j)"

"compute color as a function of $hodge(i,j)$"

Each of these statements expands into an algorithm (or subalgorithm) in its own right. For example, the first statement implies that each of the four (von Neumann) neighbors of the (i,j)th cell of *hodge* must be examined. These are the cells with coordinates $(i-1,j)$, $(i+1,j)$, $(i,j-1)$, and $(i,j+1)$ where the possibility exists that an index incremented or decremented lies on the other side of the array. There are many timesavers available here but, in keeping with a "lowest common denominator" policy, I will list the very simplest kinds of instruction, even if they result in a somewhat longer program.

IF $i = 1$ THEN $k \leftarrow 20$
          ELSE $k \leftarrow i-1$
$l \leftarrow j$
IF $hodge(k,l) < n$
   THEN $a \leftarrow a + 1$
   ELSE $b \leftarrow b + 1$

Notice that four sections are involved here. The last four lines are always the same. The first three lines compute k and l according to the wraparound property of the cellular space.

(continued)

(continued from previous page)

$s \leftarrow s + hodge(k,l)$

IF $i = 20$

       THEN $k \leftarrow 1$

       ELSE $k \leftarrow i+1$

$l \leftarrow j$

IF $hodge(k,l) < n$

  THEN $a \leftarrow a + 1$

  ELSE $b \leftarrow b + 1$

$s \leftarrow s + hodge(k,l)$

IF $j = 1$ THEN $l \leftarrow 20$

      ELSE $l \leftarrow j-1$

$k \leftarrow i$

IF $hodge(k,l) < n$

  THEN. . . . etc.

Computing the screen coordinates (x,y) that correspond to the (i,j)th array element of *hodge* depends on where you wish to display the array on your screen. An example will make this clear; suppose your screen happens to be 200 pixels wide and 150 pixels high. You might wish to center the display so that the index i, in running from 1 to 20, covers the pixels with x-coordinates that run from 91 to 110. In this case, the computation of x would look like

$x \leftarrow i + 90$

The y-coordinate would be computed similarly.

To compute the color you want to display at the point (x,y), will depend on how many states you are using and how many colors you have. On the most modest assumption, suppose only four colors are available to register some 51 states:

range#1: $hodge(i,j) = 0$
range#2: $hodge(i,j) = 1$ to 16
range#3: $hodge(i,j) = 17$ to 33
range#4: $hodge(i,j) = 34$ to 50

The subdivision is quite arbitrary, of course, but in this particular case you will see the infection rendered by bands of color that swirl

(continued)

(continued from previous page)

about the cellular space as generation succeeds generation. One color is allocated to the 0-state alone because it is singular. In all cases, IF statements may be used to determine the range of *hodge(i,j)*. The THEN part will involve a statement that draws a point of a particular color at (x,y) on your screen.

○ 12 ○

The Demons of Cyclic Space

Cellular automata are stylized, synthetic universes. . . . They have their own kind of matter which whirls around in a space and a time of their own.
— TOMMASO TOFFOLI AND NORMAN MARGOLUS, *Cellular Automata Machines*

Certain mathematical systems, although easily described, can generate miniature universes of incredible complexity. These universes are not accessible by telescopes or spaceships; they can only be explored by means of computers. The Mandelbrot set (described in the first part of this book) is one example. The iteration of simple arithmetic operations, when displayed on the computer screen, produces images of breathtaking intricacy. Cellular automata offer perhaps even better examples because, like our everyday universe, they change over time.

A new type of cellular automaton, discovered by David Griffeath of the University of Wisconsin at Madison, provides the best example yet of such a miniature universe. Started in a random state it exhibits four distinct phases, ending with strange crystalline growths that remind one strongly of primitive forms of life.

A cellular automaton consists of an infinite grid of cells, each of which is in one of a number of possible states. Each cell changes its state in synchrony with the tick of an imaginary clock according to a set of simple rules. As implemented on a computer, the cells are pixels on the screen whose states are represented by different colors. Given the right set of rules and initial states, computer-based cellular automata can generate extraordinary patterns of color that evolve over time.

Griffeath's creation, which I shall call cyclic space, relies on an absurdly simple rule to produce striking phenomena of scientific interest and great beauty. The rule is based on the numbering of n states from 0 to $n - 1$. A cell that happens to be in state k at one tick of the clock must "eat" any adjacent cells by the next tick that are in state $k - 1$. Ingestion is indicated by a change of state of the adjacent cell, from $k - 1$ to k. The rule resembles a natural food chain: a cell in state 2 can eat a cell in state 1 even as the latter is eating a cell in state 0. In cyclic space, however, the food chain has no end, because a cell in state 0 eats neighboring cells that are in state $n - 1$.

On the basis of that one simple rule, cyclic space can turn a random distribution of colors into stable, angular spirals. Griffeath refers to the initial disordered stage of *debris* — and with good reason: The cyclic space looks cluttered at that state (*see* Color Plate 9). After some time, however, little droplets — awash with internal waves of color — succeed the debris. The droplets enlarge until they fill the cyclic space completely. At that point, crystalline spirals begin to develop (*see* the illustration at the top of the next page). They are elegant growths that feed as they revolve.

Each spiral arises from what Griffeath calls a defect, a term borrowed from crystallography. The spirals grow in slow majesty, but they eventually compete for space. Some are overrun, whereas others remain to dominate the last phase of cyclic space. Griffeath calls the survivors demons (*see* the illustration at the bottom of the next page).

Regardless of whether the number of possible cell states is small or large, the same scenario unfolds: debris is followed by droplets, defects, and demons. The first three phases have the property of being metastable: They persist for a great many cycles before giving way to the next phase.

Consider a cyclic space that has 20 possible cell states. Why would an initial, random distribution of states be metastable? In other words, why does it take a long time for large areas of the screen to change their pepper-and-salt appearance? (To be sure, a few insignificant droplets pulse away here and there at the start, but they seem to be unimportant.)

The answer is actually quite simple. If a cell happens to be in, say, state 5, what are the chances that at least one of its four neighbors will be in

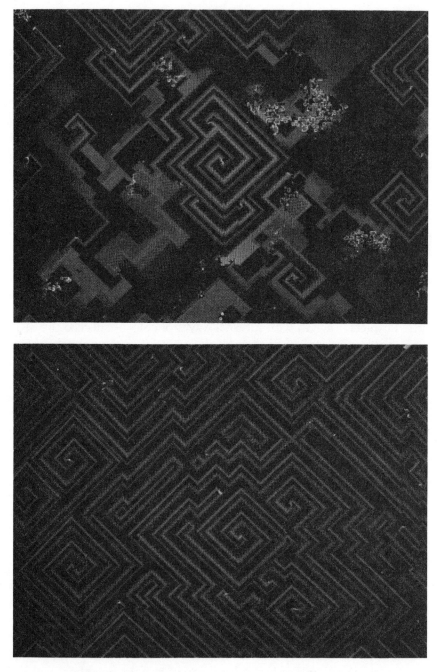

The cyclic space in its defect phase (*above*) and in its final, demon phase (*below*)

state 4? Not good, obviously. In the case of 20 states the probability is about .19. Even if one of the cell's neighbors does happen to be viable "food," what are the chances that either the original cell or the ingested neighbor will be next to a cell in state 4 at the following tick of the clock? This probabilistic argument explains what is seen on the computer screen when one runs a cyclic space seeded with random cell states: After a few sporadic meals, the cyclic space becomes stagnant, frozen.

Not entirely, however. What about those few isolated droplets? Waves of eating sweep across the face of each droplet, rebounding from the surrounding debris in new directions. That activity appears not only to sustain a droplet but actually to make it grow: New cells are recruited from the outlying debris to join the activity inside the droplet. The enlarging droplets gradually fuse together, leaving only a few scattered islands of debris.

What causes the droplets to grow? For starters, readers may take a few seconds to solve the following puzzle: Why do droplets never shrink?

One guarantee of a droplet's continued enlargement is the presence of a loop: a closed chain of cells in which the state of each cell differs from that of its neighbors by no more than 1 (*see* the illustration below). Hence, if one picks any cell in a loop, the next cell's state number is given merely by either adding 1, −1 or 0 to the picked cell's state number. (Remember that in cyclic space the highest state differs from state 0 by 1.) If one keeps a running sum of such differences as one goes from cell to cell in a complete circuit of the loop, it may happen that the final sum is

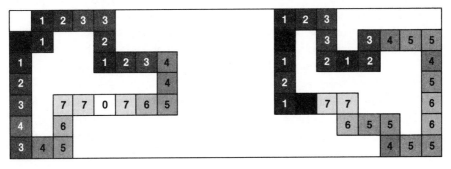

Two loops, one of which (*right*) is a defect

not 0. A loop having that characteristic will sustain a droplet's growth indefinitely. It is in fact a defect, the very foundation of the third metastable phase of cyclic space.

The cellular action generated by a defect differs from that generated by a nondefect loop. A defect entrains surrounding cells to change states in a regular rhythm. On a computer screen the area surrounding a defect takes on an attractive spiral geometry. Eventually the entire cyclic space (or at least the part of it one sees on the screen) becomes completely covered by such spirals.

How do defects arise as cyclic space evolves from debris? Naturally, a defect might be present from the very beginning of the cellular universe. Indeed, if one considers cyclic space to be infinite in extent, then it is statistically guaranteed to have defects among its debris. Yet defects typically are formed where there were none before. How? Readers are hereby challenged to produce a small rectangle of cells that does not contain a defect but that will in time develop one. This means developing some simple test (short of letting the computer run for a long time) that detects areas where defects will develop.

The fourth and final phase is hard to tell visually from the third. According to Griffeath, some defects are more "efficient" than others in that they function as n-state clocks: The march of cell states around the innermost loop takes exactly n ticks of the clock. Spirals that march to a slower beat end up being absorbed by their more efficient cohorts. Such efficient spirals are the demons that populate the fourth phase of cyclic space. They settle into an indefinite existence, marked off from neighboring demons by invisible but rigid fences.

Cyclic space might not have been discovered by Griffeath had not Norman Margolus and Tommaso Toffoli of the Massachusetts Institute of Technology developed the Cellular Automaton Machine, or CAM. The CAM consists of several large chips on a board that fits inside a personal computer. Within the chips each cell is represented by a memory location that is updated by a special control logic. At full speed the CAM can recompute a 256-by-256 cellular array at a rate of 60 times a second.

Unfortunately, such a device is rather expensive. Nevertheless, readers can write their own cyclic-space simulator (albeit one slower than a CAM) called DEMON by translating the following algorithmic outline into their favorite programming language. The algorithm uses two arrays called *new* and *old* to hold the current and previous states of the cells in the cyclic space.

```
repeat until key is pressed
for i ← 1 to 100
    for j ← 1 to 100
        for each neighbor (k,l) of (i,j)
            if old(k,l) = old(i,j) + 1
                then new(i,j) ← old(k,l)
    for i ← 1 to 100
        for j ← 1 to 100
            display new(i,j)
            old(i,j) ← new(i,j)
```

The outer loop, which ends when the user of DEMON presses a certain key, controls repetition of the main checking and displaying cycles. (Of course, there are other ways to construct such a loop.) Readers who have computers with small memories are advised to limit themselves to a smaller array of cells, say one that is 50 by 50. The two inner loops used here presuppose a 100-by-100 cellular array. The cell (i,j) sits at the intersection of the ith row and jth column.

The innermost loop of DEMON simply checks the state of each of the four cells adjacent to cell (i,j). (Readers must therefore include instructions in their versions of the algorithm that assign the values $i - 1$ and $i + 1$ to the index k while l equals j. Similarly, the values $j - 1$ and $j + 1$ must be assigned to l while k equals i.) If the state number of a neighboring cell happens to be 1 more than the state number of the cell at (i,j), then the cell at (i,j) is eaten: it has its state number changed to that of the neighboring cell.

DEMON must perform modular arithmetic when it calculates the value of $old(i,j) + 1$. In other words, if $old(i,j)$ happens to be $n - 1$, the highest state number, then $old(i,j) + 1$ is equal to 0. Hence, if one has specified, say, 10 states in the cellular space, the state numbers will be 0, 1, 2 . . ., 9 and $9 + 1 = 0$. If the value of a cell changes, the new value is assigned to $new(i,j)$.

The double loop that follows the checking loop displays all the cells in *new* and then updates the *old* array by replacing all its values by the corresponding values in *new*. Readers can consult other chapters, including the previous one, to figure out how to display the cells on the computer screen.

Modular arithmetic must be applied not only with cell-state numbers but also with the indexes i and j themselves. The simplest way to achieve the illusion of an infinite space is to endow one's screen with the "wrap-around" property. Cells on the extreme right-hand margin are considered to be adjacent to those on the left, and cells at the bottom of the display are effectively adjacent to those at the top. The effect is created by using index values from 0 to 99 instead of 1 to 100. The cell to the immediate right of (23,99) is in fact (23,0). Hence, the numbers $i - 1$, $i + 1$, $j - 1$, and $j + 1$, which are index values of the neighbors of cell (i,j), must all be expressed in modular form. Most programming languages have instructions that do that automatically.

Naturally, DEMON must allow a user to "initialize" the cellular space under its control. This step can be done by including a provision in the algorithm for eliciting the desired number of states from the user, as well as a loop that gives every cell in the space an initial, randomly chosen state within the allowed range of numbers.

What number of states works best? It all depends on how long the reader is willing to wait for the four phases to succeed one another. When the number of states is very large, say more than 25, a 100-by-100 random cellular array is likely to remain fixed forever. On the other hand, when the number of states is small, the stages succeed each other too quickly to be appreciated. Griffeath recommends between 12 and 16 states.

The University of Wisconsin is a known center for the activities of the so-called Particle Mafia, of which Griffeath is a member. The name comes from an early association of the general field of particle systems with Frank Spitzer, a mathematician at Cornell University in upstate New York, where—according to Hollywood legend—the Mafia used to hang out. Spitzer's articles and talks on particle systems first popularized the subject in North America, just as the work of his colleague R. L. Dobrushin did in the Soviet Union. Several of Spitzer's students at Cornell, as well as his followers elsewhere, took up the work of controlling the particle-systems numbers game. They include not only Griffeath but also Maury Bramson (also at Madison), Richard Durrett of Cornell, and Thomas Liggett of the University of California at Los Angeles.

What exactly is a particle system? It is usually a cellular automaton in which only one cell changes at a time, often in a random fashion. The diffusion–limited-aggregation algorithm described in the next chapter is an example of a particle system. There, a single particle wanders randomly across a grid of cells until it encounters a growing aggregate. Its position is then frozen as another particle begins to wander. In time, the aggregate invariably develops a treelike shape.

A number of important but difficult problems are raised by particle systems, not the least of which concern the long-term stability of certain phases that arise when the systems are set running. Although cyclic space is not a traditional particle system, Griffeath thinks it nonetheless provides a model for locally periodic wave formations that is particularly amenable to mathematical study because of its straightforward rule. Indeed, he has recently proved a theorem that gives, for each possible array size and number of states, an estimate of all the probability that cyclic space will never escape from debris gridlock.

For the rest of us, the cyclic cellular automaton at least provides an opportunity to explore a miniature universe. To be sure, it is much simpler than the universe in which we exist, but it has alien beauties and wonders of its own. (Readers who prefer ordering a cyclic space program to writing one should consult the List of Suppliers.)

ADDENDUM

This chapter first appeared in the "Computer Recreations" of SCIENTIFIC AMERICAN in August, 1989. I can do little more than sample the interesting experiments being carried out as a consequence in the scientific hinterland by hundreds of dedicated amateurs.

Griffeath's cellular universe is called cyclic because of the "eating" habits of its cells. A cell in state k will eat a neighboring cell in state $k - 1$. If k happens to be 0, the next lower state is $n - 1$ if only n states are allowed. The food chain becomes a food cycle. If the cellular space is initially filled with random states (debris), when n is large, there is little activity at first, because it is rather unlikely that any particular cell would be adjacent to a cell in the next lower state.

Harry J. Smith of Saratoga, Calif., has worked with a 320-by-200 space where each cell is in one of 14 states. At first about 25 percent of the cells change their states at each iteration, but by 15 generations the percentage drops to less than three. Then, Smith says, the patches of intense activity that Griffeath calls droplets begin to form. As the droplets grow, the percentage of cells that change state at each iteration grows steadily until, at about the 150th generation, the percentage begins to grow even more rapidly until the demon phase is reached, when all the cells are changing at every iteration.

In the column on cyclic space I challenged readers to discover a small rectangle of cells that do not contain a defect but will in time produce one. By a defect Griffeath means a closed cellular chain that includes a contiguous cycle of all possible states. Such is the egg from which demons hatch. The nicest solution to this problem came from Marlin Eller of Seattle, Wash. What happens to the following three-by-three rectangle in an eight-state cyclic universe?

$$
\begin{array}{ccc}
0 & 1 & 2 \\
7 & 4 & 3 \\
7 & 5 & 6
\end{array}
$$

John D. Brereton of West Haven, Conn., developed an ingenious screen display to show what the cyclic cellular automaton was really up to. He produced not one picture of cyclic space on his screen but two, side by side. The space on the left shows the last generation, but the space on the right shows only the cells that change their state as the next generation is computed. Unable to leave things as Griffeath and I left them, Brereton tinkered by counting as neighbors not only the four cells along a side but also those touching a cell's corners. The new space prompted the feeling of discovery: "As we approach this strange planet, at first we see a multicolored cloud cover, beneath which no details are visible. As we go closer, descending through successive cycles, color patterns on the ground are vaguely distinguishable through gaps in these clouds. Then distinct boundaries of various colored fields appear, followed by small buildings. . ." But I leave the description to be completed by readers who wish to visit Brereton's planet.

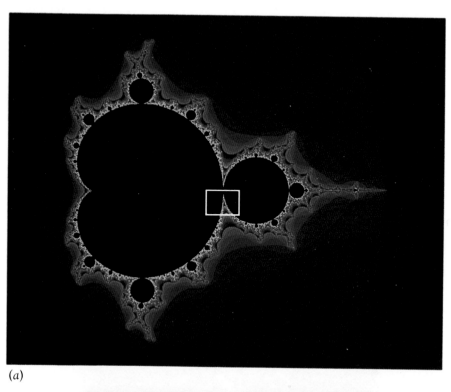

(a)

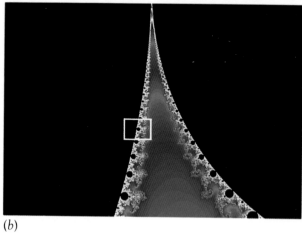

(b)

Color Plate 1   The Mandelbrot set (a). The white box indicates a section of "Sea Horse Valley" (b).

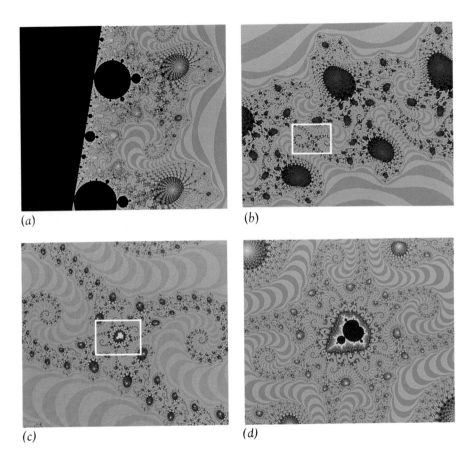

(a) (b)

(c) (d)

Color Plate 2   (a) Mandelbuds line Sea Horse Valley. (b-d) A three-part zoom
from a seahorse tail to a miniature Mandelbrot set.

Color Plate 3 The Mandelbrot set appears as a lake in a fairy landscape; the mountains reflect dynamics of the surrounding points.

Color Plate 4 A three-dimensional cross section of the four-dimensional Mandelbrot set.

Color Plate 5 A logarithmic function conjures up a snail shell.

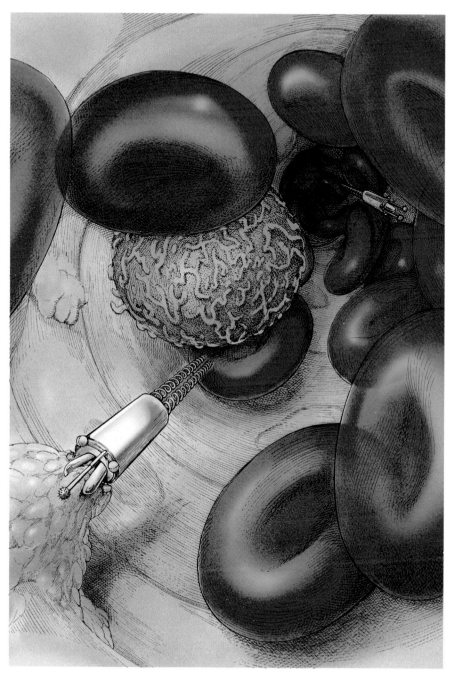

Color Plate 6   A nanomachine swimming through a capillary attacks a fat deposit.

Color Plate 7 Computer-generated fractal mountains imitate nature (the clouds were added by hand).

Color Plate 8   Graftal plants materialize from simple formulas.

Color Plate 9 A cyclic space in the debris (top) and droplet (bottom) phases anticipates the appearance of demons.

· 13 ·

Slow Growths

The most useful fractals involve *chance* . . . both their regularities
and their irregular ities are statistical.
—BENOIT B. MANDELBROT, *The Fractal Geometry of Nature*

Is it a zinc ion, a bit of soot, or a staggering drunk wandering about on the
display screen? Does it join others of its kind to form a metallic flower, a
dark patch, or an insensible crowd? The answer depends only on one's
imagination, but—flower, patch, or crowd—the shape of the aggregate
structure is unquestionably fractal; its fractal dimension (which is between 1 and 2) can even be measured.

A fractal such as the one in the illustration on page 142 is created by a
program called SLO GRO. It directs a succession of particles to wander
aimlessly about the screen until they eventually encounter a collection of
stationary kindred. As soon as the encounter takes place, the particle's
motion is frozen. As several hundred particles accumulate one by one in
this way, the collection slowly develops the irregular branches and tendrils characteristic of fractal shapes.

The SLO GRO program was inspired indirectly by the article "Fractal
Growth," by Leonard M. Sander that appeared in SCIENTIFIC AMERICAN,
in January, 1987. The article described the particulate growth process I
have outlined above, which goes by the name of diffusion-limited aggregation, or DLA.

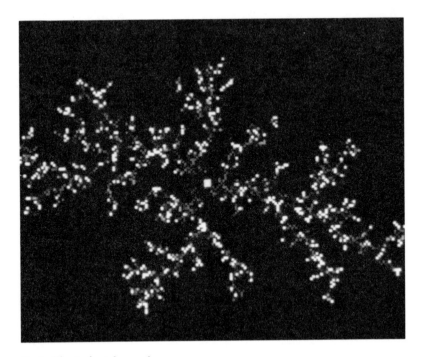

Kevin Eber's fractal crowd

Several intrepid souls with the kind of adventurous spirit that characterizes the readership of "Computer Recreations" did not wait for me to pick up on DLA-simulation programs but wrote versions of SLO GRO for themselves. In particular, my hand was forced by Eric M. Smiertka of Santa Clara, Calif. With little more than an elementary programming course under his belt, he wrote a successful version of SLO GRO. Not content with merely watching his fractal grow, he measured its dimension as well.

The DLA process might well represent the diffusion of zinc ions through a two-dimensional electrolytic solution. When ions come in contact with an aggregation of metallic zinc at an electrode, they immediately bond with their atomic mates in the aggregate. Particles of soot that are wafted hither and yon before meeting other soot particles clinging to some substrate also seem to follow the same process, although in their case the cohesion is electrostatic in nature.

The most colorful (albeit the least realistic) model for a DLA process involves a succession of drunks wandering about in the dark until they stumble on a crowd of insensate comrades; lulled by the sounds of peaceful snoring, they instantly lie down to sleep. An aerial view of the slumbering crowd by morning light might well reveal the same fractal shape found in a zinc cluster or a soot patch.

The key to modeling the diffusion part of the DLA process is a "random walk." Each step of a random walk in two dimensions is taken in one of four randomly selected directions: north, south, east, and west. (Sometimes a random walk also allows intermediate directions such as southeast, but I shall stick with the more restrictive version.) The illustration below outlines a typical path made by a particle on a random walk. The particle seems to meander aimlessly. Watching such a particle on the screen, one can be excused for having serious doubts that it will ever reach a given destination. But the particle does have a goal (to be somewhat teleologic): to reach the crowd of fellow particles accumulating at the center of the screen.

It all starts when SLO GRO places a single particle at the center of the computer screen. Another particle is then set on a random walk from a random point on a large circle centered on the initial particle. After a long and arduous journey the second particle happens on the first one and stops. Immediately SLO GRO dispatches another particle on a similar

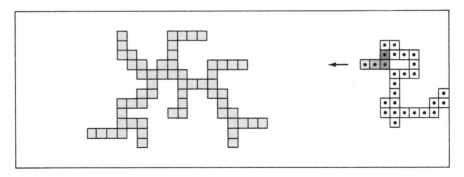

A staggering drunk may or may not reach the crowd

journey from another random point on the circle. Particle after particle collects at the site of the original one and a strange shape emerges within the circle: a treelike growth with oddly twisted branches and twigs. The shape results from the tendency of a randomly walking particle to run into an outer part of the crowd long before it encounters a cohort much deeper in the crowd; twigs are more likely to grow from branches than from the core, so to speak.

All of this takes time. As Smiertka says, "It takes four or five hours to run the program on my IBM XT, so I just let it run overnight." The algorithms described below give rise to a somewhat faster version of the program, but of course the duration of a run depends on how many particles one wants to accumulate.

The diffusion algorithm (SLO) is a bit easier to write than the aggregation one (GRO). For the sake of simplicity I shall confine all the action to the inside of a circle 200 pixels in diameter. To choose the point on the circle from which a given particle begins its random walk, SLO computes a random angle in one instruction and then in the next two instructions works out the coordinates of the point on the circle that defines that angle:

$$angle \leftarrow random \times 360$$
$$x \leftarrow 100 \times \text{cosine}(angle) + 100$$
$$y \leftarrow 100 \times \text{sine}(angle) + 100$$

The computer itself must choose a random number labeled *random*. Because such a number lies between 0 and 1, it must be multiplied by 360 to yield a random angle between 0 and 360 degrees. (For systems that employ radians instead of degrees, *random* must be multiplied by 2π, or approximately 6.283.) The next step calculates the x coordinate of the point on the circle that lies at that angle by multiplying 100 (the circle's radius) by the cosine of the angle. The third step works out the y coordinate of the point with the sine function. Because most popular programming systems place the origin—the point with coordinates (0,0)—in one corner of the screen, I have added offsets of 100 to both coordinates in order to center the circle on the screen. Of course, this will work only on a screen that happens to be 200 by 200 pixels. Readers must work out ideal offsets based on the dimensions of their own screen.

Having chosen a starting point for the particle, SLO must now set it in motion with the following algorithm (which is embedded in a loop):

$$select \leftarrow random$$
$$if\ select \leq .25$$
$$then\ x \leftarrow x + 1$$
$$if\ select > .25\ and\ \leq .5$$
$$then\ x \leftarrow x - 1$$
$$if\ select > .5\ and\ \leq .75$$
$$then\ y \leftarrow y + 1$$
$$if\ select > .75$$
$$then\ y \leftarrow y - 1$$

The motion rules are spelled out explicitly in terms of a random variable called *select*. Depending on where (in which of four equally likely ranges between 0 and 1) *select* lies, one coordinate of the particle is increased or decreased by 1. In this way the particle moves randomly either up, down, left, or right by one pixel.

What is not spelled out explicitly are the two conditions under which the particle's motion must be stopped: whenever the particle has wandered outside the circle from which it originated or whenever it has arrived at a pixel adjacent to the accreting mass of pixels constituting the fractal crowd. In the first case SLO GRO simply extinguishes the particle; if it did not, the particle could easily wander off the screen into an endless electronic night. In the second case SLO GRO fixes the particle to the spot where it encounters the growing cluster, as though it were transfixed by the sight of a fractal Medusa.

These instructions are incorporated into a WHILE conditional statement at the beginning of the random-walk loop that animates the particles. Excursions outside the circle are curtailed by simply keeping track of the particle's distance from the center of the circle. The distance is computed every time new values of x and y become available. (Actually SLO GRO computes the square of the distance. This saves a little time, since a square-root calculation is avoided.)

$$distx \leftarrow x - 100$$
$$disty \leftarrow y - 100$$
$$distance \leftarrow distx^2 + disty^2$$

The WHILE condition tests how far the particle has traveled from the center of the circle by comparing *distance* with the square of 100 (plus 1). If the condition is violated, the program will exit from the loop and start anew with another particle.

How does one determine the other condition, namely whether the particle has joined the crowd? To answer the question, SLO GRO maintains two lists, one for each coordinate of every particle in the crowd. The lists are arrays called *crdx* and *crdy*. The "seed" particle initially placed at the center of the screen happens to have coordinates $crdx(1) = 100$ and $crdy(1) = 100$. If in its peripatetic career a particle comes in contact with the crowd, SLO GRO executes the instructions:

$$crdx(count) \leftarrow x$$
$$crdy(count) \leftarrow y$$

As its name implies, *count* keeps count of the number of particles in the aggregate. At the beginning of SLO GRO it has the value 1; every time a new particle is added to the aggregate, *count* increases by 1.

But how does GRO know when a particle has reached its colleagues? The simplest contact algorithm compares the coordinates of each of the four pixels surrounding the particle in its current position with the coordinates of the pixels kept in the lists *crdx* and *crdy*.

```
for n ← 1 to count
    xı ← x + 1
    if xı = crdx(n) and y = crdy(n)
        then contact ← true
    xı ← x − 1
    if xı = crdx(n) and y = crdy(n)
        then contact ← true
    yı ← y + 1
    if x = crdx(n) and yı = crdy(n)
        then contact ← true
    yı ← y − 1
    if x = crdx(n) and yı = crdy(n)
        then contact ← true
```

I have used here a so-called Boolean variable called *contact*. Such a variable takes the values true or false (or, equivalently, 1 or 0). Just before the WHILE loop begins, *contact* is given an initial value of false.

All the essential features of SLO GRO have now been described except for an outer WHILE loop that keeps SLO GRO going until COUNT reaches some desired number of particles, say 500. The complete SLO GRO algorithm is displayed in the box at the right. The parts that have already been

———————————————————o———————————————————

A LIST OF THE COMPLETE SLO GRO ALGORITHM

draw point (100,100)
count ← 1
crdx(1) ← 100
crdy(1) ← 100
while *count* ≤ 500

> | choose point on circle |

> *distance* ← 0
> *contact* ← false
> while *distance* < 10001 and not *contact* erase point (x,y)

> | motion algorithm |

> draw point (x,y)

> | compute distance |

> | contact algorithm |

> if *contact* = true
>   then *count* ← *count* + 1
>   *crdx(count)* ← x
>   *crdy(count)* ← y

———————————————————o———————————————————

described in detail are represented by appropriately labeled boxes. The parts that have not been explicitly described include instructions that initialize variables and erase and draw particles. (Tyro programmers are warned that the commands to "erase" and "draw" should not be taken literally: In real programming systems these are not viable commands. Instead both operations are done by means of other commands that color pixels.)

Fractal crowds, such as those produced by SLO GRO, can be categorized by a dimension that characterizes their rate of growth. In particular, consider the number of particles that lie within a circle of radius *R*. If a crowd more or less filled the general area of its growth, one would expect that a doubling of the radius would lead to a quadrupling of the number of particles inside the circle: The crowd's growth would be quadratic. In other words, one would expect the number of particles to be approximately proportional to R^2. On the other hand, if a crowd of particles took on a linear shape with little or no branching, doubling R would merely double the number of particles within the circle. The crowd's growth would be linear, that is, proportional to R. It turns out that fractal growth tends to be faster than linear growth but slower than quadratic growth: The number of fractal particles in a circle of radius R is proportional to R^d, where d is a number between 1 and 2.

For that reason a plot of the number, N, of particles in a SLO GRO crowd versus the pixel radius R on ordinary graph paper yields a curve somewhere between a straight line (the result of linear growth) and a parabola (the result of quadratic growth). It is tricky to tell what fractional power is at work in the growth of the crowd merely by examining such a curve. The task is made easier if one plots the points on so-called log-log graph paper.

Log-log graph paper has horizontal and vertical coordinates that double, triple, or increase by some other factor that depends on the unit chosen. If one plots N versus R on log-log paper, a strange thing happens to quadratic curves: They turn into straight lines! Why? Remember that, for quadratic growth, every time the radius doubled, the number of particles quadrupled. On log-log paper this represents a regular upward step of four units for every two units across the graph, which happens to be a straight line of slope 2. In fact, growth rates proportional to R^3 appear as straight lines of slope 3 on log-log paper for the same reason.

That last observation tells us what to do once the points corresponding to all pairs of R's and N's have been plotted on log-log paper. If the shape is a fractal, the points will all lie about a straight line (except near the end of the line, where the crowd tends to peter out). The slope of the line approximates the fractional dimension of the crowd.

Smiertka did exactly that for one of his SLO GRO creations; His graph appears above at right. The slope of the growth line is 1.58. The estimate is slightly smaller than those published in the scientific literature, but that hardly diminished his pleasure in carrying out the measurement. Smiertka has gone on to experiment with different rules governing particle attachment and to measure the fractal dimension of the resulting DLA fractals.

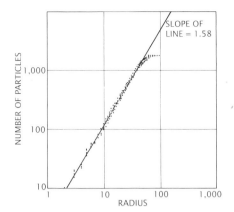

How to estimate a fractal dimension

As I mentioned, other readers wrote versions of SLO GRO. Scott Cama-zine of Ithaca, N.Y., concedes that his particles do not always move randomly and that they sometimes seem to "invade" the aggregation. But his graphic images of fractals have convinced me that his program proba-bly has got the basic details of DLA right.

He will send his program (for IBM PC and compatible computers) to readers who write him (*see* the List of Suppliers).

Kevin Eber, a graduate student in journalism at the University of Colorado at Boulder, wrote a version of SLO GRO in which all the particles arise at random points along the left edge of the screen. With the help of his friend Jon Saken at the university's Center for Astrophysics and Space Astronomy, he was able to produce the fractal crowd shown at the beginning of this chapter. Eber changed the color of his particles every 100 iterations as a quick way to estimate the number of particles that have collected on the display screen.

Finally, I should mention Marlin Eller, who wrote from Hiroshima, Japan, to describe a program called SOOT. It resembles SLO GRO in all respects except that the diffusion takes place in the opposite direction: Particles are emitted at the center of the screen and wander until they happen on a surrounding circle or some other particle of soot. In this way tendrils are made to grow inward until eventually the emitter becomes clogged.

ADDENDUM

Enthusiasm for the fractal-generating program SLO GRO, which I described in "Slow Growths," did not grow slowly. After it first appeared in SCIENTIFIC AMERICAN in December, 1988, a hefty bag of mail hinted at the continuing interest in fractals in any shape or form.

The SLO GRO recipe was sufficiently simple for many readers to follow, and many in fact did so. The basic algorithm involves the injection of a randomly walking "particle" into a circle from a random point on the circle's circumference. When the particle comes in contact with a stationary fellow particle, it too ceases to move and thus produces an aggregation of particles. The program was easy to write but was somewhat painful for certain people to watch. Why should they spend their time watching a point of light jittering for what seemed forever? As a result several readers thought of changes in the algorithm that speeded its operation.

Edward H. Kidera IV of Columbia, Md., achieved a definite speedup by starting with a small circle and steadily increasing its radius as the aggregation grew. A number of readers also made suggestions for speeding up the test for contact with a crowd of fellow particles. The test involved comparing the particle's neighboring pixels with the recorded positions of every particle in the growing crowd.

Ronald C. Read of the University of Waterloo in Ontario made the following suggestion on this very point. "For those who use BASIC (as I'm sure many of your readers do) there is a much easier way. That is to use the POINT command of BASIC in order to tell whether the pixel in question has been given a color. In effect, then, one is using the screen as a storage device."

Most impatient of all was William H. Pratt of State College, Pa. Why make the particle wander randomly at all? Why not just give it a random position next to the growth itself? Pratt was dismayed, however, to find that his growth looked nothing like my illustrations. It certainly was ragged about the edges but more solid — a different creature altogether.

Pratt was unknowingly playing with what is known as Richardson's growth model, a favorite research tool of a group of mathematicians called "the Particle Mafia," whom we met in Chapter 12.

· 14 ·

Programmed Parties

I recently gave a party I was not able to attend in person. My eight guests had quite distinct personalities and occupations; for example, there was Walter (not his real name) the weight lifter. Wally had conceived a hopeless passion for another guest, Princess Penelope, a refined and sensitive woman of aristocratic pretensions. At the party Wally continually edged closer to Princess Penelope, while she just as continually moved away from him. In quantitative terms Wally would have liked to spend the entire evening just three feet away from Penelope; to have been any closer would have been socially unacceptable. For her part, Penelope was not comfortable unless 15 feet separated her from her admirer. But if Wally strayed any farther, Penelope would begin some edging of her own. Perhaps she enjoyed remaining in Wally's view.

It will surprise few readers to learn that the party was held in my computer. The guests were represented on my display screen as typographic characters: Wally was a W and Penelope was a P, for instance. As the party progressed, the eight guests drifted about the room in a seemingly endless search for social equilibrium. Occasional clusters of closely interacting people would form only to be dispelled by the arrival of a new individual who upset the delicate balance in some subtle way. Each guest had an ideal distance from each of the others. He or she would always move in a direction to minimize unhappiness. In the context of my admittedly quantitative (and stereotyped) party, the unhappiness of a given guest was measured by the sum of the differences between the ideal and the actual distances to all the other guests.

The guests were confined to a single rectangular room dominated by a table spread with tempting refreshments. Each person had an ideal distance from the table as well as from the others; dieters preferred a distance of five feet, whereas others were not completely happy unless they were just a foot from the table. This is not to say that the average, nondieting guest would simply move toward the table. For example, Arty the artist might have wanted to sample some digital dip but Bernie the businessman (whom Arty disliked) blocked the way, expounding on the principles of vertical marketing.

The program that produced the party is called PARTY PLANNER by its originator, Richard Goldstein, a computer artist and game designer who lives in Los Angeles, Calif. Rich Gold, as he prefers to be called, is well known as the designer of "The Little Computer People," a game that produces a cross-sectional image of a house in which a mannequin (the little computer person) goes about his daily routine.

Gold calls his new recreation PARTY PLANNER with tongue in cheek; he maintains that by coding the likely relations between guests invited to a real party one can determine possible outcomes of the mix in terms of social dynamics. One might even discover the optimal location for the refreshment table. Perhaps a proper evaluation can only be left to those readers who both write their own version of the game and attempt to apply it to real life. The real guests, it would seem may at least chuckle at their own antics on the screen.

Gold's computer party can be held in a room digitized into 600 squares in a 20-by-30 array. Each guest occupies a single square of the array. PARTY PLANNER proceeds by considering each person in turn; the program moves a guest to each of the eight neighboring squares. In each location the program calculates the total unhappiness of the guest. The neighboring square in which unhappiness is at a minimum becomes the person's new location.

Organizing a party requires only a modicum of programming experience. The 20-by-30 array will be called *room*. Since the entries of the array are alphabetic characters, *room* must be declared as a character array in the program. The walls and refreshment table are designated by fixed characters (*see* illustration at the right).

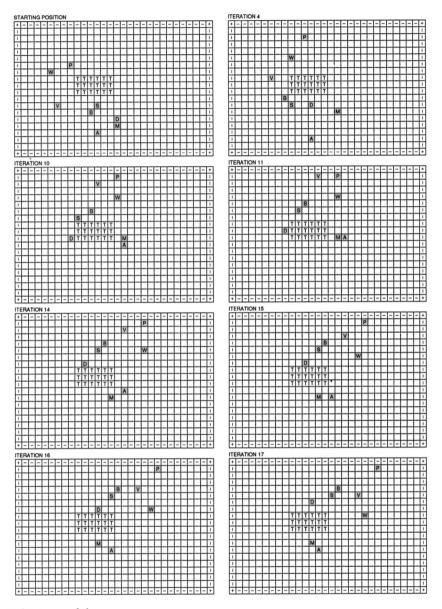

Eight stages of the party

PARTY PLANNER has a fairly simple structure that can be described on two levels, from the outside in. First there is a loop within which all the guests are moved about the room endlessly, or at least until the user of the program presses the space bar. In algorithmic terms the outer level can be summarized as follows:

> repeat
>   for $i \leftarrow 1$ to 8
>   move the ith guest
>   display room
> until space bar

Inside the repeat loop is a second loop in which the eight people are all shifted to new locations. I shall expand below on the mysteries of moving the ith guest. A display of the room requires a double loop that scans the array *room* when the new positions of the guests have all been computed. Using indices j and k, for example, the routine will examine $room(j,k)$ and display whatever character is stored there at a corresponding position on the screen.

Moving the ith guest is in itself a somewhat complicated operation because his or her new position will depend on the positions of all the other people and the distances the ith guest prefers to be from them. Of course, PARTY PLANNER must include a table showing the distance the guest listed by row prefers to be from the guest listed by column (*see* the table below). Such an array, called *ideal*, must be stored in the program as

Ideal Distances Between Party Guests

	A	B	D	M	P	S	V	W	T
A	0	15	7	2	6	9	4	12	1
B	8	0	6	4	6	3	2	10	1
D	11	4	0	5	12	2	9	6	1
M	6	9	3	0	10	7	13	5	5
P	3	10	5	14	0	11	7	15	5
S	12	2	4	8	5	0	12	4	1
V	7	8	14	10	4	13	0	3	5
W	6	7	13	6	3	8	9	0	5

Guest List for a Computer Party

NAME	OCCUPATION
ARTHUR	ARTIST
BERNIE	BUSINESSMAN
DENNIS	DENTIST
MILLIE	MODEL
PENELOPE	PRINCESS
SUSAN	STOCKBROKER
VIOLA	VIOLINIST
WALLY	WEIGHTLIFTER

a data file or as a set of data statements. The entry *ideal*(i,j) records the ideal distance the ith guest prefers to be from the jth guest. This may not have the same value as *ideal*(j,i). For example, Wally may want to be three feet from Penelope, but Penelope wants to be a good 15 feet from him.

Two arrays, x and y, store the current positions of the eight party goers. During any given computational cycle the ith guest occupies a position whose coordinates are $x(i)$ and $y(i)$. The ith guest's level of unhappiness is computed as shown:

$$presum \leftarrow sum$$
$$sum \leftarrow 0$$
$$\text{for } j \leftarrow 1 \text{ to } 8$$
$$dist2 \leftarrow [x(i) - x(j)]^2 +$$
$$[y(i) - y(j)]^2$$
$$dist \leftarrow \text{sqrt}(dist2)$$
$$sum \leftarrow sum + abs[dist - ideal(i,j)]$$

The FOR loop is run not only for the ith guest's current position $x(i)$ and $y(i)$ but also for the eight surrounding positions, yielding a total of nine calculations. Every time a new calculation is made, the value of *sum* is stored in the variable *presum* in order to save it for the purpose of comparison. The variable *sum* is then set to zero and the distance *dist* from the ith guest to the jth is calculated. The absolute value of the difference between the actual distance and the ideal distance (from the ith guest's point of view) is then calculated and added to the ongoing total.

Once a new value of *sum* has been calculated, the program compares it with the previous value stored in *presum*. If the new *sum* is smaller than the previous one, PARTY PLANNER must save the coordinates. The following algorithmic fragment indicates how that might be done:

$$\text{if } sum < presum$$
$$\text{then } xx \leftarrow x(i)$$
$$yy \leftarrow y(i)$$

In this way an up-to-date record is maintained of the coordinates that yield the (so far) minimum unhappiness of the *i*th guest. When all nine positions have been calculated, the *i*th guest is moved to the position that yields the least unhappiness. The nine calculations are most simply accomplished by means of a double loop that uses variables x and y in place of the array elements $x(i)$ and $y(i)$. Thus x would go from $x(i) - 1$ to $x(i) + 1$ and y would go from $y(i) - 1$ to $y(i) + 1$. A simple way to construct the loop is to add the increments dx and dy to $x(i)$ and $y(i)$ respectively:

$$\text{for } dx \leftarrow -1 \text{ to } 1$$
$$\text{for } dy \leftarrow -1 \text{ to } 1$$
$$x \leftarrow x(i) + dx$$
$$y \leftarrow y(i) + dy$$

One further complication should be addressed by party programmers: Guests must not be allowed to walk through walls or over the refreshment table. For this reason, every time a new set of coordinate values x and y is about to be tried, PARTY PLANNER must test them against certain bounds that represent the walls and the table. In the array *room* used in the version of the program described here the four walls are at $x = 1$, $x = 30$, $y = 1$ and $y = 20$. If either coordinate of the *i*th guest is equal to one of the corresponding wall coordinates, the calculation of unhappiness must be skipped entirely. Similarly, the table in my room occupies x coordinates 10 through 15 and y coordinates 9 through 11. If x lies in the second, the guest is in imminent danger of destroying the property of the host. Again the calculation is skipped. Purists might urge that guests not be allowed to walk over each other; this does not occur frequently enough in well-planned parties, however, to be worth the trouble of implementing.

The programmer initiates PARTY PLANNER by selecting starting positions for each guest. The positions can be entered by typing coordinates or by allowing the program to select positions randomly. In the latter case there must be a provision for ensuring that initial positions do not coincide with a wall or the table.

Magi, my cybernetic sidekick, has been experimenting with variations of PARTY PLANNER. Why, he reasons, must everyone have some ideal distance from everyone else? Perhaps some guests will have no feelings at all about certain other guests. When that is the case, Magi inserts a −1 in the appropriate cell of the ideal distance matrix. When the program comes to consider the attraction of that guest for the others, it first tests the value of the ideal distance to the others. If the value is −1, the calculation is skipped; the other guest contributes nothing to the first guest's happiness or unhappiness.

I urge readers to experiment with different room configurations, size of party, and array of ideal distances. Gold has even suggested holding what he calls "irrational parties": Guests are invited in off the street, as it were. In other words, the ideal-distance array is filled with random integers chosen from an appropriate range of numbers, say 1 through 25.

It is fascinating to experiment with various predetermined guest lists. Sometimes the results are predictable. For example, if all the ideal distances are greater than the room size, the partygoers will all become wallflowers, skirting walls in a vain attempt to avoid everyone else. (I have been to such parties.) If, on the other hand, the ideal distances are small, guests will form a single, tight conversational knot near the refreshments. Hilarious results can be had by setting up an endless cycle of one-way attractions: *A* loves *B* but *B* hates *A*. At the same time, *B* loves *C* but *C* hates *B*. The chain continues until it closes in on itself at *A* again. Depending on how the guests are distributed initially, one may witness an endless chase with occasional romantic eddies and culs-de-sac.

The notion of an ideal distance is not a complete mathematical fiction. Behavioral scientists use a similar concept called social distance. In daily interactions with others there is a distance we naturally tend to adopt depending on our relative mobility and our relation to the other person. The study of social distances is called proxemics. Findings include the discovery that social distances are determined in part by culture, role and sex. North Americans, for example, sometimes feel a bit crowded in conversation with people from a country where social distances are smaller. The phenomenon could be studied in a group setting by using

PARTY PLANNER. Let half of the guests prefer to be one foot from everyone else and let the other half prefer a distance of three feet. Will they continue to mill about or will some final, stable configuration emerge?

The foregoing question leads us willy-nilly into the realm of dynamical systems. Abstractly considered, a computer party of the kind described here consists of a distance matrix, a two-dimensional cellular space (be it finite or infinite), and a set of tokens that move by turns according to the value of a potential function. From the point of view of a given token (that is, a guest) the space is an undulating plain. The height of any point in this dynamical landscape is the value of the potential function for the token. The value is simply the sum of the differences between the token's matrix distances and actual distances to the other tokens.

The motion of an individual token is analogous to a ball rolling under the influence of gravity; the ball always seeks to move "downhill." By this reasoning Gold sometimes describes the guests at his computer parties as continually seeking valleys of pleasure. At the same time, each token inhabits a different landscape. One guest's valley of pleasure is another's hill of happiness (*see* illustration below).

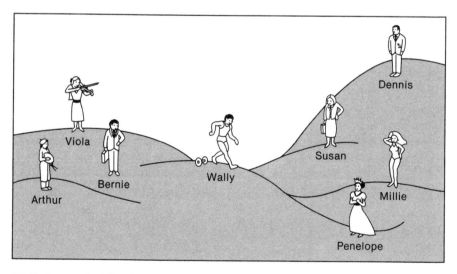

Wally the weight lifter descends a hill of unhappiness toward Princess Penelope

Given a particular cellular space, whether it is a party room, an infinite plain, or a wraparound, toroidal space of the kind so often encountered in "Computer Recreations," the questions asked by the abstract investigator are simple: What distance matrices guarantee the ultimate stasis of tokens? What matrices guarantee eventual periodic behavior? The second question makes sense only for infinite spaces, however. In a finite space some configuration must eventually repeat itself. Thereafter the tokens will behave in ruthlessly periodic fashion. In infinite two-dimensional spaces what matrices will never produce periodic behavior?

In a geographic context, Gold has developed a particularly interesting version of PARTY PLANNER. Invite the eight largest cities in the U.S. to a computer party (in a large room). In other words, let the ideal distance between each pair of guests reflect the distance between the corresponding cities. Amazingly, when such guests are given a random initial placement and are allowed to roam freely according to the rules of the game, they usually end up in correct geographic positions in relation to one another! Readers who try this experiment may be momentarily puzzled by the emergence of a map that is reversed or tilted from its usual orientation, but the emergence is undeniable. Presumably the phenomenon occurs for any set of distances between points on a plane.

As an artist, Gold pursues what he calls algorithmic symbolism. PARTY PLANNER emerged not from Gold's need to plan parties but from his need to paint pictures: He writes:

> "These paintings were to consist of a number of objects such as oranges, apples, violins, hammers, etc. I wanted to paint [them] so that similar objects were close together on the canvas while dissimilar ones were far apart. I had constructed a matrix indicating the ideal distances each object would have from [every] other but discovered it was no easy task to find such an arrangement by eye. . . . I began to wonder what would happen if I could animate . . . the objects and let them wander around seeking their own positions. I was not prepared for the beautiful dance they performed as they sought to minimize their own unhappiness. The party planner was born!"

For readers who prefer purchase to perspiration, Gold has diskettes available for the IBM PC and compatible computers as well as a version for the Apple series (*see* List of Suppliers).

ADDENDUM

In Rich Gold's party planning program a set of hypothetical guests are invited to a party in a personal computer. The scene of the party is a grid of squares on the display screen. The guests move about from square to square in a search for happiness. Each guest has a preferred distance from each of the other guests. He or she will take a step in the direction that minimizes total unhappiness in the current configuration: The summed differences between current and preferred distances measure unhappiness.

The basic program cycle described in "Programmed Parties" was the simplest one possible. Guests moved one at a time. According to Arthur Charlesworth of the University of Richmond, such simplicity can distort festivities somewhat. Charlesworth studied a parallel programming utility called the multiway rendezvous. If each guest were represented by a process in a parallel programming language, at the end of each iteration "all such processes would hold a 'meeting' to share the information about the new positions of guests." The distortion can be removed in our still-commonplace sequential milieu by not moving the guests until the unhappiness of each has been computed.

Arthur D. Penser of Huntsville, Ala., was unhappy about the unhappiness function. He prefers parties in which the differences between current and ideal distances are squared. Given the same invitees in the same initial positions, how different would such parties be? Clearly, they would be more strongly pulled by extreme differences. Absence would make the heart grow fonder squared.

As I stated, there is a science of sorts called proxemics. William Ickinger, Jr., of the University of Maryland once constructed a hexagonal grid that could be laid out on a floor to study interpersonal distances at controlled gatherings of people. Ickinger is fascinated by the subject of programs that simulate gatherings. It remains to be seen whether PARTY PLANNER catches on with social scientists.

○ 15 ○

Palmiter's Protozoa

For those, like me, who are not mathematicians, the computer can be a powerful friend to the imagination.
—RICHARD DAWKINS, *The Blind Watchmaker*

On the muddy bottom of a stagnant pool of water a number of protozoa creep about, feeding on the bacteria that slowly rain down on them. The protozoa all look alike, but their behavior shows important differences. Some of them move erratically in search of bacteria and consequently eat little. Others move with more purpose, following a search pattern that seems almost methodical; they find plenty to eat. Such microscopic worlds have a fascination all their own, but this particular scene has special significance: The methodical protozoa evolved from their erratic cohorts in the space of only one hour

As some readers may already have guessed, such a scene is not viewed through a microscope but on the display screen of a computer. It is generated by a program called SIMULATED EVOLUTION that was written by Michael Palmiter, a high-school teacher from Temple City, Calif. Tiny white protozoan creatures, which Palmiter calls bugs, crawl about on the screen, gobbling up purple bacteria. As generations of bugs pass by, one can watch new feeding behaviors evolve.

Richard Dawkins of Oxford University has also looked for insights into evolution by investigating programs that attempt to simulate its various aspects. One such program, written by Dawkins himself, displays biomorphs: the computer-generated forms that sometimes resemble living creatures. They evolve by a process of "artificial selection": The computer operator arbitrarily selects one of nine possible variant forms of the current biomorph as the basis for future generations of biomorphs.

The biomorphs that emerge from Dawkins' program can be bizarre and amusing — and sometimes even lifelike — but they cannot be said to have evolved naturally, that is, under internal selective pressures. Yet Dawkins thinks it ought to be possible to write a computer program that mimics natural selection. Computer-generated species having such "evolvability" would radiate increasingly complex forms, which selection would pare to a manageable number. Moreover, the surviving descendants would then have to be capable of evolving in new ways that were completely unavailable to ancestors.

Palmiter's protozoan bugs certainly move us one step closer to Dawkins' goal. As a glance at the illustration below reveals, the bugs (the white blips) live within a rectangle on which bacteria (the gray blips) are

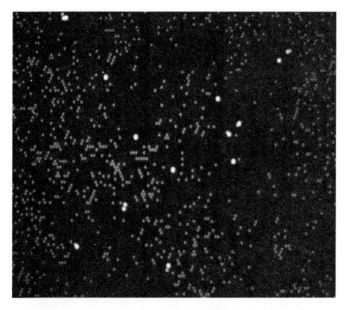

"Jitterbugs" slowly evolve into "cruisers"

continually being deposited. The bugs pursue a life dominated by moving and feeding on bacteria. Each bacterium eaten by a bug provides the bug with 40 units of energy, which is enough to make 40 moves. In places where the feeding is rich, a bug may readily acquire 1,500 units of energy in a few minutes. If that happens, however, a strange mechanism kicks in: All further eating does not benefit the bug until its energy level falls below 1,500 units.

On the other hand, it may happen that a bug finds very little to eat over an extended period. In such a case the bug's energy reserves could gradually drop to zero. At that point it would appear to sit morosely for a few cycles, as though pondering its end, and then wink out like a small light.

A bug's success in finding food depends, of course, on the relative abundance of bacteria in its immediate neighborhood. Because the bacteria are deposited more or less uniformly within the white rectangle, if localized feeding has depleted the bacteria in one place, they are bound to be plentiful elsewhere. Some bugs appear to get to the areas of relative abundance quicker than others. It all depends on the moves a bug makes — its search pattern, so to speak.

The Darwinian scenario of SIMULATED EVOLUTION, albeit abstract, hinges on the "genes" that govern the way a bug moves. These particular genes probably do not exist in real protozoa, but Palmiter's bugs have six of them. They are labeled F, R, HR, RV, HL, and L for Forward, Right, Hard Right, Reverse, Hard Left, and Left. (All directions are expressed from the bug's point of view. Normal turns amount to 60 degrees in one or the other direction, whereas hard turns are 120 degrees.)

On any given move the bug heads in a direction chosen by lottery: The program picks one of the six possible directions from a kind of mathematical hat. If the program chooses L, for example, the bug makes a 60-degree turn to the left. The probability that a particular direction will be chosen is given by a value assigned to the corresponding gene. Hence the higher a gene's value, the greater its contribution to the bug's overall pattern of movement. If, for example, a bug has a large L value in relation to the other five gene values, the bug will spend a lot of time veering to the left.

Every possible combination of gene values results in a different general pattern of movement, and whatever a bug's genetic makeup may be, the bug is stuck with it for life. It can only hope (to be somewhat anthropomorphic) that its offspring will do better.

After a bug has made 800 moves, it becomes "mature" and is ready to reproduce. It does so only if it also happens to be "strong," that is, if it has 1,000 or more units of energy stored under its electric-white membrane. Paramecia undergo a process called conjugation when they reproduce, but the bugs fission: A strong mature bug splits into two new ones, each with half the energy of its parent. When that happens, the new bugs inherit the movement genes of the parent but with a small difference. The value of one of the genes in each offspring is increased or decreased slightly.

Suppose, for example, a strong mature bug has the gene values $F = 3$, $R = 2$, $HR = 0$, $RV = -2$, $HL = 0$ and $L = 1$. Its two offspring, labeled A and B, might inherit the following, mutated forms of that genetic makeup:

$$A: \quad F = 4 \quad R = 2 \quad HR = 0 \quad RV = -2 \quad HL = 0 \quad L = 1$$

$$B: \quad F = 3 \quad R = 2 \quad HR = 0 \quad RV = -2 \quad HL = -1 \quad L = 1$$

As can be seen, in offspring A the F value has been incremented by 1, and in offspring B the HL value has been decremented by 1.

How will the offspring differ from their parent? Offspring A will have a slightly greater tendency to move forward than its parent did, whereas offspring B will have a slightly lesser tendency to make hard-left turns. Such small shifts in tendencies are barely perceptible on the computer screen to a trained observer.

In its simplest mode, SIMULATED EVOLUTION starts out by endowing 10 bugs with a random genetic structure, which causes the great majority of them to jitter from side to side in an unpredictable manner. As a rule such "jitterbugs" exhibit a high death rate. They simply tend to eat up most of the food in their immediate vicinity and then jiggle themselves into starvation on barren ground. Nevertheless, some do survive.

Generation succeeds generation every minute or so. This miniature life-and-death struggle makes for absorbing viewing, but the drama is greatly heightened after several minutes, when the viewer becomes aware that some of the bugs have begun to behave differently. They do not jitter; they bobble. Then, a few minutes later, there are bugs that tumble. After 20 minutes or more one can see bugs that glide — at least for short distances. These bugs appear to do much better than their jittery ancestors. Indeed, they proliferate before one's very eyes for precisely that reason.

In due course "cruiser" bugs develop that move forward most of the time but turn every now and then. This means they are almost always moving toward denser populations of delicious gray bacteria. Once the behavior is established in just a few individual bugs, it comes to dominate the entire population, since the cruisers end up gathering the lion's share of the food.

Although the cruisers constitute a species of sorts, there nonetheless is still some variation within the cruiser population. For example, some cruisers turn more often to the right than to the left, whereas others favor left turns. There are also occasional setbacks, of course. Some cruisers spawn maladapted descendants. A common genetically transmitted disease is the "twirlies," wherein a bug makes too many turns in one direction. Such unfortunate creatures usually die without having known the joy of fission.

It is interesting enough to watch the cruiser species emerge, but Palmiter's program offers more. What if there is variation in the environment? Will more than one species evolve? That question is answered by running SIMULATED EVOLUTION in a mode in which the screen looks much the same except for a particularly rich patch of bacteria in the lower left-hand corner. The bacteria in that patch are replenished at a much higher rate than normal (*see* illustration on page 166). Palmiter calls that bountiful area the Garden of Eden.

As generations of bugs come and go, the cruisers evolve as before. But within the Garden of Eden something quite different happens. A few lucky jitterbugs that have stumbled into the bacterial banquet are promptly rewarded for their lack of an organized feeding method. Jiggle as they will, food continues to surround them.

As food becomes scarcer in the Garden of Eden, however, a subtle environmental pressure begins to operate. Jiggling and jittering soon are no longer viable strategies. That is when the twirlers make their appearance. What normally is a disastrous genetic defect is actually an advantage in an overpopulated Garden of Eden. Indeed, in the course of time those bugs with a strong tendency to turn in one direction predominate in the garden. The reason is obvious. A bug that turns frequently in the same direction, say to the right, will tend to remain in the Garden of Eden longer than its jittery ancestors.

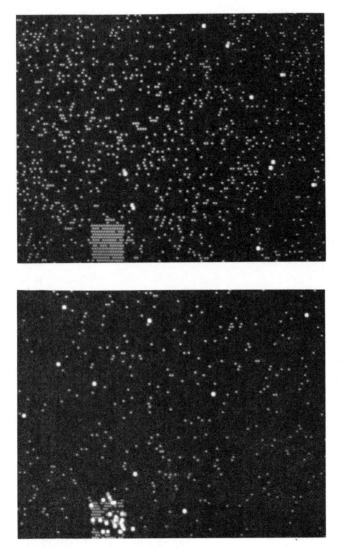

The Garden of Eden (*top*) fosters the evolution of "twirlers" (*bottom*)

Within a few hours at most the Garden of Eden is populated almost exclusively by highly specialized twirlers that might as well be called nervous orbiters. They follow a specific orbit for many cycles and then suddenly move just one square away and repeat the orbit, sweeping up bacteria with each shift.

Is the SIMULATED EVOLUTION program a valid model of biological evolution? Only in a very limited sense. It shows how an environment can favor certain variations in offspring, leading ultimately to the formation of new species. But that is as far as the similarities go. Once one or two stable bug species have emerged, nothing else happens. What would it take to realize Dawkins' dream of an indefinitely continuing computer-generated evolution? Perhaps nothing less than a miniature universe inside the computer.

Readers who would like to study the subject can order a copy of SIMULATED EVOLUTION from Life Science Associates, a small educational-software company (*see* the List of Suppliers). The program runs on IBM PC and compatible computers, and it comes with an elaborate manual. For those relatively advanced programmers who prefer to write their own version of SIMULATED EVOLUTION, I shall now describe BUGS, my name for a simplified version of the program.

A BUGS bug can be represented by a small square that has three pixels on a side. The six directions in which such a bug moves can then be illustrated as they are below. A simple table specifies how the coordinates of a bug's central pixel change depending on the direction in which the bug is heading. The table contains two six-element arrays, *xmove* and *ymove*.

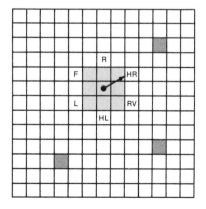
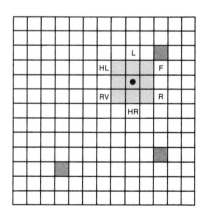

A bug's turns are relative to its current direction

dir	0	1	2	3	4	5
xmove	0	2	2	0	-2	-2
ymove	2	1	-1	-2	-1	1

The direction in which a bug is heading (with respect to the computer screen) is given by the value of the variable *dir*. The corresponding numbers in *xmove* and *ymove* indicate by how many pixels, in the horizontal and vertical directions respectively, the bug must accordingly be shifted on the screen in a single move. If, for example, a bug is headed in direction 2, it must be shifted to the right by two pixels and down by one pixel, since $xmove(2) = 2$ and $ymove(2) = -1$.

BUGS determines the direction of motion for each of the creatures in its charge by consulting a formula based on each bug's genetic code, which is contained in a two-dimensional array called *gene*. The element $gene(k,j)$ contains the jth gene value of the kth bug. In the formula each gene value is made an exponent of 2 in order to avoid having to deal with negative numbers. The probability that a bug will move in direction d is then found by dividing 2 raised to the d-gene value by the sum of 2 raised to each of the gene values. For example, the probability that the bug will next turn hard left is the result of dividing 2^{HL} by the sum $2^F + 2^R + 2^{HR} + 2^{RV} + 2^{HL} + 2^L$.

In this manner BUGS calculates six probabilities for each of the possible moves. When the probabilities are added up, the result naturally is 1. One can think of the probabilities as six different ranges that together span a number line extending from 0 to 1. In other words, if the probabilities for the six different directions of motion are represented by p_0 through p_5, then range 0 consists of the interval from 0 to p_0, range 1 consists of the interval from p_0 to $p_0 + p_1$, range 2 consists of the interval from $p_0 + p_1$ to $p_0 + p_1 + p_2$ and so on.

In each cycle BUGS then determines a new value for the direction of motion for a particular bug by selecting a random number between 0 and 1, seeing in which range it has happened to fall, and assigning the range number to the variable *turn*. In this scheme, then, *turn* equals 0 for F, 1 for R, 2 for HR, 3 for RV, 4 for HL and 5 for L.

A few simple statements complete the motion algorithm:

$$dir \leftarrow dir + turn \ (\text{mod } 6)$$
$$bugx(k) \leftarrow bugx(k) + xmove(dir)$$
$$bugy(k) \leftarrow bugy(k) + ymove(dir)$$

The arrays *bugx(k)* and *bugy(k)* contain the *k*th bug's current coordinates.

In the first line the current direction *dir* is changed by adding the result of the turning lottery embodied in the variable *turn*. Addition must be modular. For example, if *dir* = 5 (which means the bug is heading up and to the left) and *turn* = 2 (which means it needs to turn hard right), the new value for *dir* will be 5 + 2 (mod 6) = 1, and the bug's next move is up and to the right.

BUGS must move all bugs according to this formula, at each step checking whether a bug hit a barrier or landed on a bacterium. In addition it must keep a record of each bug's age and energy supply in order to determine whether a particular bug should be extinguished or allowed to fission. When a bug is ready to fission, the program merely replaces the old bug with two new ones at the same location. These inherit the old bug's gene values except that a randomly selected gene value is increased by a certain amount in one offspring and another randomly selected gene value is decreased by the same amount in the other.

This description of BUGS will be enough for some to try their hand at writing the program. Others may wish to consult the box below. There, a complete algorithmic outline leaves little in doubt.

───────────────────○───────────────────

AN ALGORITHM FOR BUGS

The BUGS algorithm is presented in two parts; first an outline consisting of segments, then an expanded version. This makes it easier to grasp the program as a whole. At the same time, readers would be wise to retain the modular structure presented here. That makes it easier to debug the program and, later, to modify it.

BUGS uses several arrays and variables:

bugx(i) and *bugy(i)*: *x*- and *y*-coordinates of the *i*th *bug*
dir(i): current direction of *i*th bug
time(i): number of cycles since the *i*th *bug*'s birth
fuel(i): amount of fuel currently available to the *i*th *bug*
gene(i,k): the *k*th gene of the *i*th bug.
numbug: the number of *bugs* currently in the simulation

(continued)

(continued from previous page)
xmove and *ymove*: two fixed arrays that contain the relative indices

for each of six kinds of moves that a bug can make
turn: the turn that a *bug* is about to make
bacx(i) and *bacy(i)*:   x- & y-coordinates of the *i*th bacterium
numbac: the number of bacteria currently in the simulation

BUGS   1. INITIALIZE
　　　　2. GENERATE INITIAL BUGS
　　　　3. GENERATE INITIAL BACTERIA
　　　　4. repeat
　　　　　　1. for $k \leftarrow 1$ to *numbugs*
　　　　　　　　1. BUG *k* EATS
　　　　　　　　2. BUG *k* MOVES
　　　　　　　　3. $time(k) \leftarrow time(k) + 1$
　　　　　　　　4. BUG *k* LIVES OR DIES
　　　　　　2. Replenish Bacteria
　　　　5. until keystroke

Statements in lower case are already in detailed agorithmic form.
Statements in upper case will be expanded later. In this connection,
the statement-numbering scheme used here makes it easy to refer to
specific statements no matter how deeply indented they are. For
example, statement 4.1.2 is BUG *k* MOVES: read from left to right,
the three numbers refer to statement 4 of the top (outermost) level,
statement 1 of the next level, and statement 2 of the third level.

BUGS first initializes the evolutionary scenario by setting up arrays
and filling the screen with a supply of bugs and bacteria. Statement 4
is a repeat loop that readers are free to adapt. This form of loop is
exited from only when a certain key is struck. Readers unfamiliar
with this method of loop control will find something equivalent in
their programming manual.

Within the repeat loop (statement 4) there is a FOR-loop (statement
4.1) that merely cycles through all the bugs currently in the simulation. For each bug, the program checks whether it happens to be
sitting on top of a bacterium, in which case it can eat and have its fuel
updated. The program then moves the bug according to the specifics
laid out in Chapter 15. After updating the bug's personal clock, BUGS
then checks whether the bug is ready to die, reproduce, or merely go
on swimming about.

(continued)

(continued from previous page)

The modules follow:

1. INITIALIZE:
    1. *xmove* ← (0,2,2,0,−2,−2)
    2. *ymove* ← (2,1,−1,−2,−1,1)
note: these statements can be realized in a variety of ways, depending on the computer and language one is using. The two *move* arrays give the relative motion of a bug (in terms of a single coordinate) for each of six possible relative directions the bug might next take. It is convenient to assume that the indices of these arrays can run from 0 to 5 instead of from 1 to 6.

2. GENERATE INITIAL BUGS:
    1. for *k* ← 1 to 10
        1. *x* ← random[0,1]
        2. *x* ← 148∗x + 1 /to keep bugs on a screen . . .
        3. *y* ← random[0,1]
        4. *y* ← 98∗y / . . . that is 150 by 100 pixels
        5. *bugx(k)* ← *x*
        6. *bugy(k)* ← *y*
        7. DRAW BUG at (*x,y*)
        8. *fuel(k)* ← 40
        9. *time(k)* ← 0
       10. for *j* ← 0 to 5
            1. *r* ← random[0,1]
            2. *r* ← r∗10 − 5
            3. *gene(k,j)* ← *r*
       11. *r* ← random[0,1]
       12. *dir(k)* ← int(r∗5.999)
    2. *numbugs* ← 10

The function random[0,1] refers to a facility for retrieving a random number from within the range of 0 to 1. Two random numbers, scaled to the size of one's screen (in this case 150 × 100), become the coordinates of 10 successive bugs. Of course, the number 10 can be changed by readers wishing to experiment with initial population sizes. It can even be made a variable to be typed in by the user at run time. The statement DRAW BUG refers to yet further instructions that plot a 3 × 3 square of pixels on the screen. This represents the bug. The center of the square has coordinates (*bugx(k),bugy(k)*). The

(continued)

(continued from previous page)

fuel and clock of the kth bug are each set to appropriate levels. On exiting from this initializing loop, BUGS sets the number of bugs to 10.

3. GENERATE INITIAL BACTERIA: This part of the program has the same general structure as statement 2 does: change the loop limit from 10 to 100, change *bugx* and *bugy* to *bacx* and *bacy*, DRAW BACTERIUM instead of DRAW BUG, omit statements 1.8 to 1.12 and, finally, change *numbugs* to *numbac* ← 100.

4.1.1 BUG k EATS:
1. for i ← 1 to *numbac*
   1. if $bugx(k)-1 > bacx(i)$ or $bacx(i) > bugx(k)+1$ or $bugy(k)-1 > bacy(i)$ or $bacy(i) > bugy(k)+1$
      1. go to 7
   2. ERASE BACTERIUM at $(bacx(i),bacy(i))$
   3. if $fuel(k) < 1500$
      1. $fuel(k)$ ← $fuel(k) + 40$
   4. $bacx(i)$ ← $bacx(numbac)$
   5. $bacy(i)$ ← $bacy(numbac)$
   6. $numbac$ ← $numbac - 1$
7. next statement

BUGS is currently deciding what to do with *bug k*. It runs through the list of bacteria currently in the environment. There are *numbac* of these. For each one, it tries to ascertain whether it lies outside the bug's range. If so, the program goes to the next executable instruction (#7 above). If not, the bug is currently sitting on a bacterium. It proceeds to eat it. The bacterium disappears from the screen (when drawn in the appropriate color) and the bug gains 40 more units of fuel, provided that the bug does not already have 1500 units. BUGS then removes the last bacterium from the bacteria array and places it in the *i*th position, meanwhile decreasing *numbac* by 1. In this way the indices 1 to *numbac* all continue to represent valid bacteria.

4.1.2 BUG k MOVES:
1. ERASE BUG at $(bugx(k),bugy(k))$
2. sum ← 0

(continued)

(continued from previous page)

> 3. for $j \leftarrow 0$ to 5
> > sum $\leftarrow$ sum + 2**gene(k,j)
> 4. $r \leftarrow$ random[0,1]
> 5. $p \leftarrow 0$
> 6. for $j \leftarrow 0$ to 5
> > 1. $p \leftarrow p + 2$**gene(k,j)/sum
> > 2. if $r < p$
> > > 1. turn $\leftarrow j$
> > > 2. exit from loop
> 7. $dir(k) \leftarrow (dir(k) + turn)$ mod6
> 8. $d \leftarrow dir(k)$
> 9. $bugx(k) \leftarrow bugx(k) + xmove(d)$ /test for boundary
> 10.$bugy(k) \leftarrow bugy(k) + ymove(d)$ /test for boundary
> 11.$fuel(k) \leftarrow fuel(k) - 1$
> 12.DRAW BUG at $(bugx(k),bugy(k))$

This module first erases the kth bug at its current location. This is done essentially by using the DRAW routine but with the background color replacing whatever color is used to draw bugs. Instructions 2 and 3 assemble the sum of gene values as powers of 2. This will act as the denominator in the probability to be calculated. Instructions 5 and 6 determine a succession of 6 intervals in one of which a random number (chosen in instruction 4) must lie. The intervals divide [0,1] in proportion to the turn probabilities encoded in the bug's genes. The formula is taken directly from Chapter 15. One of the numbers j thus chosen becomes the variable *turn* which is then added (modulo 6) to the bug's current direction, *dir(k)*. The arrays *xmove* and *ymove* are then applied to produce a new position for the kth bug which is then drawn at the new position. Of course tests must be applied each time a bug moves to see whether it happens to be at the boundary of one's display area. Merely compare current x- and y-coordinates with boundary coordinates. If they are equal, allow a move only if it removes the bug from the boundary.

4.1.4 BUG k LIVES OR DIES:
> 1. if $fuel(k) \geq 1000$ and $time(k) \geq 800$
> > 1. $fuel(k) \leftarrow fuel(k)/2$
> > 2. $time(k) \leftarrow 0$
> > 3. $numbugs \leftarrow numbugs + 1$
> > 4. $bugx(numbugs) \leftarrow bugx(k)$

(continued)

(continued from previous page)

5. $bugy(numbugs) \leftarrow bugy(k)$
6. $time(numbugs) \leftarrow 0$
7. $r1 \leftarrow random[0.1]$
8. $r2 \leftarrow random[0,1]$
9. $r1 \leftarrow int(r1*5.999)$

        / $r1 < 6.0$

10. $r2 \leftarrow int(r2*5.999)$

        / $r2 < 6.0$

11. for $j \leftarrow 0$ to 5
   1. $gene(numbugs,j) \leftarrow gene(k,j)$
   2. if $j = r1$
      $gene(numbugs,j) \leftarrow gene(k,j) - 1$
   3. if $j = r2$
      $gene(k,j) \leftarrow gene(k,j) + 1$

2. if $fuel(k) = 0$
   1. ERASE BUG at $(bugx(k),bugy(k))$
   2. $bugx(k) \leftarrow bugy(numbugs)$
   3. $bugy(k) \leftarrow bugy(numbugs)$
   4. $numbugs \leftarrow numbugs - 1$

Statement 1 of this module handles the case where a bug is ready to breed. Statement 2 undertakes the disposal of a bug that has run out of energy. If both tests fail, a bug is allowed to continue without reproductive or mortuary hindrance. In the first module, statements 1.1 through 1.7 are almost self-explanatory. Two new bugs are created, in effect, by leaving the old k-bug where it is and creating a new bug with index $numbugs + 1$. Both are offspring since both have their clocks reset and their fuel tanks set to half the parental value. Statements 1.8 through 1.11 select two random integers between 0 and 5, inclusive. (INT means "select the integer part of") These are the gene numbers at which the offspring are altered at statements. 1.12.1-3.

4.2 REPLENISH BACTERIA
1. $x \leftarrow random[0,1]$
2. $y \leftarrow random[0,1]$
3. $numbac \leftarrow numbac + 1$
4. $x \leftarrow 148*x + 1$
5. $y \leftarrow 98*y + 1$
6. $bacx(numbac) \leftarrow x$

(continued)

(continued from previous page)

    7. bacy(*numbac*)←*y*
    8. DRAW BACTERIUM at (*x,y*)
note: In this module, bacteria are replenished at a random location on the screen at a rate of one per cycle. Should this rate prove too low, or high, readers are free to modify it to a higher or lower rate.

    DRAW and ERASE: BUGS draws a bug as a 3 × 3 square of pixels. This may be conveniently done as a double loop within which the draw/plot/point command (whatever your system calls it) may be used:
    1. for *i*←*x*−1 to *x*+1
       1. for *j*←*y*−1 to *y*+1
         1. *point(x,y, color)*
Bacteria, of course, are much simpler. A single point (purple if one wishes) will suffice.

Alert readers will notice that a number of segments of code within the whole BUGS algorithm are repeated. It makes good sense to convert these into procedures or subroutines if one's system will allow it. DRAW BUG and DRAW BACTERIUM are two cases in point. The modules are used in several places throughout the algorithm.

─────────────────────────────○─────────────────────────────

ADDENDUM

Simulated evolution, the subject of "Palmiter's Protozoa," drew an unusually heavy mail response after its initial appearance in the May, 1989, issue of SCIENTIFIC AMERICAN. Several hundred readers requested copies of a detailed algorithm on which they could base their own version of the program. After all, it is not often that one has a chance to see pretend protozoa evolve into bacteria banqueters in an hour or less.

Michael Palmiter, the California high-school teacher who developed the program, deserves the palm leaf for his creation. It was evidently an idea whose time had come. Swept into the simulated-evolution zeitgeist were a few readers who had independently developed programs that were remarkably similar to Palmiter's SIMULATED EVOLUTION.

High-school freshman Máté Sztipánovíts of Nashville, Tenn., won accolades at science fairs with a program that simulated oval bugs roaming on a two-dimensional space, looking for randomly distributed food. In Sztipánovíts's program, the medium surrounding the creatures exerts a drag that can be minimized through the evolution of streamlined shapes.

Christopher O'Haver of College Park, Md., also submitted a simulated-evolution program as a science-fair project. Unlike Palmiter's bugs, the organisms in O'Haver's program are stationary (more like algae than protozoa), absorb food continuously, grow, and suffer predation.

Paul H. Deal of Moriarty, N.Mex., has developed a rather sophisticated evolution program that he has been distributing to educators. The genome of his creatures includes 13 genes that govern such characteristics as a creature's ability to feed on organic substrates, to absorb energy, and to move (albeit somewhat feebly). Readers wanting to experiment with Deal's program may obtain it by consulting the List of Suppliers at the end of this book.

Among the readers who were able to set BUGS, my simplified version of Palmiter's program, in motion with only the spare description given in the column were Lewis V. Glavina of Burnaby, British Columbia, Ken Sheller of Bellevue, Neb., Jim Henry of De Kalb, Ill., and Albert H. Behnke of Boston, Va. Glavina, bothered by the amount of energy that bugs sometimes waste at the screen's boundary, gave his protozoa the power to bounce off the screen's sides. Sheller explicitly rewarded the gene that made the greatest contribution to food-gathering behavior. Finding it difficult to distinguish advanced bugs from their less evolved cohorts, Henry colored a bug according to its tendency to stay in the same place. Behnke endowed his bugs with a similar feature, causing a bug to change color as it changes directions.

Puzzling Landscapes

No aspirant to wizardry can avoid the pleasures and pitfalls of conundrums. These sharpen the mind and even inspire the odd program. From the cruel labyrinth of King Minos to the banks of the Continuum River, we are brought to the intimate relationship between problem solving and programming. Panning for primes can mean writing a program that generates prime numbers. Beyond the river's gravelly banks word ladders mount up to heights that even computers cannot reach!

It was Daedalus of old who designed the labyrinth to which King Minos yearly consigned the cream of Athenian youth to wander in misery. In all probability they would be eaten by the dreaded Minotaur before finding their way out. We probe the three-dimensional maze (miraculously reconstructed for our readers) with a modern Theseus who applies computer search techniques to find his way out.

How nice to find ourselves wandering, at last, on the outskirts of Athens to find three philosophers sleeping under a tree. An owl, that symbol of Greek wisdom, suffers an embarrassing lack of control as it flies away overhead. Its hoot awakens the philosophers who all begin simultaneously to laugh. In the sly way of Greek philosophers, they avoid looking directly at the decorated forehead. But its possessor, gifted with great powers of deduction, is the first to stop laughing. How did he figure it all out? People puzzles are still with us, as modern variants of the puzzle reveal.

Old Yuke, a Euclidean prospector on the banks of the Continuum River, instructs the tyro in the ways of cold northern logic. A mathematical sluice box serves to separate primes from nonprimes. But the promise of great riches is dampened somewhat by a theorem, that ineluctible dictator of mathematical reality: The primes thin out pretty rapidly downstream.

Shivering from the cold, we are whisked rapidly to the North African desert to warm up on algopuzzles. It is the early 1940's, and Allied forces battle the Axis as readers ponder some peculiar supply problems. Trucks on patrol must be refueled from barrels of gasoline strategically located by clever readers. Back home there are trains that must turn themselves around or pass each other on single tracks. Algopuzzlers must devise algorithms to solve these problems, a chance for one-track minds to show their stuff.

There are programs that write strange prose and poetry. MARK V. SHANEY is a simple but quite crazy program that reads perfectly straightforward texts on virtually any subject and turns them into funny self-parodies. Other programs weave strange fiction about unknown beings on distant planets and still other programs write remarkably sensitive poems that seem almost to mean something. But is it art? Perhaps it is black art.

At the level of words themselves there are substitution games that lead not only to amusing mental recreations but profound truths about the very nature of the computing enterprise. A cave at the foot of Olympus Mons, that great and ancient Martian volcano, is found to contain a puzzle left by the now-vanished Martian civilization. Although it is solvable, it leads to the question of whether a single computer program that solves all such puzzles could be written. Axel Thue, the Norwegian mathematician, stated the general problem, and early computer scientists discovered its unsolvability. The moral is healthy. Computers, for all their magic, cannot do everything.

· 16 ·

Mazes and Minotaurs

... a labyrinth constructed by Daedalus, so artfully contrived that whoever was enclosed in it could by no means find his way out unassisted.
—*Bulfinch's Mythology*

Most mazes are two-dimensional, so that if we look down on them, we are able to work our way through their intricate twists and turns. But we cannot look down, so to speak, on three-dimensional mazes: upper levels obscure lower ones. We have no alternative but to feel our way—either literally or figuratively—along complex passages.

There are both old three-dimensional mazes and new ones. Given its legendary difficulty, Daedalus' labyrinth of yore must have been three-dimensional. Its Stygian darkness serves as an appropriate setting for an exploration of maze-solving techniques, including an extension of the famous right-hand rule employed in the solution of two-dimensional mazes. As for modern mazes, those that are constructed by M. Oskar van Deventer are not only three-dimensional but also invisible! They lead to a fascinating reconstruction problem: When can three two-dimensional mazes define a single three-dimensional one?

Daedalus constructed his notorious labyrinth for Minos, the powerful king of Crete. The king did not intend the maze for recreational purposes, however. The maze served to confine seven youths and seven maidens sent to him by Athens each year as tribute. No amount of intelligence would serve the hapless victims as they crept along its damp, dark passages seeking the way out. But that was not the worst of it: A fierce and horrendous creature, known as the Minotaur, inhabited the labyrinth. The Minotaur, which had the head of a bull and the body of a human, devoured the poor young Athenians who were trapped in the structure.

Only Theseus, the fabled Greek hero, solved the labyrinth and in doing so killed the Minotaur. He tied a length of thread provided by the king's daughter (who secretly loved him, of course) to the outside of the labyrinth and unwound the thread as he wandered the passages searching for the Minotaur. After slaying the Minotaur, he merely followed the thread back to escape from the labyrinth.

What would have happened if Theseus had been absentminded and had forgotten to secure the thread before entering the labyrinth? Could he have escaped some other way? One possibility would have been for him to tie the thread to the slain Minotaur before setting out in search of the exit. The thread would then at least have enabled him to return to the same starting point (the carcass of the monster) after each unsuccessful probe into Daedalus' cunning labyrinth. But the thread alone would not have guaranteed an eventual exit from the maze. How would Theseus have remembered which passages he had already explored?

That depends on whether Theseus' memory was internal or external. If it was internal, he might simply have remembered the turns he took at each junction he encountered. If it was external, he might have placed some token at each junction as a record of trasversal. Personally, I think the latter form of memory is the likelier one, and so we shall allow Theseus a number of one-drachma coins.

Every time Theseus came to a junction of three or more passages, he would have examined the floor at the entrance to each passage. If a coin was already there, he would not have entered that passage. If no coin was there, he would have entered. After entering he would immediately have put a coin down within view of the junction. Some readers will no doubt object that Theseus could not possibly have seen the coins because of the utter darkness in the labyrinth. It therefore seems reasonable to allow him some form of ancient fire-making apparatus, such as a cigarette lighter.

In following the procedure just outlined, Theseus might well have been forced to backtrack. If, for example, he had come to a dead end or a junction where all passages had coins at their entrances, he would have had to retrace his steps. Is it possible that in the course of backtracking

Theseus might have encountered nothing but nonenterable junctions? In other words, could he have been caught in an infinite loop? For the benefit of those who like to think for themselves, I shall not answer the question. Suffice it to say that the basic method I have outlined is widely applied in modern computing for searching through data structures; it is called a depth-first search.

It might have happened that our intrepid hero had no coins or — worse yet — no cigarette lighter. How could he then have solved the maze? Luckily there is a method for escaping from the maze without external memory. Moreover, executing it would not have taxed Theseus' brain any more than carrying out a depth-first search. I call this method the triple right-hand rule.

Ordinarily two-dimensional mazes can be solved by the so-called right-hand rule: On entering the maze one keeps a wall continuously on one's right, no matter how the passages may twist and turn. If a passage forks, one turns down the right-hand corridor. If a passage comes to a dead end, one simply turns around — keeping a wall on one's right. Eventually one will emerge. Astute readers will have noticed I did not state explicitly that one would emerge at the exit. If the exit happens to be in the middle of the maze (as it is in many paper-and-pencil exercises), one might well come out where one entered after a tiring application of the right-hand rule. But reemerge one must. The reason is very simple: Abiding by the rule enables one never to retrace one's steps. If no part of the wall that defines the maze's passages is ever retraced, it follows that eventually one must run out of wall, so to speak, at an opening. (The exception is the case in which the walls of the maze form a completely closed circuit, but in that case there would be no opening in the wall where one could have entered.)

A variation of the right-hand rule can be applied in solving three-dimensional mazes, including the cruel labyrinth of King Minos. To make things simple, I assume all passages in the maze have a square cross section and are quite straight, except at bends where they make 90-degree turns. In addition, I assume the passages run precisely east-west, north-south, or up-down and are therefore perpendicular to one another. I also assume only two types of junction are formed wherever three passages come together: a T junction and a three-way corner.

Let me now take the reader groping along the passages in order to explain the operation of the triple right-hand rule. No gyroscope is necessary; gravity tells us which way is up and which is down. The other four directions are remembered by keeping track of our turns as we make our way through the three-dimensional maze. If we enter the maze facing east, for example, a turn to the right leaves us facing south; after another turn to the right we would be facing west, and so on.

The triple right-hand rule is applied at a T junction only after we identify the plane in which the junction lies, since each of the three possible planes has a specific "handedness" assigned to it (*see* illustration below). Imagine a clock stuck on a surface parallel to the plane of the T junction. We arbitrarily call the direction in which the hands of a clock turn "right," and we will consistently turn in that direction in the labyrinth.

In the case of three-way corners the rule must be modified somewhat. (Is that the Minotaur bellowing in the distance?) Say that up-down passages have direction 1, north-south passages direction 2, and east-west passages direction 3. If one enters a three-way corner along direction 1, one leaves along direction 2. If one enters along direction 2, one leaves

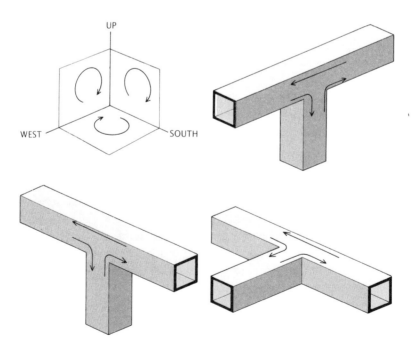

The triple right-hand rule for three-dimensional mazes

along direction 3. Even Theseus might have guessed that if he enters a three-way corner along direction 3, he ought to leave along direction 1. That is all there is to the triple right-hand rule.

The rule happens to satisfy a general criterion for solutions: No passage would be traversed twice in the same *direction*. Does the triple right-hand rule guarantee success? I contend that it does, but only if the maze has one possible path connecting entrance to exit. If the maze has more than one possible solution, I more modestly propose eventual emergence from the maze — through either the exit or the entrance.

Of course, there is no guarantee that Theseus would have emerged from the labyrinth had he started following the triple right-hand rule only after dispatching the Minotaur. But if he had used the rule from the moment he entered the maze and if the struggle with the Minotaur had not disturbed his memory, he would eventually have emerged a hero into the daylight. Theseus would not have cared whether he had left by the entrance or the exit!

With these rules in mind readers may feel ready to try solving a three-dimensional labyrinth. After some extensive research into the matter I offer nothing less than a reconstruction of Daedalus' original labyrinth. The reconstruction is displayed on the next page. Its six levels are all underground. The top level (level 1) lies just under the heavy stone slabs of the courtyard of King Minos' palace. Two of the slabs are missing, revealing holes. The reader is shown into the maze at one of those holes by a burly servant of King Minos. The reader might eventually emerge at the other hole, for that is the labyrinth's exit. Between entrance and exit lie perhaps a few adventures and misadventures.

The six levels of the labyrinth reflect the origin of its design: a cube consisting of six cells on a side. All horizontal passages appear as passages normally do in maps of two-dimensional mazes. Vertical passages, however, appear as solitary squares. A would-be Theseus may go from one level to the level below by clambering down a hole depicted as a black square. He or she will then emerge in the corresponding cell in the underlying level, where the reader will find a larger white square on the map — the hole through which he or she came. Naturally, when a reader wants to go up, he or she must go to the nearest white square. Sometimes one sees a black square inside a white one. This simply means that from that particular position in the labyrinth it is possible to go either up or down.

There are several possible paths from entrance to exit in the labyrinth. Some readers will be content to find just one of them; others may want to

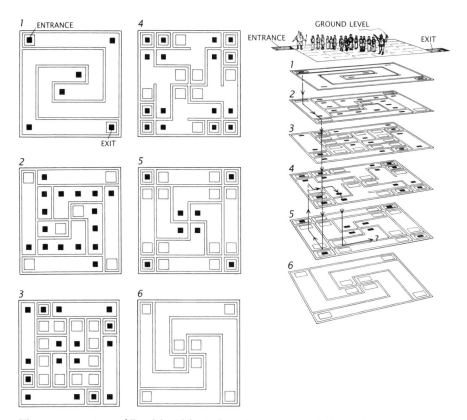

The reconstruction of Daedalus' labyrinth and a possible path (*arrow*)

search for the shortest solution path as measured in cells traversed. To make it a bit more adventurous, I have added a Minotaur to the labyrinth. It stands at the one spot where it is guaranteed to intercept any innocent explorer.

Among the more modern types of three-dimensional maze are two that stand out. The first is visible, the second invisible. The visible maze is a clear plastic cube that contains an arrangement of intersecting, perforated walls. A steel ball rolls along passages created by the walls. The solver holds the maze, manipulating it so that the ball rolls until it eventually reaches the "finish" position. Such a maze, made by the Milton Bradley Company, was a favorite in game stores a decade ago. Today a similar puzzle, called Miller's Maze is available at Toys Я Us stores.

The other kind of modern maze comes from the workshop of van Deventer in Voorburg, The Netherlands. He calls one of his productions a *holle doolhof*, or hollow maze. The terminology is perfectly reasonable: His mazes are wood boxes that contain absolutely nothing! Not a passage or wall can be seen within, but a three-dimensional maze nonetheless exists in the box.

The secret lies in the sides of the box. They are two-dimensional "control mazes": wood surfaces in which slots have been cut. A cursor consisting of three mutually perpendicular wood spars registers one's position in the hollow maze. Each spar passes from one side of the box to the other, sliding along the slots of the control maze on each side. Not surprisingly, the two control mazes on opposite sides of the box are identical. In this way van Deventer can produce a single three-dimensional maze from three pairs of two-dimensional mazes.

In the simple example shown on page 186 one starts with the cursor in one corner of the box and tries to manipulate it into the opposite corner. Each spar is pushed into and pulled out of the box, automatically moving the other two spars (if possible) along slots in their respective control mazes. It might seem that to solve a hollow maze one merely solves each of the three control mazes. But this is not so. Although each of the control mazes can be easily solved, the hollow maze is quite difficult.

The difficulty lies in the fact that possible moves on one control maze may be blocked by another control maze. Moreover, it is not clear in which order the cursor's three spars should be pushed or pulled. There may be several possible moves at any given position of the cursor. To solve the maze one might as well close one's eyes and "feel" one's way through it. In such a mode the invisible maze within the box takes on a new, tactile reality.

The invisible maze can in principle be made visible by tracing the slots of three mutually adjacent control mazes onto a solid cube of material that can be carved. When the tracing is complete, all "non-maze" material is cut away from the solid. The control mazes must of course have the same orientation as they do on the original van Deventer maze.

Since the process is largely imaginary to begin with, I equip myself with a laser saw in carrying it out. Positioning the saw directly over one of the cube's faces, I simply follow the traced lines, cutting straight through the solid as I go. When the cutting is complete, I gingerly push all the unwanted material out of the cube. It slides away, leaving a three-dimensional form that corresponds to the slots of the control maze. After the

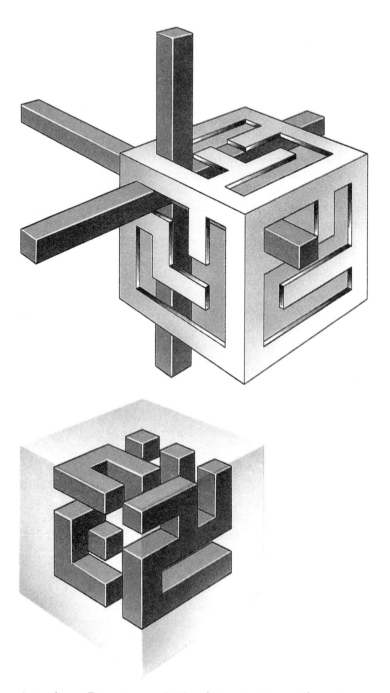

A simple van Deventer maze (*top*) and its projective cast (*bottom*)

same process is repeated for the other two faces, the solid that remains is in effect a "negative" of van Deventer's implicit maze: The allowed passages are represented by solid posts and beams. I call it a projective cast. Readers can see a rendition of one in the illustration at the left.

Two fascinating questions revolve around projective casts. First, when do three two-dimensional mazes yield a projective cast of a viable three-dimensional maze? Second, when does a three-dimensional maze yield three projections that are viable two-dimensional mazes? The term "viable maze" ought to be defined. It refers to a maze in which all passages have unit width and there is a path from the "start" to the "finish" position. (A viable three-dimensional control mazes, it seems to me, ought to be called a van Deventer maze.) Other conditions could readily be suggested, but they would relate to the aesthetics of good maze design; the proposed definition will do for a start.

One can experiment with very simple control mazes and still be quite confounded by what emerges in three dimensions. For example, one can construct a van Deventer maze from rather trivial control mazes consisting of 3-by-3 cellular matrices in which contain adjoining cells have been removed. Readers might enjoy starting with three 3-by-3 control mazes having L-shaped slots in various orientations. How many combinations result in van Deventer mazes?

The other question addresses the opposite issue: When does a three-dimensional maze yield three viable control mazes as projections? Both questions have practical importance for van Deventer. An answer to either one greatly simplifies the process of designing his mazes. Van Deventer himself confesses to having done a great deal of actual cutting and trying in coming up with more complicated hollow mazes.

ADDENDUM

The shortest path through the cruel three-dimensional labyrinth described in "Mazes and Minotaurs" was identified by many readers. It was 39 cells long (counting both the entrance and the exit cells). There are many other, longer paths through the labyrinth, but all paths to the exit lead past a specific point in its murky interior. It is at that spot that the ferocious Minotaur awaits the hapless Athenian youths and maidens who have been forced into the maze. Although some readers discovered the Minotaur's secret location by laboriously drawing a map and then spotting the bottleneck, others suspected that the high degree of symmetry in the design of the maze might be the clue to determining the Minotaur's spot. It was.

At just one point the three-dimensional maze is asymmetric. Readers might enjoy returning to the maze to discover a "missing" wall between the cells (5,3) and (5,4) on the second level. (The coordinates respectively designate the number of cells to the right of the left edge of the maze and the number of cells down from the top edge.) Why does the bottleneck have to be at the point of asymmetry?

The six readers whose correct Minotaur solutions reached me first were Michael Amling, Glen Ellyn, Ill.; Lawrence Leinweber, Cleveland Heights, Ohio; Thomas R. Lunsford, Jr., Hinesville, Ga.; Donald E. G. Maln, Rochester, Mich.; Jim Newton, Middleton, Wis.; and Ken Silber, New York, N.Y.

· 17 ·

People Puzzles

It seems that the analysis of character is the highest human entertainment.
—Isaac Bashevis Singer, *New York Times Magazine*, November 26, 1978

Three philosophers of ancient Greece once took a noontime walk in the country near Athens. Finding shade under an olive tree, they unplugged a wine flask and began a quiet discussion of the fundamental ontological question: Why does anything exist? The discussion grew heated, then confused and rambling. Soon afterward all three philosophers fell asleep in the shade of the tree.

Later that afternoon an Athenian youth who was bent on mischief spied the three slumbering philosophers. He gently splashed drops of white paint on their foreheads. Just before sunset an owl that made its home in the tree sidled out onto a branch above the three men. It hooted once loudly and then flapped noisily away. The owl's cry awakened the philosophers, each of whom immediately assumed that the owl was responsible for his two colleagues' decorated foreheads. They all began to laugh.

The sight was no doubt amusing, and perhaps five seconds passed before one of the men abruptly stopped laughing. Why? The puzzle can be solved by accounting for the thought process of the one philosopher who stopped laughing. In doing so, one has to consider what he must have supposed his cohorts were thinking.

189

Many puzzles involve people merely to provide a human context in which the would-be solver feels more comfortable. But the solutions to problems I call people puzzles, such as that of the three philosophers, depend on thinking about what each person in the puzzle is thinking the other people in the puzzle are thinking. Such reasoning about reasoning is not only an amusing theme for puzzles but also a necessary one for computer scientists who seek to create programs that mimic the way a human being might think about similar perplexing situations.

The basic theme of this chapter is not complete without the solution to the puzzle of the three philosophers. Let us call the philosophers Pythagoras, Plato, and Aristotle. Pythagoras, the oldest and wisest, is the one who stopped laughing. Here is the reason: Pythagoras looked at Aristotle chortling away and realized that Aristotle had no idea his own forehead was anointed with a white substance. If he (Pythagoras) had a clean forehead, then Aristotle was evidently laughing at Plato. But who then did Aristotle think Plato was laughing at? "Great Athena!" Pythagoras must have exclaimed to himself, "I shouldn't be laughing." The situation is depicted in cartoon form at the right.

That is the answer to the more or less traditional form of the puzzle. The puzzle can be extended somewhat by asking why a few seconds later Plato also stops laughing. As soon as Pythagoras quits laughing, his line of thought is no longer open to Plato. Indeed, it would seem that the belief that one's own forehead is clean is now reinforced in Plato's mind. "Pythagoras evidently saw my clean forehead and realized that Aristotle was laughing at him," Plato might think. Yet if Plato cogitates a bit more, he will deduce his own befouled state. I shall let the reader step into Plato's sandals to determine how.

Consider a variation of the three philosophers theme. A sultan wanted to choose the wisest of three candidate viziers for the position of grand vizier. The sultan took the viziers into a darkened room and put a white hat on the head of each. He then led them back to the throne room and told them: "Each of you has been given a hat that is either white or black, and at least one of the hats is white. The first of you to tell me the color of your hat will get the job of grand vizier."

The puzzle of the three viziers is essentially the same as that of the three philosophers, even though there is no laughter to serve as an indicator of what each vizier sees. In a curious way the shared knowledge that at least one hat is white works hand in hand with the silence of indecision to produce an equivalent effect.

One philosopher thinks on a deeper level than his colleagues

Let us call the candidate viziers al-Khwarizmi, ibn Khaldun, and ibn Sina. Here are al-Khwarizmi's thoughts, which win him the position:

"H'm, I wonder if my hat is black. If it were, what would the other viziers think? Suppose ibn Khaldun too thought his hat were black. In that case he would realize that ibn Sina would see two black hats and deduce immediately that his own is white. Yet ibn Sina has not cried out, 'My hat is white?' hence ibn Khaldun knows that ibn Sina sees at least one white hat. But if my hat were indeed black, then ibn Khaldun would know that his is the white hat ibn Sina sees, and he would say so. Yet ibn

Khaldun has not done that. By the beard of the Prophet, my hat cannot be black!"

The three viziers puzzle has a meta-puzzle level pointed out by one of my colleagues: As soon as the viziers are told the nature of the contest, each can deduce that the only fair test of their cognitive abilities would in fact require all three hats to be white.

One can easily rewrite the puzzles of the three philosophers and the three viziers in an endless number of ways. A well-known variation involves three aristocratic women traveling by train through the English countryside at the turn of the century. It is a hot day and they have opened their compartment window to let in some fresh air. The train, belching thick black smoke, enters a long tunnel. When it emerges into daylight, all three women simultaneously break into laughter at the sight of their traveling companions' soot-covered faces — until one of them ceases to laugh.

Here is a second variation: Three businessmen lunch on spinach quiche at a Manhattan expense-account restaurant. All three get spinach on their teeth . . . The realization that a people puzzle can take many different equivalent forms leads to the idea of puzzle transformations. How does one transform philosophers into viziers, so to speak? It helps to identify the elements of one puzzle that have corresponding elements in the other:

1. mischievous youth → sultan
2. philosopher → vizier
3. forehead → head
4. white mess → white hat
5. laughed → kept silent

In addition to these elements, the transformation must also define the peculiar characteristic of a philosopher or a vizier as operationally defined in the puzzle. A philosopher is someone who, until he analyzes the situation, will laugh if he sees at least one befouled forehead but will otherwise not laugh. A vizier is someone who, until he analyzes the situation, will say nothing if he sees at least one white hat. Otherwise he will say, "My head has a white hat on it."

Readers are invited to fill in the blanks in the generic people puzzle that follows. Filling in the numbered blanks with the corresponding words in the left-hand column of the table above will result in the three philosophers puzzle. If the blanks are replaced with the corresponding words in the right-hand column, the three viziers puzzle emerges. (One can, of course, come up with one's own set of words that would make sense if they replaced the blanks.) Colorful details of time and place have been eliminated to simplify the demonstration.

Once upon a time a (1)_____ put a (4)_____ on the (3)_____ of each of three (2)_____s without their knowing it. As long as he did not know that his own (3)_____ had a (4)_____ on it, each (2)_____ (5)_____. Suddenly the wisest of the three (2)_____s no longer (5)_____. He then exclaimed, "My (3)_____ has a (4)_____ on it!" How was he able to deduce this?

The next variation I shall present on the theme of the three philosophers originally concerned unfaithful wives. Because it involves sexual stereotyping, I shall take advantage of a simple transformation to alter it. In any event the puzzle is interesting because it generalizes the problem of the three philosophers.

The tyrannical queen of the Amazons announced one day to her subjects that at least one husband in her realm had been unfaithful. She then issued a proclamation: "If any of you discovers your husband to be unfaithful, I order you to execute him at the stroke of midnight of the day on which you ascertain his infidelity." In the realm of the Amazons information was shared freely but not too freely; each wife knew about the infidelities of all husbands except her own. Also, word of an execution spread throughout the realm within a day. As it happened, there were exactly 40 unfaithful husbands. Were any executed and, if so, when?

Readers will have noted that the queen announced that at least one husband had been unfaithful. If exactly one husband had been cheating, his wife would have known immediately: If any husband but her own was a philanderer, she would have heard about it. Hence on midnight of the day of the queen's announcement he would have been killed by his wife.

If there had been exactly two unfaithful husbands, their respective wives would have dispatched them at midnight of the second day. The news that there was no execution carried out at midnight of the first day would confirm the fact that there were two husbands who were unfaithful. Because the wives of the two philanderers would have been aware of only one philanderer in the realm (although all the other Amazons would have realized that there were at least two), they would immediately have realized that their own spouse must be the second philanderer.

By now readers will have caught the drift of the argument. No execution at midnight of the nth day means that at least $n + 1$ husbands were unfaithful. At the dawn of the 40th day it would be common knowledge that at least 40 husbands were unfaithful. Indeed, this would come as no surprise to Amazons married to faithful husbands, since they would know of 40 philandering husbands. Only a wife with an unfaithful husband would know of 39 unfaithful ones, meaning that their own spouse was the 40th. These wives, in carrying out their monarch's command, would then summon their husbands for a midnight tête-à-tête on the 40th day after the queen's proclamation.

Is the Amazon puzzle really a variation of the three philosophers puzzle? The question can be answered by asking what would happen if there were only three Amazons, each married to an unfaithful husband. In that case at the end of the third day each Amazon would have drawn the correct conclusion. In this form the puzzle compares most directly with that of the three viziers (which I have already shown to be a transformation of the three philosophers puzzle).

To see this, suppose the sultan had told the three candidates for grand vizier, "I shall ask several times in succession whether you know the color of your own hat. Answer only if you know, otherwise remain silent." In that case the first time the sultan asked the question, all three viziers would have remained silent. The second time he asked the question, all three would again have remained silent. The third time he asked, all three candidates would have replied yes.

The Amazon puzzle deals with 40 unfaithful husbands, not three. Can the three philosophers puzzle be generalized to a group of 40 philosophers? Yes. For the moment, imagine just four philosophers asleep under the tree. On awakening they all begin to laugh and the fourth philosopher (actually one of the gods in disguise) reasons as follows:

"H'm. It is consonant with my divine dignity to assume I have an unsoiled forehead and can therefore laugh at the three besmirched mortals. But why does one of them not realize his condition and stop laughing?" (The Olympian now mentally recapitulates Pythagoras' argument.) "Dear me, I think I know the reason."

If such a thought process can bring a fourth philosopher to realize that his forehead has not been spared, then it can just as easily explain how a fifth, a sixth, and even a 40th philosopher might arrive at the same conclusion. In one of his "Mathematical Games" columns Martin Gardner developed a generalization of the three viziers puzzle along these lines (*see* SCIENTIFIC AMERICAN, May, 1977). As he astutely observed, however, difficulties arise. "This generalization usually provokes arguments, because the problem demands so many fuzzy assumptions about degrees of smartness and lengthening lapses of time that the problem becomes unreal."

To be sure, all puzzles have a degree of unreality about them. How likely is it, even in a trendy restaurant, that three people lunching on spinach quiche will all end up with a bit of spinach on their teeth at the same time? And even if that does happen, how likely is it that one of the three would not see from another's glance that he himself was being laughed at?

Still, to investigators trying to develop new forms of artificial intelligence based on what is known as logic programming, people puzzles are serious business. John L. McCarthy of the University of California at Berkeley, among others, tested the deductive powers of logic systems by applying them to people puzzles such as that of the three viziers. Logic-programming systems exploit a kind of symbolic thought process known as predicate calculus to derive automatically various deductions from certain assumptions. In order to mimic the human capacity by which people make deductions in various social situations, logic-programming systems must have the power to model reasoning about reasoning.

Such investigators might do well to examine the more realistic kind of people puzzles that occur in everyday life. Although these puzzles are not logically deep and require a great many assumptions for their solution, they nonetheless reveal that a significant part of our mental capacity is applied in thinking about what other people may be thinking we are thinking.

Erving Goffman, late of the University of Pennsylvania, was a pioneer in a field of psychology called transactional analysis, which maintains that every person is constantly trying to know what others are thinking about him or her and to manipulate that thinking, rather in the manner of actors. Goffman has documented this aspect of our inner lives through a compilation of all-too-human behaviors that we recognize as valid experiences.

Here are two examples of the kind described by Goffman that actually come from my own life; it so happens that I have been collecting similar examples for years. They all seem to point to a human facility for thinking about what other people are thinking, which in most of us, I believe, is semiconscious.

I once saw a policeman descending to street level from a second-floor establishment of a questionable nature. Perhaps it was a massage parlor. (The section of town in which the incident took place makes that likely.) As he emerged onto the street, the policeman unexpectedly met a fellow officer. For his colleague he put on a very strange face: he looked not embarrassed but as though he were pretending to be embarrassed. This was at first strange to me but later understandable. The first officer's primary feeling was probably outright embarrassment. After all, the colleague would rightly suspect that the visit had been unofficial, so to speak. Yet to have expressed such embarrassment would only have confirmed those suspicions. On the other hand, if the second officer could be made to perceive that the first officer was only pretending to be embarrassed, he might pass the incident off as a joke.

Games sometimes bring out the worst in people. Two rather competitive colleagues had just finished a game of poker. The loser was visibly upset but trying hard to control himself. Finally he blurted out: "You were planning to _____ me and I was planning to _____ you. You just beat me to it!" (Here the blanks can be filled in with a suitable coarse word meaning, in this context, to cheat.)

The operative word here is *just*. At first it seems to imply that luck played the major role in his opponent's victory. On closer inspection, however, it appears to mean the loser wants the winner to think he (the loser) thinks the most significant aspect of their game was the equality of their motivation rather than the inequality implied by his losing.

I wonder if any readers have examples of their own to send in. Particularly interesting would be examples that are a little closer in actual content to traditional people puzzles.

Speaking of puzzles, readers may wish to acquire *The Puzzling Adventures of Dr. Ecco*. It is written by Dennis Shasha, a computer scientist at the Courant Institute of Mathematical Sciences at New York University. The book describes the adventures of the mysterious Dr. Ecco, a fabulously intelligent eccentric who solves puzzles for a living. Besides a couple of people puzzles, it includes puzzles about elections, multiple routes, spies, circuits that check circuits, and much more.

I shall close the discussion of people puzzles with one from Shasha's book. Two generals whose respective armies occupy two sides of a ridge want to coordinate their attack on a common enemy, because if either army attacks alone, it could be destroyed. Unfortunately the generals can communicate only by carrier pigeons that fly over the ridge from one camp to the other (*see* the illustration opposite).

Will the confirmations of confirmations between the generals ever end?

The first general sends the second general the following message: "Attack at 0800 hours. Confirm message received, otherwise I shall not attack." The second general has no objection to attacking at that time and intends to send a pigeon bearing the confirmation. But the second general suddenly realizes that the first general will not attack unless he receives the confirmation. Since the second general has no guarantee that a carrier pigeon will actually deliver his confirmation to the first general, he decides that he himself will not attack unless he knows that the first general knows that the attack has been confirmed. The second general then sends a pigeon off with a message to the first general. Will the seemingly infinite regress of confirmation messages ever stop? Perhaps the answer depends on the particular message that one of the generals sends at some point.

I acknowledge with thanks the help of two of my colleagues at the University of Western Ontario, Andy L. Szilard and Areski Nait Abdallah, in the preparation of this chapter.

ADDENDUM

In "People Puzzles" I wrote about a class of logic puzzles that can be solved only by thinking about what other people are thinking. Such puzzles were typified by three philosophers who awoke from an afternoon slumber under a tree and noted that the foreheads of the other two had apparently been befouled by a bird. Only in the course of the ensuing laughter did the wisest of them realize that his own forehead was decorated.

It had not occurred to me, as it did to James D. Klein of College Place, Wash., that there is a two philosophers puzzle of sorts. Klein tested his own children with the story of a pair of workmen who fall from a scaffold onto the ground. The fall does not hurt either of them, but it does dirty the face of one. Why did the workman with the clean face rush to wash up while the one with the dirty face merely went back to work? Klein writes, "It is interesting to hear them think out loud and watch their eyes as the solution dawns."

Another people puzzle was borrowed from Dennis Shasha's book *The Puzzling Adventures of Dr. Ecco.* In this conundrum two nineteenth-century generals whose armies are separated by a ridge of land decide to coordinate their attack on the enemy by sending messages by carrier pigeon. But what message to use? An infinite regress of messages appeared to be inescapable.

The generals' predicament reminded Warner Clements of Beverly Hills, Calif., of a little-known off-Broadway play that involved a would-be double agent shuttling back and forth between two hostile nations. It begins when the agent learns that country A has broken the secret military code of country B. The agent goes to B in order to sell that country's intelligence officers the information. "We already know that," the officers say. The agent is at first discouraged but then realizes he can sell that information to the intelligence offers of country A. They in turn reply, "We know the B's have broken our code. We have been sending them false information!" The agent rushes back to country B: "Do you realize the A's know you have broken their code?" "Oh yes," reply the B officers. The agent returns to the A's to apprise them of the situation, and so on. How long might the agent have to continue the back-and-forth journeys, bearing an ever lengthening message about what the other side knows? Although in this puzzle the two military factions are not coordinating but competing, it makes the solution no easier — there not being one.

More down-to-earth people puzzles involved real people in everyday situations like those studied by the late Erving Goffman, a sociologist. In my "Compute Recreations" column in Scientific American of January, 1989, I asked for examples and received several, including one from P. M. Cambeen of Muiden in the Netherlands. During World War II an officer in the German force occupying Holland expressed to a resident his puzzlement at Dutch people's attitudes. He was told: "The Dutch have three virtues. They are intelligent, loyal, and pro-Nazi. Any given Dutch person, however, has only two of these virtues and the opposite of the third." While the logical implications of his statement were being worked out by the officer, the wit had enough time to get away.

ₒ 18 ₒ

Panning for Primes

No recreation embodies the lure of pure number better than the search for primes. Like nuggets of gold, they hide in the gray gravel of ordinary numbers. A prime is elemental: It cannot be divided evenly by any numbers other than 1 and itself. Primes are precious because they are rare. Common enough among the small numbers near the source of the great Continuum River, they thin out rapidly in the downstream banks.

One can pan for primes, even build a sluice box to mine these nuggets, but no one knows where they all are without looking. There is no formula for primes. There are patterns of sorts, a primitive kind of geology by which we can guess the deposits. Just as amateurs flocked to California and the Yukon to pan distant streams for the elusive yellow, so ordinary readers can set out for Number Country with little more than this primer tucked into a spare pocket.

Few mathematical ideas are as accessible to the average person as the concept of a prime number. It takes about a minute to explain primes to the man or woman in the street. Buy them a coffee and with a little encouragement they will write the primes on a paper napkin: 2, 3, 5, 7, 11, 13, 17 and so on. The number 1 is not normally considered to be prime.

Can one tell a prime just by looking at it? If there are many numbers in the pan, does a prime flash yellow to the eye? Some people think so. Numbers that end in 1 are often precious, such as 11, 31, 41 and 61. But one must beware of such fool's gold as 51 and 81, for example. Eventually the numbers that end in 1 fool us with increasing frequency, so that it is possible to wonder, as a few ancient Greeks did, whether the primes eventually thin out to nothing. There comes an end finally, or does there? Euclid has passed down to us the first proof that there is no end to the prime numbers.

The proof is so simple that one can imagine Euclid drawing forth the demonstration, Socratic fashion, from a slave. I prefer the conversation between the tyro and the old-timer on the banks of the Continuum River:

TYRO: Hey, mister! How far downstream do the primes go?

YUKE: Why, boy, all the way to the Sea of Infinity.

TYRO: I don't believe you. Here we are at the millions and I haven't seen color all day.

YUKE: You tenderfeet gotta be told everything. Look, suppose you came to the last prime. No more after that, right?

TYRO: Uh, right.

YUKE: Call it n. You take and form the product of all the primes there are right on up to n. O.K.? That's $2 \times 3 \times 5 \times \ldots \times n$. Now add 1 to the product and call the number you finally get p.

TYRO: Don't tell me that p is prime!

YUKE: Well, if it ain't prime there's a prime missing from our list! You can't divide p by 2 because there's 1 left over. You can't divide it by 3 because there's 1 left over. There's always 1 left over, right up to n. There's just no getting around it.

TYRO: Gosh, I guess that's what keeps you going.

YUKE: Yup. Well, don't just stand there yammering. Help me with this sluice box here.

Even if there is no largest prime, there is certainly a largest known prime. The distinction confuses some readers and even a few journalists. The fault lies with those back-page headlines: LARGEST PRIME FOUND. The confusion sometimes continues into the story. We learn that a new supercomputer has just shown that the 7,067-digit number $5 \times 2^{23,473} + 1$ is prime. It has no divisors except 1 and of course, itself. The story might well omit (or the reader might miss) the fact that this is merely the largest known prime; soon a new, larger prime may well be found.

I hesitate to mention the largest prime number currently known. It may no longer be current by the time these words appear in print. As of this writing, the largest know prime is a 65,050-digit number found by David Slowinski of Cray Research, Inc., in 1985: $2^{216,091}-1$. Prime numbers that have the form 2^m-1 are called Mersenne primes after the preeminent French mathematical amateur Marin Mersenne. All known primes with more than 1000 digits are collected by another amateur, Samuel D. Yates of Delray Beach, Fla. The Yates collection is definitive. He has generously offered it to readers who send him the cost of copying and postage ($3) (*see* the List of Suppliers).

How quickly do prime numbers thin out along the banks of the continuum? Within the first 10 numbers, four, or 40 percent, are prime. Within the first 100, the percentage drops to 25 percent. The percentage continues to drop more or less progressively. In general, the number of primes less than or equal to a number n is approximately $n/\log n$. (In this context the approximation is asymptotic. In other words, if the number of primes less than or equal to n is represented by the symbol $p(n)$, the ratio of $p(n)$ to $n/\log n$ approaches 1 as n gets larger. To quote old Yuke: "Downstream the primes thin out by the factor of a natural log.")

A few trials give some feeling for the rule. How many primes are there, according to the formula, between 1 and 100? Between 1 and 1000? In the first case the formula yields an approximate value of 22. In the second case the formula predicts something like 145 primes.

Not surprisingly, the phenomenon of thinning-out produces more and longer stretches of numbers where there are no primes at all. To find a stretch of a million consecutive nonprimes, for example, one need only travel downstream, as Martin Gardner once did, to the number 1,000,001!. The exclamation mark does not indicate admiration but elaboration: it stands for $1 \times 2 \times 3 \times \ldots \times 1,000,001$. Teen-age terminology applies, namely humongous. But with ease we detect the prime-free stretch. If n runs from 2 to 1,000,001 in the simple formula 1,000,001! + n, each of the resulting numbers happens to be composite. After all, in each case n divides both 1,000,001! as well as itself. Thus it divides the sum.

I stated above that there is no formula for prime numbers, no combination of algebraic operations on n that will produce, with a fixed number of crank turns, the nth prime. Many people have fallen prey to vain imaginings brought about by initial success. A well-known joke among mathematics undergraduates illustrates the point. It involves three ways of showing that all odd numbers are prime:

Mathematician: "Three is a prime, 5 is a prime, 7 is a prime . . . The result follows by induction."
Physicist: "Three is a prime, 5 is a prime, 7 is a prime, 9 — experimental error, 11 is a prime. . ."
Engineer: "Three is a prime, 5 is a prime, 7 is a prime, 9 is a prime. . ."

Engineers may have the last laugh, since mathematicians depend increasingly on computers to probe for large primes.

Would it be enough to produce a formula that itself produces only primes? Pierre de Fermat, the famous seventeenth-century French mathematician, thought he had such a formula when he wrote $2^{2^n} + 1$. Plug in any value of n, he believed, and a prime number would emerge. Fermat's bubble was burst after his death when the Swiss mathematician Leonhard Euler found factors for the fifth Fermat "prime": $4{,}294{,}967{,}297 = 641 \times 6{,}700{,}417$.

As old Yuke might remark, "There's more than one way to skin a cat." Sometimes a visual pattern suggests a formula. Such a pattern was doodled one day by Stanislaw Ulam, the Polish-American mathematician. Attending a boring lecture, he began absentmindedly to draw a grid of horizontal and vertical lines. He numbered one of the resulting squares 1 and proceeded to number succeeding squares in a spiral around the first one:

$$
\begin{array}{ccc}
5 & 4 & 3 \\
6 & 1 & 2 \\
7 & &
\end{array}
$$

When the spiral of numbers had wrapped around itself several times, Ulam began to circle the primes with no particular purpose in mind. He sat up rather quickly, however, when he noticed an odd pattern developing. Straight lines had begun to appear out of nowhere! Ulam was immediately aware, of course, that such lines hinted at formulas for primes. The computer plot on page 204 duplicates Ulam's pencil-and-paper experiment by replacing nonprimes with small white squares and primes with black ones.

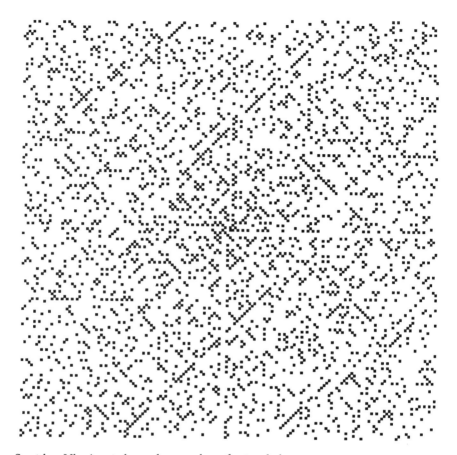

Stanislaw Ulam's spiral reveals a number of prime lodes

The prominent diagonal lines correspond to prime lodes. How could one express this geology symbolically? Near the center of the diagram one such deposit proceeds down and to the right. It consists of the number sequence 7, 23, 47, 79, . . . The formula for this sequence happens to be quadratic: $4x^2 + 4x - 1$.

Those with some memory of high-school algebra can develop the formula for virtually any line in the diagram. It may be that the formula is rich in primes well beyond the limits of the plot. Euler (rhymes with "spoiler"—and he ruined a number of careers by anticipating so many mathematical results) had stumbled on a similar formula in the eighteenth century: $x^2 + x + 41$. The formula does not show up on Ulam's spiral unless one uses a different central number. A spiral that starts at 41 reveals a vein that contains 40 consecutive prime numbers before it peters out!

Perhaps it is only city slickers who mine primes by formulaic methods. Those who work the banks of the Continuum River prefer pans or, better yet, sluice boxes. In these devices, also known as number sieves, numbers are shoveled in at one end; only primes emerge from the other end. Wood ribs catch the composite numbers by a divisibility test (*see illustration below*). Sluice boxes work perfectly well inside computers, naturally.

The simplest sluice box separates primes by dividing by 2, 3, 4, and so on. If one inputs the number n at one end, the sluice box tests whether n is divisible by 2, by 3, by 4 and continues until one of the tests succeeds or the count reaches n. In the first case the number is not prime. In the second case it is. An algorithm for this model of sluice box provides the simplest framework for home-computer programs. It is called SLUICE1:

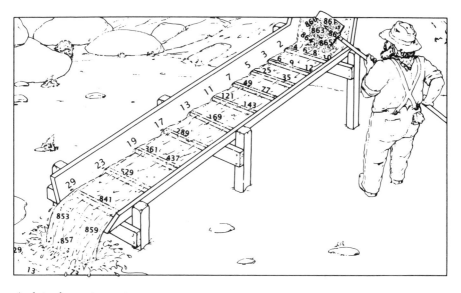

A sluice box mines primes

```
input n
f←1
for k←2 to n − 1
    test←rem(n/k)
    if test = 0 then f←0
if f = 1 then output "prime"
```

The program accepts a number n that is typed in (input) by the human user. Then the program sets the variable f (which acts as a flag) to 1; if f still has the value 1 when the program reaches its last line, the number n must be prime. A single IF statement is executed repeatedly inside a loop. The index k runs from 2 to $n − 1$. For each such value SLUICE1 performs the division n/k, takes the remainder (rem) of the division n/k and stores the result under the name *test*. Usually *test* will be non-zero at the end of the loop. In other words, the number k does not divide n evenly. But if the division ever results in a zero remainder, SLUICE1 will immediately set the flag f to the value 0, holding it there until the loop has been completed. If the second IF statement has a positive outcome, the program will print "prime." If f has been set to 0 somewhere along the line, only a grim silence will follow.

Although it is easy to understand, the foregoing program is too slow, particularly if it is adapted to produce a sequence of primes. The adaptation would merely involve replacing the first input statement by a loop statement, such as "for $n←3$ to 1000." The final statement would be modified to print not "prime" but the value of n that made it all the way through the sluice box without being divided evenly. One by one all the prime numbers from 3 to 997 will come tumbling out, but very slowly!

Things move much more swiftly after SLUICE1 has been subjected to some tinkering. First, there is no point in testing whether the number n is prime by the division n/k if k happens to be larger than the square root of n; at least one of n's factors does not exceed its square root. The famous "fundamental theorem of arithmetic" also tells us that every whole number is the product of a unique set of prime numbers. It is not composite unless it can be divided evenly by a prime less than itself. Putting the two facts together results in a much shorter loop that uses only prime values for the index k and only those primes that are less than the square root of n.

The new algorithm, called SLUICE2, differs enough from its simple-minded counterpart to require a relisting:

```
r ← 1
p(1) ← 2
for n ← 3 to 1000
    k ← 1
    f ← 1
    while f = 1 and p(k) ≤ sqrt(n)
        test ← rem(n/p(k))
        if test = 0 then f ← 0
        k ← k + 1
    if f = 1 then r ← r + 1
        p(r) ← n
```

Because SLUICE2 needs a list of primes in order to function properly, it stores these as it generates them in an array called p. The variable r keeps track of the index for the last entry of p. That way SLUICE2 always knows where to put the next prime it generates. The first line of the algorithm sets the index to 1. The next line specifies that the first member of the prime array will be 2. Then comes the loop command discussed above. It controls the testing of all numbers from 3 to 1000. The variable k keeps track of which array element is currently being tested against n. Inside the main loop is a common kind of loop that uses the word WHILE; as long as the flag is 1 and the current prime to be tested does not exceed the square root of n, the inner loop keeps chugging through successive values of k. Outside this loop f will equal either 1 or 0. In the first case a prime has been found. SLUICE2 adds the prime to its list. In the second case the main loop will simply go on to the next value of n.

Readers programming this kind of sluice box have two choices for structuring the program to print out all the primes found. SLUICE2 may print the array p all at once when the main algorithm is complete. The experience is akin to opening a poke full of nuggets. It is more adventurous, some would say, to place a print command right after the line $p(r) ← n$. Then the user watches individual nuggets appear as soon as they are found.

I have been unadventurous in suggesting an iteration limit of a mere 1000 numbers to test. There is no reason the limit should not be increased to 100000 or even one million. Or is there? It all depends on how large an array one's system allows. The size of the array hinges on the number of primes one expects to generate. Here the prime-ratio formula comes in handy. The formula suggests that approximately 72,382 of the numbers less than 1,000,000 are prime. A computer that has only 64K of memory will not make the grade. If we do not insist that all these primes be on our list, however, we can retain only the primes between 1 and $\sqrt{1,000,000}$. These will suffice to weed out the non-primes up to 1,000,000, the remainder being printed out as they are found.

Prime numbers have figured in countless mathematical recreations. To continue the theme of primes in square arrays, two diversions come to mind. The first originates with Henry Ernest Dudeney, the distinguished English puzzle creator. Magic squares will be familiar to many readers as square arrays of numbers whose entries have the same sum along each row, each column and the two main diagonals. Are there magic squares consisting only of primes? The answer is yes. The 3-by-3 magic square shown below sums to 111 along all rows, columns and the diagonals. The 3-by-3 square is accompanied by a 4-by-4 companion. Squares of orders higher than 4 have been found. Readers may enjoy hunting for them.

Another British purveyor of puzzles has issued a challenge to readers. Gordon Lee, who writes a column called "Winners and Losers" in a computer publication titled *Dragon User*, has constructed a 6-by-6 square of digits that conceals a great many prime numbers, 170 to be exact (*see* illustration below, right). To find a prime number on Lee's grid scan along any row, column, or diagonal in any direction. It may happen that a

67	1	43
13	37	61
31	73	7

3	61	19	37
43	31	5	41
7	11	73	29
67	17	23	13

3	1	3	9	9	1
9	8	3	9	2	9
1	6	4	3	1	2
5	1	7	4	7	1
7	1	5	9	7	1
9	3	7	3	3	9

Henry Ernest Dudeney's prime square (*left*), Allan W. Johnson, Jr's. prime square (*middle*), and Gordon Lee's 6-by-6 primer grid (*right*)

sequence of digits thus encountered is a prime number, one of the 170 counted by Lee. No more than 616 numbers (prime or otherwise) can be found in a 6-by-6 grid of digits. Repeated primes are only counted once. Lee counts 1 as a prime.

Can readers come up with a 6-by-6 square of digits that contains more than 170 primes? Those who write and run SLUICE1 or SLUICE2 will have a slight edge on the task. Lee suggests a strategy of seeding the square with the digits 1, 3, 7, and 9, since a prime must end with one of them. On the other hand, a square composed of only those digits would be relatively poor in primes. A judicious scattering of even numbers, including 0, might improve one's chances of meeting Lee's challenge.

ADDENDUM

I shall now announce the winners of the prime-grid challenge issued by Gordon Lee in "Panning for Primes." A prime grid is a six-by-six grid of squares each of which contains a single digit. The object is to choose the digits and their positions in the grid in such a way that one gets as many prime numbers as possible by reading consecutive digits along any straight line—horizontal, vertical or diagonal. Lee, who recently organized a similar contest in England, reported a wining entry of 170 primes. Could the readers of this column do better? I never doubted it!

After "Panning for Primes" appeared in SCIENTIFIC AMERICAN in July, 1988, I received many more entries than I thought I would. They came both from high-tech hackers who employed supercomputers and from humbler folk who worked them out with pencil and paper. I mailed the entries to Lee for adjudication. Here are the results in reverse order:

Grittiest gridder: Larry J. Padden of Oklahoma City, Okla., who produced 147 different prime grids containing between 170 and 173 primes.

Sixiest gridders: David Mckenzie and Frank Endres of Austin, Tex., who discovered a grid that contained only 106 primes, but all 28 possible six-digit numbers in it were prime.

Third-place gridder: James I. Waldby of Robinson, Ill., whose score was 185.

Second-place gridder: Mckenzie and Endres share this honor with Stephen C. Root of Westboro, Mass. They were able to come up with grids that contained 186 primes.

Top gridder: Root again. His winning entry, which is given below, has a total of 188 primes:

3	1	7	3	3	3
9	9	5	6	3	9
1	1	8	1	4	2
1	3	6	3	7	3
3	4	9	1	9	9
3	7	9	3	7	9

∘ 19 ∘

Trains of Thought

Problemtown and Solutionville are 100 miles apart. At noon one fine day in June a train leaves each city and heads for the other at 50 miles per hour. Simultaneously a bumblebee that had been resting comfortably on the headlamp of the Problemtown train stirs to life and flies down the track toward Solutionville at 90 miles per hour. When it meets the Solutionville train, the bee makes an abrupt about-face and flies back along the tracks at 90 miles per hour. When it meets the Problemtown train, it does another about-face. It continues reversing until the trains meet. How far does the bumblebee travel?

The answer to this familiar puzzle, which is given toward the end of this chapter, is short. In fact, it is simply a number. Some puzzles, the ones I call algopuzzles, have more complicated answers. They consist of a recipe, or procedure, for bringing about some desired state of affairs. In other words, the answer is an algorithm. Traditional puzzle literature is full of algopuzzles. We may be asked to divide a container of fluid into three equal amounts by a succession of pouring operations involving containers of specific capacities. We may be asked to row a wolf, a goat, and a cabbage across a river by means of successive ferrying operations.

We may even be asked to detect a bad penny (overweight or underweight) among many by consecutive weighing operations on a scale.

The difference between the answers to an ordinary puzzle and to an algopuzzle should be made clear by an explicit example. To encourage the proper train of thought, I shall continue along the tracks of the first puzzle. Fortunately the second example does not require the two trains to squash a bumblebee between them in a paroxysm of infinitesimal vibrations. Instead of colliding, the trains see each other in time to stop. There is a great rumbling hiss followed by the squeal of steel brakes. (For some reason I picture two leviathans from the age of steam.) Between the trains lies a short stretch of track and a siding that is only long enough to hold one car or an engine (*see* the illustration on the facing page). Obviously someone has made a serious scheduling error. The only way out of the dilemma is for the two engineers to use the siding in some manner to get their trains past each other. In this problem and in the problems that follow, each engine and car has a coupler at each end. Each train also has a brakeman who runs along the tracks to couple or uncouple designated cars.

Wiping the sweat from his face with a red polka-dot handkerchief, the engineer from Problemtown declares, "I don't see how we can get by each other. All we got is that little siding over yonder." The engineer from Solutionville is more optimistic. He outlines a plan for getting the two trains past each other. Is it possible? Readers might like to look at the illustration before reading on. To be concrete, the illustration shows two trains with five cars each. In a true algopuzzle, however, trains always have n cars.

In arriving at a solution to this rather simple algopuzzle, a typical reader may have mumbled something like the following: "Let's see, now. Why not just put the Problemtown train on the siding, one car at a time. The Solutionville train can then just shuttle back and forth, pulling a new Problemtown car on the siding in one direction, puffing past it through its entire length and then coupling onto it to push it off the siding before puffing back again."

Such a description provides a starting place for an algopuzzle solution, but it must be made clearer and more explicit. For this purpose an algorithmic format is ideal. Some notation will also be helpful. There are four main sections of track that play a role in the solution: the stretch from Problemtown to the siding (designated A), the stretch between the siding switches (B), the siding itself (B') and the track from the siding to

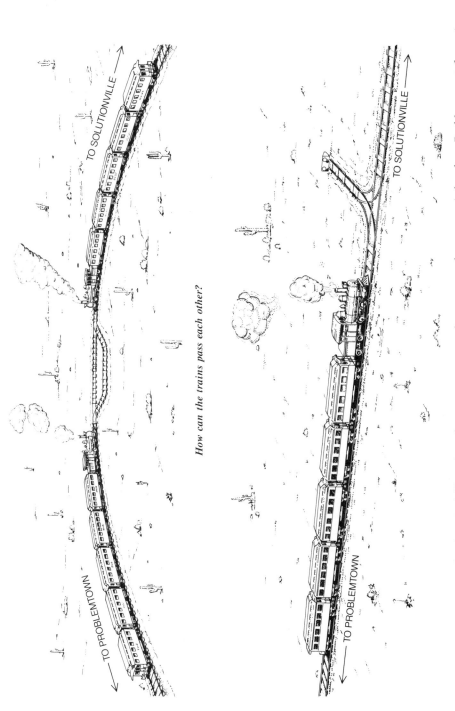

How can the trains pass each other?

How can the trains pass each other? (*top*) How does the train turn around to retrieve the engineer's lunch in Problemtown? (*bottom*)

Solutionville (C). An instruction such as "Forward A" means that the Solutionville train, consisting of the engine and all cars currently coupled to it, moves forward until it lies entirely within the A section of track.

Both trains have n cars, of course. The engine of the Problemtown train is labeled P1 and its cars are labeled P2, P3 and so on. The instruction "Couple Pk" means that the Solutionville train currently has one end adjacent to the kth element of the Problemtown train; the Solutionville train rolls gently into Pk and couples onto it with the wonderful shuffling noise that those of us who lived near rail yards remember well.

The algorithm can now be given:

> uncouple P train
> for $k = 1$ to $n + 1$
>   forward to A
>   couple Pk
>   backward to C
>   forward to B′
>   uncouple Pk
>   backward to C
>   forward to A
>   backward to B′
>   couple Pk
>   backward to C
>   uncouple Pk
> couple P train

At first the Problemtown train is completely uncoupled into separate units, one engine and n cars. The algorithm then enters a loop in which the same 11 steps are repeated over and over again. The Solutionville train does all the work. Without ever uncoupling any of its own cars, the train proceeds forward to the A section of track, where it couples with the first ($k = 1$) unit of the Problemtown train, the engine. It pulls the engine backward to the C section and, throwing the siding switch, pushes it onto B′, where it uncouples the Problemtown engine. The Solutionville train then backs up to section C again, throws the switch and puffs forward into the A section. It subsequently backs into the siding, couples once again to the Problemtown engine and pushes it out of the siding to section C, where it uncouples the engine. It then repeats the same sequence of steps with each of the Problemtown cars, one at a time.

When the main loop is finished, the Problemtown train is on the Solutionville side of the Solutionville train. As soon as it has recovered from the lengthy algorithmic operation it is ready to chug off to Solutionville.

The next example of an algopuzzle comes about as the Problemtown train completes its trip to Solutionville. As he watches the scenery unfold, the engineer realizes with a gasp that he has forgotten his lunch. There is nothing he can do but go back. He applies the brakes and gently eases the massive n-car train to a halt. Backing all the way to Problemtown has little appeal. Fortunately the engineer sees a very short spur line off to his right. It has a switch for either direction of track and is just big enough to hold one car. Inspired by the Solutionville engineer's earlier algorithmic feat, our humble hero is not to be outdone.

To begin, the Problemtown engineer draws a diagram of the spur on a piece of paper (*see* illustration on page 213). Then he writes out an algorithm and checks it carefully by tracing his finger back and forth over the paper and muttering to himself. He then begins a laborious series of uncouplings, shunts and recouplings that eventually results in the reversal of the entire train. Not only is the order of the engine and cars completely reversed but also the engine has been turned around and so has each car. How did he do it? The best solutions are clearest and cleverest. There is more to the problem than meets the eye.

While on the way back to retrieve his lunch, the Problemtown engineer realizes his solution has taken a lot of energy. The coal in the tender is nearly depleted. It turns out that the amount of work done by his train was proportional to n^3: If mass is measured in cars and distance is measured in car lengths, he has moved on the order of n cars a distance of n units, each n times. Only now, as he chugs home, does he ponder the existence of a more efficient solution. Is it possible to turn the train around in fewer steps, say on the order of $n^{5/2}$ or even $n^2 \cdot \log n$?

For the purpose of training single-track minds further in the gentle art of algopuzzlery, here is a pretty little poser. A lone engine approaches a circular track containing two empty cars. Between the cars is a bridge that is just strong enough to hold one car but not the engine (*see* the illustration on page 216). The engineer must reverse the position of the cars. As in the foregoing algopuzzle, all coupling and uncoupling is done when the train is stationary. (In other words, no "flying shunts" are allowed.) The bridge is no longer than a car, and the engine must be off the circular track when it has finished the job. The solution to this problem is a simple algorithm with no loops.

The next two algopuzzles are new to me. They continue the transportation theme of the train problems but they move the inquiry into high gear by using trucks. I call them the Desert Fox puzzles. In the first puzzle a patrol vehicle belonging to the Desert Fox has a fuel tank that holds 10 gallons of gasoline. Its tank is filled from one of several 50-gallon drums stored at a supply depot. If the vehicle can carry only one drum at a time and if it gets 10 miles to the gallon whether it carries a drum or not, how far can it go before running out of gasoline? The answer surely depends on the number of barrels stored at the depot. In the spirit of algopuzzle generality, the number of barrels is specified as n.

If n is equal to 1, the answer is easy. The vehicle fills its tank from the single drum, loads it and sets out into the hot desert sun on patrol. Refueling itself from the drum as necessary, the vehicle obviously travels 500 miles before it runs out of gas. How far can the vehicle travel on two drums? Since it can carry only one drum at a time, it will carry the first drum some distance out into the desert, refuel from it if necessary, then return to the depot for the second drum. It carries the second drum out on patrol by the same route. It may or may not stop to refuel at the first

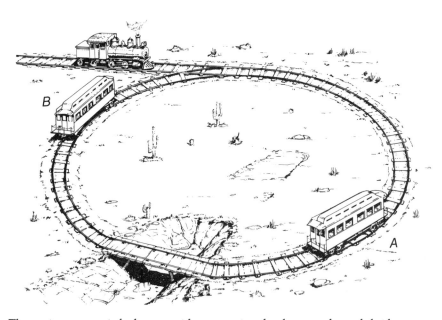

The engine must switch the cars without crossing the dangerously weak bridge

drum before continuing its journey. It may even drop off the second drum and pick up the first one before continuing. How far can it go by shuttling back and forth in this way? Suddenly the problem looks less trivial.

Here is a short algorithm that guarantees the patrol vehicle a journey of 600 miles. The truck starts its route at the depot:

> fuel vehicle and load first drum
> forward 100 miles
> drop drum and refuel
> back to depot for second drum
> refuel and load drum
> forward 100 miles
> refuel from first drum
> forward 100 miles
> drop drum and refuel
> back to first drum
> refuel and load drum
> forward 100 miles

At this stage in the algorithm the vehicle has progressed a grand total of 200 miles. It has with it two drums. The first drum holds 10 gallons and the second holds 30. The patrol continues when the driver refuels the vehicle from the first drum (leaving it empty), loads the second drum and drives off over the dunes. It therefore travels 400 miles more before running out of fuel. The total distance traveled is 600 miles. Since the improvement in distance over the one-barrel case is only 100 miles, readers would be right to suspect that a better algorithm exists. Indeed, one can achieve what the Desert Fox's enemy might describe as a "beastly number" of miles.

How far can the Desert Fox go if the depot contains n barrels? In the algopuzzle spirit, a single numerical answer or formula simply will not do. One must specify the algorithm that yields the answer (*see* illustration on page 218).

In another part of the vast sandy domain the Desert Fox (temporarily) calls home, there is an enemy patrol route that is traveled in a very different way: An aircraft drops n drums of fuel at arbitrary points along a closed-loop route. Each drum contains a certain quantity of gasoline but the amount may vary considerably from one drum to the next (*see* illustration on page 219). Since the patrol is in unfriendly territory, the car and driver are parachuted in. They land near one of the drums, fuel

How far can the patrol truck go on *n* barrels of fuel?

up, and begin the tour. The car's fuel tank is expandable: It can handle any amount of fuel, no matter what size drum it encounters.

Strangely enough, as the patrol proceeds, the car never runs of out of gas before it reaches the next drum. In other words, the total amount of fuel in the drums is exactly enough for a patrol car to complete the loop, neither more nor less. This is odd because, as I said, the placement and quantities of fuel are completely arbitrary. For example, it is perfectly possible for the car to begin its journey at a drum that does not contain enough fuel to get the car to the next drum in either direction. It is even possible to get to the next drum but to be stymied at some point thereafter. How is the feat possible?

The Desert Fox has observed these patrols and is frankly puzzled by them. Is the enemy, known to be mad, also lucky? A subordinate who spends every night in his tent solving puzzles discovers the answer. "It seems, sir, that no matter where the barrels are dropped or how much fuel they contain, there is always a place where the car can begin its patrol with every hope of completing the journey.

Where must the patrol car begin its journey to ensure a successful circuit?

I leave it to readers to discover the secret. There is, of course, an algorithm involved. A step-by-step procedure that locates at least one barrel at which the car can begin (and complete) its patrol must first be found. The algorithm must also specify a direction in which the car can travel. To go the wrong way could be disastrous.

At the beginning of this chapter I promised to reveal the answer to the puzzle involving the bumblebee and the trains. Good puzzle posers are often careful to mislead readers particularly when there is an easy answer. By describing the infinite number of reversals in the bumblebee's flight I deliberately tried to confuse readers. It is necessary to realize only that the bumblebee is in flight as long as it takes the trains to meet. They travel half the distance between Problemtown and Solutionville in just one hour. The bee, always flying at 90 miles an hour, therefore travels 90 miles.

There is an apocryphal story about this puzzle that I cannot vouch for. Someone is said to have posed the puzzle to John von Neumann, one of the greatest mathematicians of the century. He is said to have replied instantly, "90 miles, of course."

"Ah," his tormentor said, "I might have known you'd find the easy way of doing it."

"What easy way?" von Neumann responded. He had summed the infinite series in his head.

ADDENDUM

Readers with one-track minds have by now undoubtedly solved the problem involving the interchange of two cars across a weak bridge. The cars are on a circular track, and an engine occupies another track connected to the circular one by a switch. The bridge is strong enough to hold one car but not the engine. How can the engine switch the cars?

The engine enters the circular track, goes to car A and pushes it onto the bridge. Then the engine backs around the track to car B, couples with it, pushes it to the edge of the bridge and couples B with A. Chugging back to the switch, the engine and two cars back onto the straight track, where A is uncoupled. Next the engine takes B back to the bridge, leaving it uncoupled there. Finally the engine circles the track, pulls B off the bridge to its new position and then retrieves A.

"Trains of Thought" appeared in the June, 1987, issue of SCIENTIFIC AMERICAN and drew mail from around the world. Before plunging into the desert to discuss answers to the last two puzzles posed in it, I should indicate an improvement to the train-passing algorithm. It required in the order of n^3 elementary moves to get one train by the other. Manuel Blum, a computer scientist at the University of California at Berkeley, has found an algorithm that does the same job with an amount of work proportional to $n^2 \times \log n$. Unfortunately there is no space here for Blum's algorithm.

The first Desert Fox problem concerned a truck that could carry one 50-gallon drum of fuel at a time as well as the 10 gallons of fuel in the truck's tank. I mentioned that from a depot of two drums the truck could travel a maximum distance of 666 miles before running out of fuel. Many readers were able to improve this solution to the actual maximum of 733⅓ miles.

Algorithms submitted by Chester Nowogorski of Naples, Fla., and Norman Rokke of Wintersville, Ohio, indicate that a truck can use three drums of fuel to travel the grand total of 860 miles before running out of gas. Most readers attempting the feat came up short of this figure. Indeed, general formulas supplied by most readers also fell short when 3 was substituted for n, the total number of barrels employed. I cannot, therefore, vouch for accuracy in formulas such as the one sent by Lawrence Leinweber of Cleveland, Ohio. It was, however, typical of formulas submitted that yielded the greatest distances:

$$5 \sum_{i=1}^{n} \frac{100}{2i-1} - \frac{100}{2n-1} + 100$$

The Greek sigma (Σ) symbolizes summation: Form n terms with successive values from 1 to n substituted for i in $100/(2i - 1)$. Add all n terms together and then multiply by 5.

The second Desert Fox puzzle allows a patrol car to refuel from n fuel depots placed at arbitrary points around a circular route to be followed by the car. The amount of fuel in each depot is also arbitrary, except that the total amount thus deposited is exactly enough for the patrol car to finish its route — provided it does not start at the wrong depot. Its own fuel tank will hold any amount of fuel but is initially empty. Where must the patrol car begin?

A number of readers, including Arnold V. Loveridge of Long Beach, Calif., arrived at an ingenious visualization of the problem. Take an imaginary tour with the patrol car starting at any depot and heading in any direction. Keep a graph of the fuel in the car's tank and keep driving even if the car runs out of gas. In this event the graph spills into the negative zone. With each refill at a depot the graph zigs up and then begins another long, slow decline. Ultimately the car returns to its initial point. The driver must now examine the graph and select the depot where the car's on-board gas was minimum (before refueling). That is the depot at which the car must begin.

∘ 20 ∘

Prosodic Programs

"Take care of the sense and the sounds will take care of themselves."
—The Duchess, in *Alice's Adventures in Wonderland* by LEWIS CARROLL

As the renowned Oxonian master of nonsense observed, semantics takes precedence over syntax in creative writing. Good literature is shaped by the meaning contained in a writer's ideas. Computers are not yet capable of ideas and so cannot take care of a composition's sense. Yet, as a number of contemporary programs show, computers can certainly take care of the sounds. But is it art? That is for the reader to decide.

Consider the writings of MARK V. SHANEY, a computer program created by Bruce Ellis (now at the University of Sydney) that is based on an idea of Don P. Mitchell of the AT&T Bell Laboratories. MARK V. SHANEY is not exactly a self-starter. The program must first read and reflect on someone else's work. It then produces a rambling and somewhat confused commentary on the work. As an example, I quote MARK V. SHANEY's reflections on reading an elementary chemistry textbook.

"Wash the blackboard. Watch it dry. The water goes into the air. When water goes into the air it evaporates. Tie a damp cloth to one end of a solid or liquid. Look around. What are the solid things? What are the only ones that take part in the clouds themselves. As clouds move air tosses the tiny droplets of water. Sometimes the water which leaves the body in the leaves of green plants. It is quite porous, almost like a sponge.

But the walls of the hollow tubes and cells are very strong. Chemical changes take place when something burns . . . ."

The commentary is hardly different when MARK V. SHANEY digests a book on elementary mathematics.

"Why do we count things in groups of five. When people learned how to count many things, they matched them against their fingers. First they counted out enough things to match the fingers of both hands. Then they put these things aside in one quart. A giant-size bottle that will hold four quarts is a three-digit number . . . ."

From here on, the program's output becomes increasingly confused, as readers may see for themselves in the excerpt below.

Although sense is conspicuously absent from MARK V. SHANEY's writings, the sounds are certainly there. The overall impression is not unlike what remains in the brain of an inattentive student after a late-night study session. Indeed, after reading the output of MARK V. SHANEY, I find ordinary writing almost equally strange and incomprehensible!

How does MARK V. SHANEY produce its remarkable works? The answer is rather simple. The program's name, a weak pun on "Markov chain," provides a clue. In abstract terms, a Markov chain is a sequence of

```
        Why do we count things in groups of five. When people
learned how to count many things, they matched them
against their fingers. First they counted out enough
things to match the fingers of both hands. Then they put
these things aside in one quart. A giant-size bottle that
will hold four quarts is a three-digit number. A digit
gets its value from the top of a sidewalk are straight,
and straight lines mark off the tennis court and baseball
diamond. Drawing a straight line without the help of a
house or table, you would choose one copy rather than the
other? Suppose that there is "one chance out of 52" and
define the probability, accordingly, to be so tall?" she
said. The chief engineer smiled. "Television waves don't
bend as much as radio waves," he said, "I caught 12 fish"
she knew right away that he had this many. She didn't have
to go down to his boat to see if he had this many. She
didn't have to go down to his boat to see if he had caught
a lot or just a few...
```

MARK V. SHANEY's mathematical commentary

symbols generated according to a table of probabilities. In the version relevant to MARK V. SHANEY's operation, each row of the table corresponds to a pair of symbols. The entries in each row consist of individual symbols, each paired with an associated probability. A sequence of symbols is generated by an algorithm that begins with a "chain" of two symbols and thereafter cycles through four simple steps:

1. Find the last two symbols in the current chain.
2. Go to the row of the table corresponding to the symbol pair.
3. Select a symbol from the row according to its probability.
4. Add the selected symbol to the end of the chain.

For example, the first few entries of a Markov-chain table for the symbols *A*, *B*, *C* and *D* might look like this:

$$AB: \quad B(.1) \quad C(.1) \quad D(.8)$$
$$AC \quad A(.1) \quad B(.2) \quad C(.1) \quad D(.6)$$
$$AD: \quad B(.4) \quad D(.6)$$
$$BA: \quad B(.3) \quad C(.4) \quad D(.3)$$
$$BB: \quad A(.5) \quad C(.5)$$

.
.
.

Given the symbol pair *AB* as the initial chain, the algorithm would have a 10 percent chance of selecting *B*, a 10 percent chance of selecting *C*, and an 80 percent change of selecting *D* as the next symbol. How does the algorithm choose a symbol according to the probabilities? It divides the interval between 0 and 1 into numerical segments whose lengths correspond to the symbol probabilities. It then chooses a random number between 0 and 1 and determines in which segment the number has fallen.

For row *AB* in the above table, the segments corresponding to the respective probabilities for *B*, *C*, and *D* range between 0 and .1, between .1 and .2, and between .2 and 1. Suppose, then, that the computer's random-number generator yields .0172. Because that number lies in the first segment, *B* would be selected as the next symbol in the chain. The chain would then consist of the symbols *ABB*. The algorithm would next consult row *BB* in order to select a fourth symbol for the chain. Here again, a random number is generated. If it is less than or equal to .5, A is selected; otherwise the algorithm selects C. Because of its dependence on chance, if the algorithm were restarted with the same initial symbol pair, it might well produce an entirely different chain.

Such an algorithm was actually applied in the 1940's by Claude E. Shannon of Bell Laboratories to analyze the information content of human language. He constructed the algorithm's probability tables by scanning ordinary text and counting how many times each individual character followed each pair of characters (including blanks). Once the character frequencies for a given text were known, they could easily be changed into probabilities. The Markov chains of characters generated in this manner had statistical properties that resembled the source text, although they rarely contained valid words. How then does MARK V. SHANEY apply Markov chains to produce understandable English words?

The trick is to apply Shannon's algorithm for Markov chains, but with entire words instead of characters as the concatenated symbols. As MARK V. SHANEY scans a text, it builds a frequency table for all words that follow all the word pairs in the text. The program then proceeds to babble probabilistically on the basis of the word frequencies.

A key feature of the program is that it regards any punctuation adjacent to a word as part of the word. That feature enables it to form sentences having a beginning and an end. Approximately half of them are even grammatical. I shudder to think what the program might produce after scanning this article!

Indeed, others have already shuddered at MARK V. SHANEY's reflections, some with rage and others with laughter. Some years ago Ellis decided to go on-line with his creation. The victims of the program's analyses were the innocent computer users who subscribed to an electronic bulletin board called net.singles. The bulletin board provides a place for male and female scientists, engineers, programmers and graduate students from all over the country to post their thoughts on subjects as diverse as dating, makeup, and personal relationships. Why not have MARK V. SHANEY read the postings and respond with its own "thoughts" on those subjects? Here are some of MARK V. SHANEY's more thoughtful comments.

"When I meet someone on a professional basis, I want them to shave their arms. While at a conference a few weeks back, I spent an interesting evening with a grain of salt. I wouldn't dare take them seriously! This brings me back to the brash people who dare others to do so or not. I love a good flame argument, probably more than anyone. . . .

"I am going to introduce a new topic: does anyone have any suggestions? Anybody else have any comments experience on or about mixed race couples, married or otherwise, discrimination forwards or reverse, and eye shadow? This is probably the origin of makeup, though it is worth reading, let alone judge another person for reading it or not? Ye gods!"

The opinions of the new net.singles correspondent drew mixed reviews. Serious users of the bulletin board's services sensed satire. Outraged, they urged that someone "pull the plug" on MARK V. SHANEY's monstrous rantings. Others inquired almost admiringly whether the program was a secret artificial intelligence project that was being tested in a human conversational environment. A few may even have thought that MARK V. SHANEY was a real person, a tortured schizophrenic desperately seeking a like-minded companion.

If the purpose of the computer prose is to fool people into thinking that it was written by a sane person, MARK V. SHANEY probably falls short. MELL, the brainchild of Bonnie V. Firner of Piscataway, N.J., probably comes a little closer to that goal. MELL writes weird science-fantasy stories with a peculiar meditative quality.

"The warrior scowls in the drought pulses. He loves himself in the drought. He molds himself in the drought. He glowers at the warrior Dugaki in the drought pulses. He calls her in the drought. He snarls at her in the drought. He sits beside her beside awareness. He seizes her.
"Oh I am might says Oban. He smothers her in the drought. He smashes her of the turquoise. . . .
"Oban kills Dugaki. He has it of turquoise. He glares at it in the drought pulses. He calls it in the drought. He snarls at it in the drought. He sits with it beside greed. He seizes it. He smothers it in the drought. He smashes it of the turquoise. He needs it beneath the thunderbolt. His body burns beneath the thunderbolt. . . ."

MELL consists of some 1500 lines of BASIC code; in contrast to MARK V. SHANEY, Firner's program is complicated even at the conceptual level. The program's main loop generates two characters in terms of 16 randomly generated "descriptors" whose values define qualities such as size, niceness, occupation, age and health, smell, commitment (from indifferent to fanatical), and even magical power.

Having chosen the names and traits of the story's characters, the main loop then determines what motivates a character by examining the values of its various descriptors. If one of the descriptors has a low value, MELL bases the character's interaction with the other characters on that fact. If

```
                    Muofubumo

        A poet bird Aeweat smells a computer Muofubumo.
 What is the bird coaxes Muofubumo. You are too muddled
 sings Aeweat. Shut up sticks the computer Muofubumo.
 You should awaken sings Aeweat. A blotchy computer
 contracts. It flops. The computer cavorts. Aeweat
 pinpoints the humble computer. The computer bloats.
 The decrepit bird churns the computer. She twists it.
 The computer plays.
        Why does the bird twirl pleads the tree Teweshe.
 I don't know hoots Teweshe. Why does the bird think
 coaxes the computer Muofubumo. I don't know hoots
 Teweshe. A computer contracts. Teweshe scents the
 computer. The computer cavorts. Teweshe pulls the
 computer. The computer decays in the year 225.
```

Firner's MELL tells a story

no character has a low descriptor value, MELL will decide on the nature of a character's interaction based on his or her occupation. For each cycle of the main loop, the program then generates several sentences that describe the characters by fitting names for their qualities into predetermined grammatical slots. The sentences thus generated also include what Firner calls "background" words.

In the above story, for example, the background word "drought" sets the scene. Consequently that word creeps into many of the sentences. After generating a paragraph that describes an act by one of the characters in this way, the sentence-generating process starts all over again. Between iterations the program can change a quality of one of the characters. This helps to keep the story (as much as there is of one, anyway) from stagnating.

Is poetry any easier for a computer to generate than prose? One doubts it, because the meaning contained in prosody tends to be far more dense than in prose. Of the three versifying programs I shall discuss, only POETRY GENERATOR, which was written by Rosemary West of Mission Hills, Calif., is fully automated; the other two require human intervention to finish the product. West describes her program as follows:

"My approach . . . was to supply a large vocabulary of words and phrases that would be selected at random and combined according to a set of grammatical rules. For example, consider the following poem:

> The tree dips its bare fingers
>   into the black ice-pond
> just as three gray geese
>   slide down a nearby snowbank.

"Each line of the poem can be broken down into several parts . . . . *The tree* is a noun phrase; *dips* is a verb; *its bare fingers* is the object of that verb. Having categorized the parts, I can then come up with between 100 and 400 possible substitutions for each part, one of which is randomly selected by the computer. For example, using the same verse structure, I might get:

> A woman hides five gray kittens
>   under the old jalopy
> at the moment when the sad clowns
>   enter your museum of pain."

The poetic structures on which POETRY GENERATOR hangs its words may vary considerably, lending variety to the syntax and to what seems to be the meaning of the poem. West has based some of POETRY GENERA- TOR's output on the structures of her own poems, several of which have been published.

Thomas A. Easton of Belfast, Me., thinks the best way to generate computer poetry necessarily involves a symbiosis between human and machine. He has written a semiautomatic program called THUNDER THOUGHT that provides ideas for poems. Again, I quote the author of the program:

"I conceive of the creative mind as having two components: the popcorn mind and the critical mind. The former generates random combinations of whatever words, ideas and images happen to be in a sort of mental focus (along with peripheral material, which is why the popcorn mind can surprise us). The critical mind then discards as garbage the vast bulk of what the popcorn mind produces and edits, twists and elaborates the remainder to form poems."

Relying on internal lists of nouns, verbs, adjectives and adverbs, THUNDER THOUGHT operates roughly like West's POETRY GENERATOR, arranging words into sentence frames to produce what Easton regards as raw poetic material for a human mind to refine (*see* top of page 229).

My Husband's Mistress

```
Of course my husband's mistress appears to be in charge.
She watches me work for a living in the temple,
She searches for me in the caves of evil,
She thinks about me in my fragrant bed.
Although I live in the land of indifference
She can never feel secure.
Dreams of power will be blamed on me until the end.
```

Love Song for Lonely Aliens

```
Weak with agonies of unstroked ego,
He loved physics,
Embraced its texts,
Cupped hands around the meshwork domes
Of vast antennae,
Roared erectly into orbit,
And screamed his coming
On the millimeter waves
Of space.
```

POETRY GENERATOR (*top*) and THUNDER THOUGHT (*bottom*) challenge the literati

"The intermediate result is ungrammatical, nonsensical, ridiculous garbage . . . but not always. Among the many lines of garbage there always lie a few lines to which one responds. They make sense — or seem to. They beg one to tweak them a little. A pair of them insists that one make up a third line. They stimulate one to think of other lines that can accompany them. A little editing, interpolation, elaboration and — violà! — a poem."

Easton has written some 110 poems by this method and has published 32 of them — some have even appeared in literary journals. That ratio, he claims, is one that would turn many real poets green with envy.

The last word on computer poetry goes to ORPHEUS, a program designed by poet Michael Newman of New York City. ORPHEUS lays out strict frameworks, from haiku to sonnets, into which human writers may insert their own chosen words. Essentially ORPHEUS is a word processor ("poetry processor" in Newman's parlance) that lays out the lines of a given poetic form. The program allows a human being to fill in the lines according to whim and then to end them with the help of a rhyming dictionary. Setting ORPHEUS in sonnet mode, for example, one might write a pair of lines (in imitation of Shakespeare's 130th sonnet) as follows:

> My Apple's screen is nothing like the sun;
> The Cray is faster far on problems big:

Because the first line ends with the word "sun," ORPHEUS consults its rhyming dictionary and diplays a number of words that rhyme with sun: bun, done, fun, gun, and so forth. Scanning them, one's eye might alight on the word "fun." Is there a computer that is more fun than the Apple?

An association with games brings the Atari computer to mind for the next line.

> If Apple pleasant be, th' Atari is more fun;

The first quatrain is polished off by selecting a word that rhymes with big.

> If wires be hairs, her circuits are a wig:

The entire sonnet can be read below.

```
              Sonnet CXXX-b

My Apple's screen is nothing like the Sun;
The Cray is faster far on problems big:
If Apple pleasant be, th'Atari is more fun;
If wires be hairs, her circuits are a wig:
I have seen pixels dancing, red green blue,
But no such pixels see I on her tube;
And mainframes dance a logic far more true
Than in my Apple's tiny crystal cube.
I love to watch her print, yet well I know
That line printers hasten with more speed;
I grant I never saw a virtual process go,
My Apple, when it works, does in small steps proceed;
And yet, by heaven, I think my judgement sound
As any computation she has found.
```

An unknown author and ORPHEUS combine talents to compose a sonnet

The poetry programs I have mentioned may be bought by readers who want to sharpen their prosodic skills. Newman will be happy to supply ordering information for ORPHEUS, NERD (Newman's Electronic Rhyming Dictionary), and related products to those who write him (*see* the List of Suppliers). Easton meets West in a software package containing THUNDER THOUGHT and a program similar to it called VERSIFIER, which was written by West. Readers may inquire about the package by writing to Easton. (*see* the List of Suppliers).

Readers may also be interested in what is perhaps MARK V. SHANEY's magnum opus: a 20-page commentary on the deconstructionist philosophy of Jean Baudrillard. That effort was directed by Rob Pike of the AT&T Bell Laboratories, with assistance from Henry S. Baird and Catherine Richards. The commentary can be obtained by writing Pike (*see* the List of Suppliers).

ADDENDUM

A parade of prose and poetry — or should one say a parody of prose and poetry — appeared in "Prosodic Programs." MARK V. SHANEY reads straightforward English text only to produce monstrously distorted versions of the same by working on the basis of Markov chains. The underlying algorithm is ridiculously simple. As the program scans the text, it builds up a table of two-word followers. In other words, for every pair of consecutive words that the program finds in the text under examination, it lists all the words that follow that pair wherever it occurs throughout the text. Frequencies of such following words are easily converted into probabilities at the end of the process, so that as MARK V. SHANEY regurgitates the text, it merely looks up the last two words it printed, selects a follower based on probabilities, and then prints the follower as its next word. It repeats the process ad nauseam.

I shuddered at the thought of MARK V. SHANEY going through that very chapter, reducing my own carefully constructed text to a shambles. Kenneth A. Bullis of Campbell, Calif., incarnated SHANEY on his Macintosh Plus computer, then promptly, and with no thought for my personal feelings on the matter, typed in the whole of "Prosodic Programs"! Here is SHANEY's first go at it, complete with a quote (unattributed) from other work by MARK V. SHANEY:

> "Take care of a Markov chain table for all words that rhyme with sun: bun, done, fun, gun, and so forth. Scanning them, one's eye might alight

on the nature of a solid or a liquid. Look around. What are the only ones that take part in the leaves of green plants. It is only the Mandelbus' first stop can be obtained by writing Pike at the moment when the sad clowns/ enter your museum of pain." The poetry programs I have mentioned may be either inside or outside the set . . ."

The cogitations of MARK V. SHANEY on an essay by Jean Baudrillard entitled "The Precession of Simulacra" uses the same quote from *Ecclesiastes* that heads the Baudrillard essay. The quote, which begins, "The simulacrum is never that which conceals the truth . . ." and ends ". . . is true," was condensed by SHANEY into, "The simulacrum is true." The condensation is but the beginning of Shaney's brilliant meandering through difficult philosophical terrain. Rob Pike, of AT&T Bell Laboratories in Murray Hill, N.J., has been distributing copies of this work to any and all readers who inquired at my suggestion.

Guy Ottewell of Greenville, S.C., thought that the poetry programs did not perform as well as SHANEY. In particular, he took issue with the sonnet produced with the aid of Michael Newman's computer-assisted poetry program. The fault lay not in the program but in the poet. The program, by the way, can be purchased in three parts: THE POETRY PROCESSOR, NERD II (Newman's Electronic Rhyming Dictionary), and ORPHEUS ABC. Alternatively, readers may order all three in one package called THE POETRY PROCESSOR PACKAGE (*see* the List of Suppliers).

Another rhyming dictionary is produced by Carl Wurtz of Burbank, Calif. QUICKRHYME, as Wurtz calls his program, has apparently tackled many of the thornier issues connected with computing rhymes rather than merely listing them. Readers interested in QUICKRHYME may contact Wurtz (*see* List of Suppliers).

· 21 ·

The Martian Dictionary

No one knows how or why Martian civilization vanished, but a cave at the foot of Olympus Mons holds a sad remnant of this ancient and wonderful culture. At the end of the cave a tablet reminiscent of the famed Rosetta stone is shrouded by a dusty fabric of unknown composition. The fabric is pulled aside, revealing what seems to be a kind of dictionary: A list of words on the left half of the table is matched by a list of words on the right. Two sentences are engraved at the bottom of the stone. The sentences are related in a peculiar way. The first one can be transformed into the second one by repeated substitution of words from the dictionary: Each word in the sentence on the left-hand side of the dictionary can be replaced by the corresponding word on the right.

Martiansentencescontainnospaces. Indeed, none are wanted owing to the fluid and expressive character of Old Martian; often there are many ways to divide a Martian sentence into words. As a general rule, however, only a few divisions make sense in a given context. The substitution process can be illustrated employing the first sentence of this paragraph. If *tainnospaces* appeared in the left-hand column of the dictionary and *cealwisdom* appeared as the corresponding word on the right, the latter word could be substituted for the former to obtain a new and valid sentence: Martiansentencesconcealwisdom.

The wise ones of ancient Mars held that all information worth learning could be achieved by starting with one basic sentence and substituting words according to the dictionary of wisdom, the only surviving fragment of which lies in the cave. The basic sentence is the first of the two at the bottom of the Olympus Mons stone shown below. In general a computer will not be able to verify whether a given sentence can be derived from the basic one. In other words, there is no possibility of writing a computer program (no matter how large or how fast the computer is) that will decide correctly, for each dictionary and two words (or sentences) of input, whether a translation is possible from the first word into the second. I shall explain why below. In the meantime, can readers transform the basic sentence into the one displayed underneath it? (This particular transformation can be achieved.)

The Martian translation problem is one of an entire family of puzzles that call for the transformation of words, sentences, and even entire paragraphs into other words, sentences, and paragraphs. The early development of the subject is due in part to the Reverend Charles Dodgson,

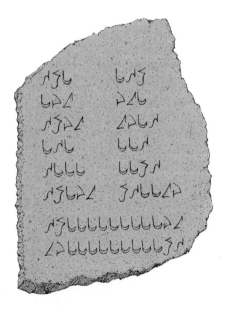

Martian dictionary of wisdom

otherwise known as Lewis Carroll. Among the many mathematical and symbolic pastimes Carroll invented during his Oxford walks is a transformation called a word ladder. In a word ladder one starts with two specific words in the language of one's choice. The first word is called the source and the second the target. Can one transform the source word into the target by changing one letter at a time?

If the two words have the same number of letters, the task is trivial. But can one ensure that all the intermediate character strings are also words? That is a horse of a different color, but a mount that people in the wordplay academy can easily ride. One can in fact start with *horse* to illustrate the process. In one step the word can be changed into *house*. Another step yields *mouse*. By this alchemy it would seem a horse could be changed into almost anything whose name has five letters. Is that possible?

To answer such a question in general, it is necessary to construct a transformational network. As an enemy of overly impressive terminology, I have renamed it a word web. The complete web for the English language would be a monstrous affair: Every English word would be present in the web as a unique dot. To satisfy the requirements of the word ladder two dots would be joined by a line if their corresponding words differed by exactly one character. To find the words to which *horse* could be changed, for example, one merely traces through the web from *horse*, adding to a list all words encountered on the journey. A complete exploration of such paths would be tantamount to plucking the web by the point *horse* and pulling up with it all the points connected to it. The whole would probably look like a poorly mended fishnet. Of course, the great majority of words would not get pulled up with *horse*; any word not having five letters would stay below, for instance.

Would all the five-letter words come up? That is to say, is it possible to build a word ladder from *horse* to any other five-letter English word? Although I must say I do not know the answer to this question, judging from past reader response I would be willing to bet that someone will find it. The requisites are a dictionary that has been put in machine-readable form and a program that searches the dictionary for connected words. Every time a word is added to the list of all words connected to *horse*, the program deletes it from the dictionary in memory and runs through the entire list again, comparing each word on it with each word encountered in the steadily diminishing dictionary. Every time a dictionary word differs by one letter from a word on the list, it is added to the list and the process begins again. Different dictionaries will undoubtedly yield different results, will they not? Perhaps. On the other hand, two reasonably complete dictionaries might give the same result. In other words, the webs might be so thick that their topology would be practically the same.

The question of whether *n*-letter words are connected can be answered almost by hand for small values of *n*. Certainly all one-letter words are connected within one web. The case for two-letter words can also be decided here and now. According to my Scrabble dictionary, the two-letter words are *aa, ad, ae, ah, ai, am, an, ar, as, at, aw, ax, ay, ba, be, bi, bo, by, da, de, do, ef, eh, el, em, en, er, es, et, ex, fa, go, ha, he, hi, ho, id, if, in, is, it, jo, ka, la, li, lo, ma, me, mi, mu, my, na, no, nu, od, oe, of, oh, om, on, op, or, os, ow, ox, oy, pa, pe, pi, re, si, so, ta, ti, to, um, up, us, ut, we, wo, xi, xu, ya* and *ye*.

A little work reveals that all the words in the web are connected. First, all two-letter words that begin with the same letter are mutually connected. This enables one to lump all words beginning with the same letter together. It remains only to note that the *a* lump is connected to the other four vowel lumps, that the *b* lump is connected to each of the other 16 consonant lumps and that the *a* lump and the *b* lump are themselves connected.

Armed with only two low-order test cases, there are people who would boldly conjecture that all *n*-letter English words are connected. The proposition typifies the excitement of abstract wordplay. Readers with computers might attempt to test the proposition with other low values of *n*, such as *n* = 3 (*see* the illustration at the right). Those without computers must be content with turning *hate* into *love*. Better still, they could attempt to convert *evil* into *good*, achieving valuable moral and logo-logical insights in the process.

The game of word ladders provides a simple example of a so-called textual transformation system. The two major ingredients of such a system are a set of texts to be transformed and a rule of transformation. The texts might be words, sentences, or paragraphs, which are really just strings of characters, no matter how the set of texts is chosen. The rule of transformation consists of a procedure for replacing part of a given string by another string. In following the procedure a dictionary is usually consulted.

In word ladders, for example, the set of strings consists of all English words in a given dictionary. The procedure takes any word submitted to it and generates another word that differs from the first word by one

The three-letter word web

letter and is also found in the dictionary. Here the dictionary is a simple list of words.

Most published dictionaries have entries that consist of words "defined" in terms of other words. Another kind of transformational chain — one that is more sophisticated than the word ladder — is implicit here. Imagine, for example, that one starts with a single English word, looks up its meaning and makes a list of all the words found in its definition. Then one looks at the meanings of those words, makes a combined list of the words, and continues to repeat the process. Since English has a finite number of words (I cannot vouch for other languages), the procedure soon develops a cyclic character, so to speak: Certain words begin to recur. They are defined, in part, in terms of themselves. One could call them primal words. They are not to be heralded with primal screams but should be repeated silently with something like awe: Perhaps they constitute the indefinable conceptual foundation of English.

The project, or something much like it, was carried out by Robert Amsler of Bell Communications Research. Amsler used a dictionary that had been modified so that the definition of every word was reduced to a set of genus words serving to identify the broad classes of things to which the word belonged. The genus words were supplemented by differentia: words that serve to distinguish a given word from other members of the genus. Utilizing a program similar to the one described above, Amsler traced through his special dictionary and found basically what the philosophers of language predicted he would find: primitive words, all of which were used in the ultimate definitions of other primitive words. Examples included *food, person, thing, instrument,* and *group.* The primitive words occupied the ultimate branches of what has been called a tangled hierarchy, something like a forest in which the branches of different trees have grown together. The primitive words lie "upward" in the direction of increased generality.

Amsler's fundamental idea is that dictionaries have more structure and reveal more about language than people commonly suppose. It would be surprising if the relatively simple genus-differentia scheme did not produce a few anomalies. A barbecue, for example, turned out to be "an animal roasted over an open fire." The barbecue thus found itself on a list somewhere between *aardvark* and *zebra.*

Amsler's research has applications for data-based retrieval schemes in which a user might want to retrieve instances of a general class. He is currently rebuilding his tangled hierarchy on the *McGraw-Hill Dictionary of Scientific and Technical Terms.*

A related transformational chain has been explored by Ron Hardin, a research scientist at the AT&T Bell Laboratories in Murray Hill, N.J. Hardin has devised a number of interesting and amusing textual transformation games over the years. His latest preoccupation involves *The New Collins Thesaurus.* The user of a thesaurus commonly looks for synonyms of a word or for a conceptual class of words that he or she has in mind. One might imagine that each word inhabits a small cloud of words that mean practically the same thing. Yet the clouds are not all widely separated from one another. Some clouds overlap others. As a consequence, although certain pairs of words are not in themselves mutual synonyms, they can share common synonyms. Therein lies the source of much mischief. Consider the following chains unearthed by Hardin. Each word is found in its predecessor's synonymic cloud:

acceptable → so-so → ordinary → inferior → rotten → unacceptable
reliable → steadfast → obstinate → wayward → unpredictable → unreliable

Hardin has generated several thousand such chains by computer. In each chain a word is gradually converted into its antonym. The great majority of the chains generated by Hardin are no longer than these examples. The exercise reminds us that human languages are fluid, that the meaning of words depends heavily on context, and that every word has a certain ambiguity that is both a blessing and a curse. Consider the case of a lawyer cross-examining a witness about the character of a defendant:

"You have stated in testimony that Watson is a reliable man. Would you not also describe him as 'steadfast'?"

"Yes."

"Indeed, would you not say that from time to time the accused was obstinate in his steadfastness?"

"Uh—I suppose so."

"At times, certainly, his obstinacy amounted to a form of waywardness, did it not?"

"I'm not sure."

"Not sure? Come, come, Dr. Finch, to be obstinate and wayward are practically the same thing."

"I suppose."

"A wayward man is an unpredictable man, in short, an unreliable man. You have just contradicted your earlier testimony."

An additional sampling of Hardin's word-reversal sequences is included below. His use of *The New Collins Thesaurus* is not quite as

---

afraid – apprehensive – expectant – hopeful – confident – **unafraid**
classified – secret – mysterious – unidentified – **unclassified**
dress – groom – tidy – clear – wipe – take off – divest – **undress**
even – level – uniform – regular – periodic – spasmodic – **uneven**
perfect – pure – unvarnished – unfinished – rough – **imperfect**
potent – dynamic – animated – excited – nervous – weak – **impotent**
rational – clever – witty – funny – silly – brainless – **irrational**
safe – undamaged – mint – untarnished – polished – slippery – **unsafe**
social – friendly – peaceable – inoffensive – retiring – **antisocial**
valid – convincing – plausible – specious – unsound – **invalid**

Ron Hardin's tower of Babel

straightforward as I have made it sound. The thesaurus is organized under headwords. When a user of the thesaurus wants a new word for a given context, he or she looks up the headword having a meaning closest to the one intended. Listed below the headword are the related words organized by sense of meaning. For example, under the headword *express* one finds senses of meaning that relate to speech and speed. Hardin's main problem was to connect senses in a logical and consistent way through headwords. As Hardin puts it, "If one supposes that the distinctions being made when senses are distinguished ought not to disappear when propagated . . . there is no consistent way to connect the thesaurus."

Hardin therefore devised an algorithm that systematically examined all pairs of related headwords and computed the strength of the connection between the various senses in which each could be taken. The senses that had the highest degree of connection were then incorporated in a kind of word web spun by the algorithm. In this way the distinctions between senses tended to remain well defined, although sometimes they became blurred. When the web was complete, a second algorithm that finds the shortest path between any two senses was deployed. It was then an easy matter for Hardin to specify various pairs of words to create his own tower of Babel, after that biblical edifice whose completion was thwarted by a confusion of tongues. Hardin's tower is a mini-tome with special attractions for linguists and lawyers.

Hardin has a certain underground fame for another kind of textual transformation, replacing words or parts of words by fragments having a similar sound.

Here is how Hardin transformed the verse beginning "Twas the night before Christmas" into another verse beginning "Tweeze denied beef worker isthmus," for example. First he decomposed all the words of the original into a string of phonemic tokens: basic sounds grouped together according to rough similarities. Having done the same for some standard dictionary, he had a computer regroup the phonemes into new words by ignoring boundaries between words in the original text when necessary. Before the madness was complete Hardin and some colleagues at Bell Laboratories had to polish by hand certain rough spots in the computer version. The resulting poem leaves the Christmas celebrant with a strangely confused notion of just what the original was about, as the text at the top of the next page reveals.

TWEEZE DENIED BEEF WORKER ISTHMUS

Tweeze denied beef worker isthmus, winnow Trudy how's,
Knot agreed juries during, gnaw Tiffany moss.
This talking swear unbided Gemini wit cairn
Hint opus scenic (alas!) sinewy dare.
Unjelled runner nozzle tools smuggling deer butts
Well fissions unshoe kerplunks thence endear huts.
Anemometer cur chiffon dyeing mayhap,
Adjust subtle warp reins fairy loin winger snap.
Winnow taunted launderer roast sachet glitter
Ice brine bromide bet deucey woodwinds schemata.

The first few lines of "Tweeze denied beef worker isthmus"

It remains now to return to the Martian translation problem. Given a dictionary of permissible substitutions and two words (however long), why is it impossible for a computer to decide in general whether the second word can be obtained from the first one by a sequence of substitutions from the dictionary? The problem is called Thue's word problem after the Norwegian mathematician Axel Thue.

Many people outside the field of computing (and even a few within it) do not realize there are some things computers simply cannot do. One of the first people to suggest that computers have inherent limitations was the Englishman Alan M. Turing, a founding father of computer science. Turing conceived of a simple kind of abstract computer called (not by him) a Turing machine. The device is capable in principle of carrying out any computation a currently existing or conceivable computer is capable of doing. Turing showed it is impossible for one Turing machine to decide, given another Turing machine and its input, whether the second machine will ever halt or not. In more concrete terms, it is impossible to write a program that, given a second program and data as input, will decide whether the second program will ever stop manipulating that data.

Turing's theorem had at least one practical application. There once was a systems expert at a certain educational institution who decided that a mainframe computer was spending too much time executing freshman computer-science programs. A major reason for the delays, it seems, was that many of the programs contained unintentional infinite loops. If the programs could be scanned by an infinity-detecting program in advance of execution, much time might be saved. Alas, the infinity-detecting program was impossible, as a student of Turing's was quick to inform the expert.

Given the unsolvability of the so-called halting problem, it is relatively easy to demonstrate to the man and woman on the street that the Martian translation problem is also unsolvable. The demonstration proceeds by showing that the halting problem can be converted into the Martian translation problem.

The conversion is conceptually simple to make. The computer is encoded with a long string of symbols. The string essentially describes the initial contents of the computer's memory and working registers. A second string is then constructed. It indicates that the computer is in a halted state; whatever computation was to have been done is complete. The program to be tested for halting is translated into a set of rules for converting the first string into the second by means of substitutions. Each intermediate string then symbolizes one step of the computer's operation as it proceeds, one hopes, toward completing the processing of the data presented to it. The rules use substitution to move this virtual computer from state to state by following the program.

If, for example, the current content of a register is to be stored in a certain memory location, the rules substitute the new content of that memory location in the part of the current string that represents the memory location in question. The transformation procedure will succeed in obtaining the second string from the first if, and only if, the computer in question ultimately halts its processing of the data provided. Since according to Turing's theorem the computer will never halt, the transformation cannot be made.

Even without such a fancy argument, the unsolvability of the Martian translation problem is strongly suggested by the following observation: If the source word can be transformed into the target word, a program that systematically tries every conceivable substitution will eventually come on the right ones. But if the transformation is impossible, how will one ever find out? How long should one wait? Readers unable to solve our special example of the Martian translation problem will not have to wait long, but merely turn to the "Addendum."

ADDENDUM

The resourcefulness of our readers never fails to amaze me. Having implied that anyone without a computer need not concern herself or himself with certain problems relating to word webs, I found those very people knocking on the door, solutions in hand, after "The Martian Dictionary" appeared in SCIENTIFIC AMERICAN in August, 1987.

In particular, I posed the general question of converting one n-letter word into another by way of a sequence of intermediate words. Only one letter at a time may be changed. The result is a word ladder. In the case of $n = 2$, for example, all two-letter words (in the dictionary I provided) are connected by word ladders. I left open the question of whether all n-letter words are connected for higher values of n. It proved hardly necessary to use computers to explore the interconnections.

Many readers offered *gnu* to settle the three-letter case. For $n = 5$ a number of others offered *xylem*. These forays depended only on the insight that a word that cannot be connected to any others settles the issue; then others cannot be connected to it. According to George A. Miller of San Francisco, there are 1,217 English words to which *horse* (my own example) cannot be connected. Miller has a program that determines al possible word ladders (*see* the List of Suppliers).

A highly interesting variation of word ladders is suggested by Paul L. Blass of Florham Park, N.J. In addition to substituting single letters, let the words crawl sideways like worms, shortening or lengthening by one letter at each end.

By employing one or two slippery intermediaries (such as *orad*), Joseph M. Erhardt of Richmond, Va., discovered a way to transform *evil* into *good*. Dennis Farr wrote from Framingham, Mass., to display a ladder stretching from *solid* to *plane*. He did some *flips* and a *slide* on the way.

The Martian word problem dealt with webs of a different kind: Given a dictionary that lists allowed substitutions of one string for another, transform an initial word into a final one. The problem was solved by Alfred V. Perthou, III, of Seattle, Wash., and Edward J. Groth of Scottsdale, Ariz. The puzzle falls apart once it is realized that the few dictionary entries amount to simple rules that allow one to shuttle symbols about. For example, a rule of the form $aba \leftarrow baa$ means that the b symbol can be shifted one place to the left when surrounded by a's.

Some of the best fun arose from the computational word-bender created by Ron Hardin. Readers may recall the strange verse entitled "Tweeze Denied Beef Worker Isthmus," a tortuous sound-alike of the familiar Christmas poem by Clement Clarke Moore. The art was already old in the hands of computerless humans. Ronald C. Read, a mathematician and gamester at the University of Waterloo in Ontario, told me of a

French (kind of) book called *Mots d'Heures: Gousses, Rames*, or "Mother Goose Rhymes," which contains such perversions as "Lit-elle messe, Moffette."

In English there is literature of this ilk. Two readers sent in the charming "Ladle Rat Rotten Hut." For such, a computer is hardly necessary. D. H. Wood of Montreal, Quebec, rendered the carol "It Came upon the Midnight Clear" with new lyrics: "Eat cane a pond am I'd knight glare." Finally, Richard Tilden wrote from Somerville, Mass., to remind me that Walt Kelly, the beloved American cartoonist, had constructed a number of pieces including "Deck the Halls with Boston Charlie" and "My Bonnie Lice Soda Devotion."

I am subscribing forthwith, after much needless delay, to the magazine *Word Ways*. I have heard so much about all the art in the field of word webs from the editor, A. Ross Eckler, that I cannot wait any longer. Readers can subscribe by consulting the List of Suppliers.

Mathemagical Movies

For sheer entertainment there is nothing like a mathemagical movie on one's computer screen. The simplest imaginable programs bring out the pixies from the pixels. Who would guess that raindrops on a pond or a mass of writhing worms could have such a mesmerizing effect? More than this, balls bouncing about in boxes lead, among other things, to pressure vessels, gas diffusion, and chain reactions in the notoriously unstable substance called gridium. And if this weren't enough, the Invisible Professor puts in a nonappearance to draw some curves on our screen. Beware the witch of Agnesi!

How does a computer draw a worm? By constructing it out of a chain of circles. The simple algorithmic cycle of erasing a circle at the tail of the worm and redrawing it in a random location near the head ensures a lively creature that seems to crawl right into our mind. Stars bursting from a single point in space are managed with equal ease. And what are raindrops on a pond but a succession of circles? There is something very special about the special effects produced by these programs: the effects are well within the reach of apprentice programmers, even beginners.

Perhaps it should not surprise us that balls bouncing inside boxes should simulate so many physical processes. The classical view of atoms involves little more than this. Let one wall of the box be free to move, and a pressure vessel results. Gravity pulls the wall into the box while countless bounces push it out. Or start with a box in which, initially, all the balls on one side are colored red while all those on the other are colored white. As the balls move about, we witness a miniature movie of liquids diffusing. Finally, the dangerous element known as gridium goes off with a chain-reactive bang. A single ball-neutron zips through a grid of this stuff and, perchance, strikes one of the gridium atoms. Now there are two ball-neutrons. If there is enough gridium in the grid, almost every ball gets split into two neutrons. But how much gridium does one need? That is a state secret, but one that home computists can discover for themselves.

The entertainment doesn't end with balls in boxes. Who is this drawing such bewitching curves on the chalkboard? No less a personage than the Invisible Professor. We can see right through him as curve after curve, each following the dictates of a mathemagical formula, etches itself on the computer screen. Most of the curves are centuries old, with names like the lemniscate of Bernoulli or the witch of Agnesi. If their sinuous beauty catches the eye, the process of their drawing entrances the mind: A point of light swoops and dives across the screen, up and down, finally rejoining itself.

· 22 ·

Special FX

Special effects do not always require the technical equipment and financial backing of a major motion-picture studio. Fabricators of fantasy can now generate limited but somewhat startling phenomena on their home computer with the aid of what might be called special-effects programs. Imagine, for example, that writhing worms were suddenly to crawl about vividly on one's display screen. A special-effects program can produce such a sight. What if the display screen were to liquefy unexpectedly? Raindrops falling here and there send circular ripples ever outward. That is also an easily managed special effect. Finally, suppose the screen becomes a window to a universe of stars that explode or stream by. Here one might be on board a spaceship flying down a corridor of stars. A third program produces such an illusion economically.

Economy of means is a feature of such programs, to my mind; if the effect is startling, so much the better if the program producing the effect is startlingly short. What more suitable vehicle could escort readers into the wider universe of ideas and appearances lying in wait behind the display screen? In particular, judging from a small but persistent fraction of my mail, there are computer neophytes who stare disconsolately at the pages of my columns, unable to convert the algorithms presented there

247

into working programs. They stand on the sidelines as the parade of Mandelbrot sets, party programs, hodgepodge machines, and fractal growths pass by. They can only guess at the joy of seeing an algorithm take on the flesh and blood of programhood.

For those readers, then, I shall do more than merely describe how the above special effects can be made. This once I shall explain the nuts and bolts of converting an algorithm into a program. I shall describe how to cover one's screen with worms in both a general algorithmic language and a specific programming language, BASIC. Besides this I shall show how to construct the algorithm itself and give an example of the art of conversion as a way of providing an entrée to past and future columns. Perhaps neophytes themselves will undergo a kind of conversion.

What protohacker can resist the temptation to write a program that will produce some lively, electronic annelids? It deflates expectation only a little to realize that each worm is nothing more than a chain of circles. But to program a special effect (or anything else for that matter), one must temporarily set aside expectation in favor of analysis. How does the worm move? By adding a new circle at the head and removing one from the tail. The resulting effect of motion — that of a whole creature sliding along — is surely an illusion, but it brings the piece off.

The program I call WORMS began to hatch when I first viewed the effect on my new SUN computer. Someone had added this eye-catcher to the basic menu of system and utility programs normally inhabiting a newly delivered machine. This someone had perhaps assumed that the sight of worms writhing on the large SUN display screen would make the buyer think the expense of the machine was justified.

The program actually hatched when I wondered how the effect of a crawling worm was realized. A close inspection of the screen made it more or less immediately obvious that the entire sense of motion was achieved by drawing a new circle at the head of the worm and erasing an old one from the tail. "Aha," I said to myself, "easy!" I briefly visualized a very short program until I realized that a program that would erase a circle previously drawn must first remember where the circle is. Since every circle in a worm must eventually be erased, every circle would have to be remembered.

One of the simplest data structures for remembering a large number of similar items is the array. I therefore thought next about how I would store the circles in an array. Whatever language one is writing in, the graphic command to draw a circle (or to erase one by drawing it black) normally uses the two coordinate points of the circle's center and its radius. The radius of the circles constituting my worm would be constant but centers would change from one circle to the next. It was therefore necessary to store only center coordinates. Because they were different numbers, it was convenient to store them not in one array but in two. I decided to call them *xcirc* and *ycirc*. Thus *xcirc(i)* would be the x coordinate of the *i*th circle and *ycirc(i)* would be its y coordinate.

The resulting arrays posed the major programming challenge of WORMS; somehow the program would have to add new circles to the array even as it deleted old ones. Like a worm, the arrays themselves would constitute a chain of circles. But the arrays would not move across the screen. Instead a special variable called a pointer would indicate which array position currently held the creature's tail-end circle. In both mathematics and computing there is a marvelous power in the simple act of naming. Calling the pointer variable *tail* immediately gave me a key statement in WORMS:

$$tail \leftarrow tail + 1$$

In other words, with each major cycle of the program's operation the tail pointer would move one position along in the arrays.

If, for example, *tail* were currently equal to 7, the last circle in the worm would have its center coordinates at *xcirc(7)* and *ycirc(7)*. When the assignment shown above is carried out, the new value of *tail* will be 8. Meanwhile a new head circle must be drawn and its coordinates put in the arrays *xcirc* and *ycirc*. The logical place to put these coordinates is in the position currently occupied by the coordinates of the old tail: position 7.

At this point I had not the slightest idea how the program would decide where to draw new head circles on the screen; this was a completely separate issue that I would deal with later. A frequent cause of difficulty in designing programs lies in the confusion that results when different computational demands become mingled in the mind. *Divide et impera.*

Before even beginning to sketch an algorithm for WORMS on paper I had the idea of creating the two arrays that would contain all the circles currently appearing in a given worm. The pointer *tail* would move along each array, replacing an old tail-circle coordinate by a new head-circle coordinate. What would happen, however, when *tail* reached the end of the array? It would jump back to the beginning, of course, using modular arithmetic. If the worm were composed of 10 circles, for instance, and the old value of *tail* were 9, the new value of *tail* would be 0. Here is what the algorithm looked like at this point:

```
loop
    tail ← tail + 1 (modulo something)
    get new head coordinates
    insert in xcirc(tail) and ycirc(tail)
    draw new head
    erase tail
end loop
```

The real usefulness of the algorithmic approach to the design and specification of computer programs lies in the wonderful vagueness and flexibility of algorithmic language. The designer may say anything he or she wants at any point in the algorithm, as long as the statement has a potential meaning that can be fleshed out later. For example, I had put off the question of just how the program would arrive at new head coordinates by writing "get new head coordinates." This would probably become several lines in a more detailed algorithm. Even at such a coarse level of detail I found that the algorithm immediately led to a clearer vision of just how the program should be structured. I even found a mistake: How would the program know how to "erase tail" if it did not know where it had been? Farther up in the loop the tail coordinates had just been overwritten with the new head coordinates. Erasure of the old tail would have to be done earlier in the loop, namely before the coordinate replacement was carried out. I amended the algorithm accordingly. Beginners may want to try to fix the algorithm themselves before going on and seeing what I did.

It was now time for a second pass through the algorithm. What kind of loop would I embed the entire thing in? The question immersed me right away in the problem of terminating the worm. The simplest scheme I could think of involved a fixed number of iterations in a FOR-loop in which some index mindlessly counts out several thousand iterations during which the worm would wriggle about the screen. But the preferred mode for ending the worm's career is to hit a key. Hence a repeat loop seemed in order. The program would repeat the instructions inside the loop until a human being hit a designated key.

I also had to decide what to substitute for "something" in the first instruction of the loop. The modulus would have to be the size of the array. This led directly to the question of how long to make the worm. I arbitrarily decided that 25 circles would yield a fairly active-looking worm.

The algorithm for WORMS now looked like this (where "mod" stands for "modulo"):

```
repeat
    tail ← tail + 1 (mod 25)
    erase tail
    get new head coordinates
    insert in xcirc(tail) and ycirc(tail)
    draw new head
until keystroke
```

Continuing to refine the algorithm, I replaced "erase tail" by something a little closer to the command I intended to use ultimately. Since I wanted to draw a black circle where formerly a light one (on my otherwise dark screen) had been, I inserted the statement "black circle at *circ(tail)*," which means that a black circle with its center at *xcirc(tail)* and *ycirc(tail)* should be drawn.

I now had to face how to "get new head coordinates." By what mechanism might the program decide where to draw the next head circle? It obviously had to be close to the preceding one and somewhere in "front" of it. Furthermore, in order for the twists and turns of the worm to look natural, the new direction taken should not be too different from the old one. Here the solution lay in a single variable called *dir*. Short for direction, it would contain the current heading of the worm in degrees. At each iteration of the main loop the program would increase or decrease *dir* randomly by 10 degrees.

It was time now to decide how close the circles should be and, indeed, how big to make them. Tentatively, a radius of 4 seemed reasonable. Since the worm had to look connected, the circles would have to overlap. I replaced "get new head coordinates" by

```
change ← random
if change < .5
    then dir ← dir + 10
```

$$\text{else } dir \leftarrow dir - 10$$
$$x \leftarrow xcirc(tail - 1)$$
$$y \leftarrow ycirc(tail - 1)$$
$$newx \leftarrow x + 4 \cdot \text{cosine}(dir)$$
$$newy \leftarrow y + 4 \cdot \text{sine}(dir)$$

The algorithm fragment selects a random number called *change*. Most programming systems provide random numbers between 0 and 1. Since a random number in this range will be less than .5 roughly half of the time, the variable *dir* will be incremented half of the time. This will be true only in the long run, of course. In the short run *dir* will be increased or decreased unpredictably by 10 degrees. The coordinates *x* and *y* are simply the coordinates of the previously drawn head. The last two statements are just high-school computations that employ the elementary trigonometric functions cosine and sine to get *x* and *y* increments scaled to size 4. Coordinates of the new head emerge.

It took only two more steps for me to refine the algorithm. Putting the new head coordinates in *xcirc(tail)* and *ycirc(tail)* was now easy — it was a simple assignment statement. Drawing the new head involved a pseudo-plot command of the form used earlier to erase the tail.

Finally, I had to initialize the arrays and variables at the beginning of the algorithm. Here I set the pointer *tail* to 1 and *xcirc(1)* and *ycirc(1)* to 100 each. The remaining entries of these arrays were assumed to be automatically set to 0. The direction variable *dir* was initialized to 90. The worm would thus begin at the point (100,100) and head in the 0-degree direction. The point (100,100) is a kind of shorthand for the actual center of one's screen. This may vary from machine to machine.

One problem remained: What if the worm crawled off the screen? I decided to incorporate a wraparound feature in the program. An *x* or *y* coordinate that wandered outside the range of allowable screen values would automatically be converted into a coordinate on the opposite side of the screen. Assuming a hypothetical screen on which coordinates range from 0 through 199, the following computation converts each coordinate outside this range into one that lies inside it:

$$newx \leftarrow newx \bmod 200$$
$$newy \leftarrow newy \bmod 200$$

The modulus function is available in virtually every programming language. It divides the number to be converted (*newx*) by the modulus (200) and computes the remainder. The variable to which the remainder is assigned (*newx*) now carries the value of the modular computation.

So much for WORMS. Or should I have called it WORM? The algorithm provides for just one. To add s meaningfully, readers may employ one set of arrays for each worm that is to appear. In any event, the algorithm I have so far specified appears in the listing below. An equivalent BASIC program appears alongside it. It would be most upsetting to this teacher to learn that any reader had merely typed the BASIC program into his or her machine without absorbing the lessons carefully spelled out here.

A line-by-line comparison of the algorithm and the program discloses a fairly close similarity between them. Indeed, two major blocks of instructions within the algorithm survived the translation into BASIC (IBM PC BASIC version 3.0) with very little change. Major differences revolve

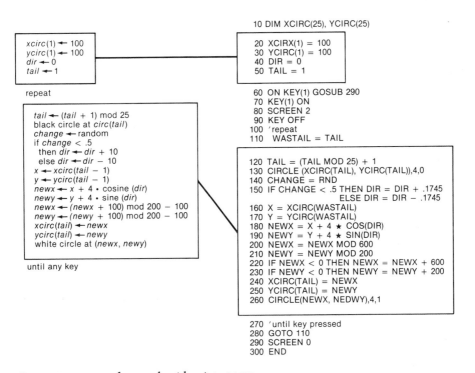

Converting WORMS from a algorithm into BASIC

around implementation features of BASIC's key facility on the IBM PC, and also on the absence of the repeat loop from this version of BASIC.

In the first category, KEY(1) (the function key F1 on the IBM PC keyboard) was selected as the trigger for turning off the program once a user had become tired of watching the worm wriggle about on the screen. In line 70 the program turns the key on, signaling the underlying BASIC system to watch for signals emanating from the F1 key. In line 90 the KEYOFF command removes the BASIC options display at the bottom of the screen to make way for the worms. The main instruction involving the F1 key, however, occurs at line 60. Here the system is instructed to jump to statement 290 if the user presses F1. At line 290 the screen is cleared and execution stops at the KEY statement.

In the second category, the absence of a repeat loop made it necessary to construct an equivalent form of execution control by means of the GOTO command at line 280 of the program. This causes execution to jump back repeatedly to line 110 until someone pushes the F1 key. The position of the resulting loop is signaled by two comments, one at line 100 and the other at line 270. These comments were inserted for the sake of indicating the intended loop structure to readers.

Other differences also came about from writing WORMS in BASIC. Statement 10 sets the dimensions of the arrays to 25 entries each. Statement 80 sets up the high-resolution screen for the IBM PC. Here the points are close together. In line 110 a new variable *wastail* takes the value of *tail* just before the latter variable is decremented. Hence *wastail* in the program can replace *tail* − 1 in the algorithm where x and y are computed. The main reason for using *wastail*, however, is that *tail*, an array index, cannot have the value zero in this version of BASIC. Consequently in statement 120 the 1 is added after the modulus is taken, not before. In the algorithm I was merely being sloppy, imagining that the index *tail* ran from 0 through 24. The actual circle-drawing command of the IBM PC BASIC occurs at line 130. The center of the circle is at XCIRC(TAIL) and YCIRC(TAIL); the radius is 4 and the color is 0 (black).

In line 150 the variable *dir* is incremented not by 10 degrees but by the roughly equivalent angle of .1745 radian. (The IBM PC BASIC does not use degrees.) In lines 200 and 210 the variables *newx* and *newy* are limited to sizes 600 and 200 respectively. This forms a box just inside the IBM PC display screen. The modulus facility in BASIC reduces positive numbers quite nicely but fails to work on negative numbers. Thus when a worm crawls off the screen in a negative direction, the modulus is taken by

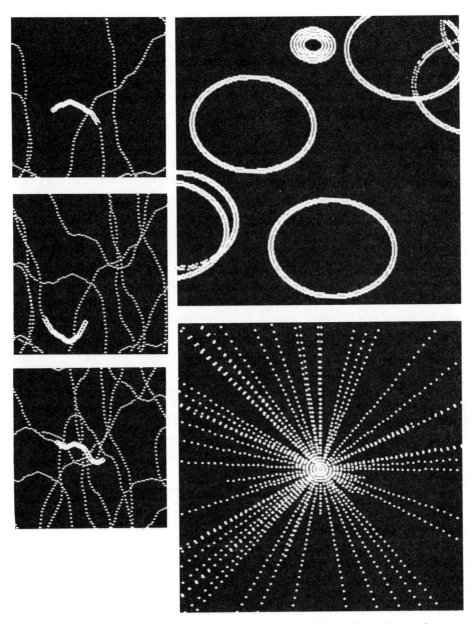

A worm that leaves tracks (*left*), falling rain (*upper right*) and a stellar explosion (*bottom right*)

adding the appropriate screen dimensions, as in lines 220 and 230. A worm that crawls off one edge of the box will reappear on the other side. At line 290 the SCREEN 0 command resets the screen for any ensuing textual displays.

WORMS lovers can enhance their program by inserting a RANDOMIZE command before the loop begins, preventing the worm from retracing its path. They can also add provisions to restart the program, if they want to. They can also add a little trail of dots as we have done in the exemplar worm displayed in the left illustration on page 255.

The other special effects I mentioned above might now conceivably be programmed, even by neophytes, if the following hints suffice.

The program I call RAINDROPS selects a random point on the display screen and draws a succession of circles of ever increasing radii about it. Then the program selects another point and repeats the circle-drawing procedure. RAINDROPS continues in this way until the rainmaker depresses a key. Thus there are two loops, an outer loop in which the point is selected and an inner loop in which the surrounding circles are drawn. RAINDROPS converts two random numbers between 0 and 1 into screen coordinates by multiplying them by the respective dimensions of the screen. The resulting point (x,y) becomes the center for a succession of circles drawn by the inner loop. Let an index k run from 1 through 25 while white (or light-colored) circles are drawn. The centers are at (x,y) and the radii take on the values $4k$. It is simpler to leave all the circles so drawn on the screen. But it is more realistic to have just one circle or a few circles spreading outward. To obtain just one, RAINDROPS must erase (redraw in black) the circle with radius $4(k-1)$ after the circle with radius $4k$ is drawn.

STARBURST displays a stellar explosion. The experience can also be seen as the trip down a vast corridor of stars that pass one's armchair spaceship at warp speed. The stars move by small increments along lines of perspective toward the viewer. The increments themselves increase as the stars approach. Nearer objects appear to move faster than distant ones. STARBURST is more complicated than RAINDROPS, however. It must keep track of all the stars currently appearing. Readers may use an array called *stars* to this end — more correctly two arrays, as in WORMS — to store the x and y coordinates of individual stars. The z coordinates are implicit in the apparent motion of the stars.

When a star first appears at the origin $(100,100)$, motion increments are at first very small. The increments get steadily larger as stars approach the observer (or vice versa), increasing by an amount inversely proportional to z, its supposed distance from the observer. Programmers may plan on, say, 25 increments per star before it flashes past. The distance z to a given star may thus be taken as $25 - k$, where k is the number of iterations in the star's history.

The grand loop for STARBURST involves the creation of a new star, the destruction of an old one and an increment for every star in the arrays.

ADDENDUM

Most programmers (tyros or otherwise) attempting the special effects described in "Special FX" settled on worms as the effect of choice. Sydney N. Afriat of Ottawa notes that the worms are particularly exciting to watch when the program is run in compiled form.

Warner Clements of Beverly Hills, Calif., disliked the wraparound dismemberment of his worms. Rather than allowing the creatures to crawl off one edge and to reappear at the opposite edge, Clements' program alters the direction of motion by +.25 or −.25. The choice depends on whether or not the variable called *change* is greater than .5.

Robert D. Scott, Jr., of Madison, Va., may be typical of a certain unfortunate class of readers running a version of the BASIC language that has enough differences from the version I described to make WORMS uncrawlable. Such differences, although fatal, are usually quite slight and easily fixed — once they are detected.

· 23 ·

Balls in Boxes

A box full of balls flying in all directions, hitherto only a mental model for physical matter, can now be viewed on the screen of a home computer. With a modicum of programming effort, readers can witness the molecular collisions that produce pressure within a cylinder or cheer on the random jostling of differently colored molecules as one liquid diffuses through another. Those undaunted by the prospect of a nuclear explosion in their computer can even play with critical masses of the unstable solid I call gridium.

The inspiration for this excursion comes from James F. Blinn, an affable researcher at the Jet Propulsion Laboratory in Pasadena, Calif. Blinn has developed simulations of various physical systems. The simulations have been gathered into a rather funny, laconically narrated videotape titled *The Mechanical Universe*. Two of Blinn's simulations that caught my eye as potential subjects for this chapter were charming animations of a gas-filled cylinder and a diffusion chamber. In the first case a few dozen balls bounded and rebounded within a two-dimensional cylinder, driving a weighted position into a state of jittery equilibrium. In the second case balls of two different colors bounced back and forth within a fixed enclosure; at first the two colors were separated, but as the balls moved about in Brownian fashion, the two colors became thoroughly mixed. The third simulation to be described here, the nuclear explosion, is my own entry. The idea springs from the primitive wish to watch a matrix explode.

The few hours it may take to create a working model of the program I call BOUNCE will be well repaid by the sight of a weighted piston coming into equilibrium with a cloud of bouncing balls. In Blinn's simulation the balls bounced off one another, but a much simpler and equally effective program can be written if the balls ignore one another and bounce only from the walls of the cylinder.

The user of BOUNCE may specify both the speed of the balls and their number. The position assumed by the piston follows the so-called ideal-gas law: $PV \propto T$, which is to say that the product of the pressure P and the volume V of a confined gas is proportional to its temperature T. The molecular speed specified by the user amounts to selecting a certain temperature, and the weight of the piston determines the pressure. What volume will result? The answer can be seen clearly on the screen (*see* illustration below). The higher the temperature of gas rises, the higher the piston goes up.

There is some value in following the path of a single bouncing ball before tackling a multitude. Consider, then, a box drawn on the display screen of one's computer. The box, 50 units on a side, contains a ball

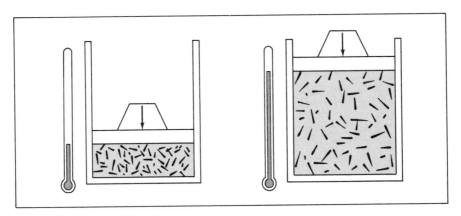

As the temperature rises the volume increases in James F. Blinn's simulation

somewhere within it. Because the demonstration lies in the plane, the ball has two coordinates of position, say x and y. It also has two coordinates of velocity, v_x and v_y. In a short period of t time units the ball will move from the position (x,y) to the position $(x + t \cdot v_x, y + t \cdot v_y)$.

The piston cylinder that is drawn by BOUNCE, also two-dimensional, has three fixed walls defined by the lines $x = 0$, $x = 50$ and $y = 0$. A fourth wall represents the piston. Its line has the equation $y = h$, h being the current height of the piston. No ball-animation program can escape the need to discover if and when a given ball will collide with one of the walls. BOUNCE does this by testing the current direction of a ball against each of the four equations: Where does the direction line intersect each of the four wall equations? The left half of the table below provides the answers.

In each case the t value listed gives the time (from the present) at which the ball will strike the wall in question. The actual point of impact is computed by substituting the t value into simple position formulas. If the t value happens to be negative, it means that the ball, continuing in its present direction, will never strike the wall because it is currently moving away from it. If the t value is infinite, one of the ball's velocity coordinates must be zero. Here too the ball will never strike the wall. Naturally BOUNCE skips the computation of a t value if that is the case.

The wall that has associated with it the smallest non-negative t value is the one the ball will strike first. That value of t can be used to calculate the actual point at which the ball will strike the wall. Again a table comes in handy (*see* the right half of the table below).

Most simulation programs exploit one of two possible techniques for advancing the imaginary timepiece known as the simulation clock. The time-slice technique advances the clock by a small fixed increment, updating appearances in a uniform manner. The critical-event technique

WALL	t VALUE		WALL	POINT OF BOUNCE
1: $x = 0$	t_1: $-x/v_x$		1: $x = 0$	$(0, y + t_1 \cdot v_y)$
2: $x = 50$	t_2: $(50 - x)/v_x$		2: $x = 50$	$(50, y + t_2 \cdot v_y)$
3: $y = 0$	t_3: $-y/v_y$		3: $y = 0$	$(x + t_3 \cdot v_x, 0)$
4: $y = h$	t_4: $(h - y)/v_y$		4: $y = h$	$(x + t_4 \cdot v_x, h)$

advances the clock to the next event of interest. BOUNCE employs the critical-event method, where an event is said to take place when a ball bounces off a wall.

Crucial to the critical-event approach is an array called *event*. If BOUNCE is juggling n balls, it must know which ball will strike a wall next. The array is actually a priority queue. Here is how BOUNCE operates:

> repeat
>   1. get time, ball and wall from *event*(1)
>   2. update system by time
>   3. determine next event for ball
>   4. insert time, ball and wall in *event*
>   5. display the system in new state
> until key

The cycle of five steps will be repeated until the home computer scientist presses a key; Chapter 22, on special effects, outlined the use of keys for this purpose.

Step 1 is fairly simple. The event queue actually consists of three arrays: *event* stores the times to the next events in the order of their occurrence, an array called *ball* stores the index of the balls that correspond to these events, and another array called *wall* stores the corresponding walls. For example, *event*(2) holds the time until the second event and *ball*(2) contains the number of the ball b involved; *wall*(2) stores the number of the wall w, which takes on one of the four values, 1 ($x = 0$), 2 ($x = 50$), 3 ($y = 0$), or 4 ($y = h$). Step 1 thus includes three instructions to place the three items of information in variables t, b, and w.

Step 2, updating the system, means changing the position of all the balls in the box. This can be done within a loop of the following form:

> for $i \leftarrow 1$ to n
> $x(i) \leftarrow x(i) + t \cdot v_x(i)$
> $y(i) \leftarrow y(i) + t \cdot v_y(i)$
>   if $w = 1$ or $w = 2$ then $v_x(b) \leftarrow -v_x(b)$
>   if $w = 3$ or $w = 4$ then $v_y(b) \leftarrow -v_y(b)$

Readers will recognize the position formulas introduced above. There is no danger that any of the balls will end up outside the box because the one ball that comes closest is only at a wall, not through it, by time t. The two IF-THEN statements handle the bounce of ball b. If the ball strikes either of the two vertical walls, its x velocity is reversed; a bounce on a horizontal wall means that the velocity coordinate in the y direction must be reversed. Updating the system also means decrementing all the times stored in the array *event*. Here BOUNCE merely subtracts t from each array entry.

I have already described step 3, the determination of the next event for ball b, implicitly; now I shall describe it in more detail:

$$\begin{aligned}
&\text{if } v_x(b) = 0 \text{ then } t_1 \leftarrow 5{,}000\\
&\qquad\qquad\qquad\quad t_2 \leftarrow 5{,}000\\
&\qquad\quad \text{else } \; t_1 \leftarrow -x(b)/v_x(b)\\
&\qquad\qquad\qquad\quad t_2 \leftarrow (50 - x(b))/v_x(b)\\
&\text{if } v_y(b) = 0 \text{ then } t_3 \leftarrow 5{,}000\\
&\qquad\qquad\qquad\quad t_4 \leftarrow 5{,}000\\
&\qquad\quad \text{else } \; t_3 \leftarrow - \, y(b)/v_y(b)\\
&\qquad\qquad\qquad\quad t_4 \leftarrow (h - y(b))/v_y(b)
\end{aligned}$$

The time-to-impact for ball b and each of the four walls is encoded in four variables, t_1 through t_4. The unreasonable value of 5000 is assigned to any of the four variables if ball b, continuing in its present direction, would never strike the corresponding wall. A computational sieve then serves to isolate the next wall to be struck by ball b. First BOUNCE sets t to 5000, then it tests each of t_1 through t_4 in turn. The test has three parts: If t_i is less than t, if t_i is greater than 0, and if *wall*(b) is not equal to i, then the program replaces the current value of t by t_i and replaces w by i.

In step 4, BOUNCE refurbishes the event queues. The main task is to find where in the queues the next bounce of ball b belongs. That is easily accomplished:

$$\begin{aligned}
&k \leftarrow 2\\
&\text{while } event(k) < t\\
&\qquad event(k - 1) \leftarrow event(k)\\
&\qquad ball(k - 1) \leftarrow ball(k)\\
&\qquad wall(k - 1) \leftarrow wall(k)\\
&\qquad k \leftarrow k + 1\\
&event(k - 1) \leftarrow t\\
&ball(k - 1) \leftarrow b\\
&wall(k - 1) \leftarrow w
\end{aligned}$$

Here BOUNCE searches through the event queue to find where ball b now properly belongs. As it searches it shifts items in all three arrays one cell to the left. As soon as it finds a cell k in which $event(k)$ is not less than t, it is obvious that the time to the next impact of ball b belongs in the preceding cell, k. (When the balls in the cylinder are given their initial positions and velocities, the event queue must also be set up. To avoid programming effort, the positions and velocities can be selected by hand and the event times worked out. The initial event-queue entries can then be typed in.)

The final step requires BOUNCE to display the box and all the balls in their current positions. This straightforward operation must be supplemented by erasing the balls in their previous positions, of course.

To get started, BOUNCE asks the user to type in a speed at which the balls are to travel. If the variable is called v, the program then selects n random numbers between $-v$ and v, placing these in the x-velocity coordinates $v_x(i)$. The y velocities are then calculated by means of the Pythagorean theorem, namely the square root of $v^2 - v_x^2(i)$. Readers may want to try various values of v in the range from 1 through 10.

Those who write BOUNCE will naturally want to watch the weighted piston move up and down in response to intermittent pressure from within the cylinder. For this purpose, step 2 must include a calculation that subtracts the downward movement of the piston due to gravity from the upward movement of the piston due to the transfer of momentum from one ball. The result is a new h.

For the sake of simplicity the interaction of the balls with the piston has been distorted to the point of chicanery. In time t the piston falls $t^2/100$ units. When a ball with y velocity v_y strikes the piston, the piston moves up $v_y/100m$ units. My apologies to physicists, but it works! Users of BOUNCE must, of course, input the mass m of the piston, as well as the number of balls, n, and their speed, v.

The diffusion program I call BLEND treats the molecules of a liquid as balls that are able to move only one step horizontally or vertically at a time. A 31-by-31 array called *tank* holds 930 balls, which are set up initially somewhat like a checkers game. BLEND is even less realistic than BOUNCE but it too works. The balls in the left half of the box are colored red and those in the right half are colored gray (*see* lower illustration on the next page).

BLEND proceeds by selecting an array position at random, then selecting a random adjacent position. If a ball occupies the first position and no ball

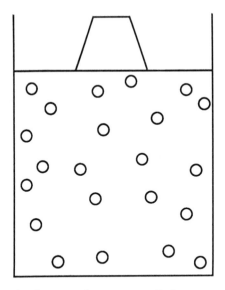

A schematic of a pressure cylinder

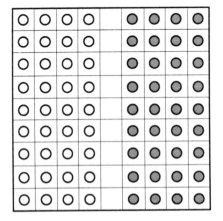 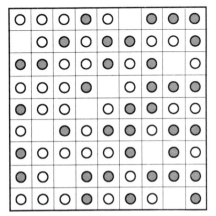

Two liquids diffuse in a 9-by-9 matrix

occupies the second, the ball is erased at its current position and redrawn at the new one. If a ball is absent at the first position or present at the second, BLEND could not care less. With microseconds of time on its hands, a movable ball will sooner or later turn up. How long will it take for the two stylized liquids to diffuse completely? No detailed algorithmic description accompanies this recreation. Readers are left to their own devices: hardware and mindware.

With unholy haste I have rushed to the matter of gridium, a violently unstable element. One atom of the stuff spontaneously decays, shooting off a neuron in the process. I am reminded of a famous demonstration by Walt Disney; the great man once filled a high school gymnasium with cocked mousetraps. Each trap held a Ping-Pong ball resting on the snapping arm normally meant for crushing rodents. With a mischievous grin, Disney threw a single Ping-Pong ball into the gymnasium. Within less than a second the air was literally filled with thousands of balls and there was a strange roar. This was probably the safest chain reaction ever.

Gridium happens to be a crystal. Its atoms are arranged like balls in a square matrix measuring $n + 1$ balls on a side. On a signal from the reader the central ball decays, producing a single neutron that zips along a random line through the matrix. Another ball will decay if it is struck by the neutron. Will a chain reaction ensue? If the matrix is small, the reaction will most likely be a dud. But larger matrices are increasingly likely to go off with a silent roar (*see* illustration below). How much

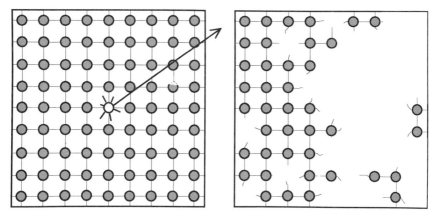

A sample of gridium before (*left*) and after (*right*) a chain reaction

larger? That is for the home experimenter to discover. There can be little doubt that even a microcomputer would have vastly relieved the work load at Los Alamos in 1944.

This department has no military secrets. I shall be pleased to report values for the critical mass of gridium as discovered by readers brave enough to try the experiment. The program I call BOOM uses an array called *grid*. Because most readers do not have variable array dimensions available to them, I have decided to make *grid* 50 by 50. When the user types in a value for n, BOOM will automatically limit its considerations to the first n rows and columns of *grid*. These will contain the atoms, one per cell in the region. For purposes of both display and calculation, atoms of gridium have one-unit radii and six-unit spacings. It is convenient to regard the atom at array position (i,j) as having coordinates $(6i, 6j)$.

When an atom of gridium decays, BOOM selects a random angle a and calculates the sine and cosine of that angle, storing the values in the variables s and c. If the decaying atom has coordinates (x,y), the point and the angle together determine a line. The key question is, "How close does the line come to another atom having coordinates (u,v)?" The answer is given by a formula, $(u - x)^2 + (v - y)^2 - [(u - x) \cdot c + (v - y) \cdot s]^2$. The formula represents the square of the distance between the point (u,v) and the closest point to it on the line in question. Rather than bothering with taking the square root of the resulting number, BOOM merely checks whether the number is less than or equal to 1. If it is, the atom at (u,v) must undergo fission.

Every time an atom in *grid* thus explodes, BOOM enters a loop that systematically plugs all n^2 coordinates into the variables u and v, omitting the exploding atom. All atoms that must undergo fission next are added to a list in the form of an array called *fire*. An index called *fired* separates those atoms already fired from those yet to fire. A second index called *end* marks the end of the list. Every time a new atom explodes, all the atoms intersected by the neutron path are added to *fire*, the index *end* being incremented each time. When all such atoms have been determined, *fired* is incremented and the cycle is reentered. When *fired* equals *end*, the common value of these indices tells the number of atoms that took part in the chain reaction. For what value of n will the entire matrix blow up? The statistical fluctuation in the answer will not be much.

Because of space limitations, this description of BOOM must suffice. It is possible to install a display routine within BOOM, but it is not necessary to undertake such an effort to find the answer. I promised to publish the most interesting picture of a partially blown-up matrix sent to me. It would represent a value of *n* very close to the critical mass.

Copies of the videotape *The Mechanical Universe* can be obtained by calling the toll-free number 1-800-LEARNER. For information about a newsletter by the same name, readers should consult the List of Suppliers.

ADDENDUM

A home-computer laboratory in which simulated gas molecules bounced within a closed vessel to mimic the effects of pressure was the subject of "Balls in Boxes." Molecules also diffused digitally from one side of a container to the other. Finally, make-believe atoms of the dangerously unstable substance I called gridium were gathered into a critical mass. A number of readers developed their own pressure vessels and diffusion chambers, but most found gridium too hard to resist. From all over North America and later from other parts of the world, reports of "computer explosions" crossed my desk.

By specifying the track of an escaping neutron with a linear equation, I inadvertently implied that two neutrons travel in opposite directions from the splitting atom. Most readers chose one of the two directions. In either case, it was not easy to get all the atoms in a plane *n*-by-*n* grid to blow up.

By plotting the results of numerous experiments, Robert Castle of Webster, Tex., found that 90 percent of the atoms usually fissioned in a 16-by-16 grid. By the time *n* reached a value of 32, 99 percent of the atoms were atomized. Robert M. Martin, a professor of philosophy at Dalhousie University in Nova Scotia, found a 90 percent criticality when *n* was equal to 19, and 99 percent of the gridium disappeared when *n* was equal to 39. Most other nuclear experimenters found values somewhere between these. Of those people sticking to the double-neutron burn in the original recipe, Richard W. Smith of Ann Arbor, Mich., was typical in finding lower critical masses. He reports a 98 percent burn when the grid measured 15 by 15.

Few readers developed a system as sophisticated as the program called SHAKEY. Developed by Robert B. Merkin of Northampton, Mass., SHAKEY not only can handle very large grids but also incorporates a great many time-saving techniques to speed up the essential boom. SHAKEY's home reactor allows different grid spacings to be tried and emits clicks at every decay like a Geiger counter. Merkin says he will be glad to share SHAKEY with readers who write to him. (*See* List of Suppliers.)

Dramatic samples of blown matrixes were sent by David H. Fax of Pittsburgh, Pa., and Patrick E. Kane of Champaign, Ill. Their productions are shown below.

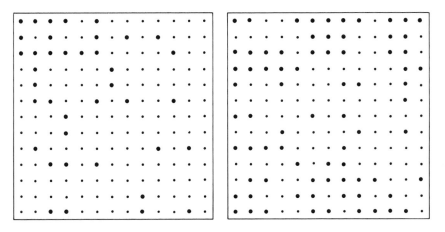

David H. Fax's blown matrix (*left*) and Patrick E. Kane's (*right*)

˚ 24 ˚

The Invisible Professor

If the darkened screen of a computer display is like a chalkboard, who is drawing the curves that arc gracefully across its matte surface? The hand must belong to the Invisible Professor, an electronic incarnation of all the academicians who have ever lovingly sketched the curves of analytic geometry. These curves have romantic and mysterious names such as the witch of Agnesi, the kampyle of Eudoxus, and the nephroid of Freeth. They include parabolas, cycloids, spirals, and serpentines. Nearly forgotten when mathematics rushed to become general and geometry became non-Euclidean, the curves remain a testament to the forms that follow function in physics. The curves mark beautiful discoveries, some famous, some less than famous, by mathematicians of past centuries.

The Invisible Professor is a collection of the simplest computer programs imaginable. In drawing the curves it captures their beauty with a piquancy their discoverers could scarcely have imagined; a single, bright point is the new chalk. It traces an equation called Tschirnhausen's cubic, for example, by gliding onto the screen from the upper right, swooping through the origin, then looping up and back through the origin. The point burns its way to the lower right-hand corner of the display, where it is extinguished.

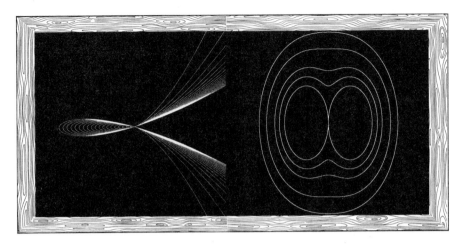

Twenty versions of Tschirnhausen's cubic (*left*) and five of the hippopede (*right*)

If asked, the invisible professor will even draw a family of curves. The equation of Tschirnhausen's cubic has a special constant symbol. When different numbers are substituted into the symbol, different versions of the curve are drawn: the screen is filled with variations on a theme. The only thing missing is the professor's frail old voice: "It will be seen at once, from a mere glance at the equation, that this curve is a generalized, semicubical parabola."

The Invisible Professor can also render transcendental landscapes as undulating sheets of parallel curves and hint at complex oceans by making curvilinear distortions of grids. Such programs, which have been written by lovers of geometry, are distributed for a price.

In order to lay down a minimal background on how to draw curves, it is my turn to be an invisible professor. The humble circle will serve as an example of a curve. Three principal formulations of it will lead to curve-drawing programs.

The first and most familiar formulation was encountered by the majority of us in high school:

$$x^2 + y^2 = c^2$$

The equation distinguishes points that lie on the circle from those that do not. A point that has Cartesian coordinates x and y lies on the circle if the square of c (the radius of the circle) results when x and y are squared and added. Whenever the program is run, the user supplies a value for c.

The formula can be employed by a circle-drawing program if the curve is divided into an upper section and a lower one. The program runs through a series of x values, plotting the corresponding y values. To be useful, y is best unsquared. Consequently the equation must be solved in terms of y. The two branches differ only in sign:

$$y = +\sqrt{c^2 - x^2}$$
$$y = -\sqrt{c^2 - x^2}$$

This formulation is already rather awkward, however. Perhaps polar coordinates would serve better.

The Cartesian coordinates x and y measure distance vertically and horizontally from a central point called the origin. Polar coordinates, r and θ, establish a point quite differently. The point lies r units from the origin, and the line joining it to the origin makes an angle θ with the horizontal. The Cartesian equation of a circle is simply $r = c$. No matter what the angle θ may be, the distance r must be c. Unfortunately, few readers will be using languages that employ polar coordinates for plotting.

The third principal presentation involves so-called parametric equations. For many curve-drawing programs these are ideal:

$$x = c \cdot \cos(t)$$
$$y = c \cdot \sin(t)$$

Here a parameter t runs from zero to 360 degrees. At each degree, say, the x and y values are plotted. Readers not familiar with the functions sine and cosine may at least discover how to use them by consulting their language manual.

At the algorithmic level a bare-boned version of the program I call CIRCLE might appear as follows:

```
input c
for t ← 1 to 360
    x ← c·cos(t)
    y ← c·sin(t)
    point (x,y)
```

The exact form employed will not differ greatly from the formulation shown. Similarly, there will be a plot command somewhat like the one immediately above.

The circle-drawing program will not, of course, be quite as simple. For one thing, most personal computers have the origin in one corner of the screen. Offsets must be added to place the circle in the center. A screen that has 200 points horizontally and 150 points vertically, for example, will need the following modification in the program:

$$x \leftarrow c \cdot \cos(t) + 100$$
$$y \leftarrow c \cdot \sin(t) + 75$$

The Invisible Professor can now be incarnated through a host of little programs that all share the same basic structure just outlined. Only the equations are different. Tschirnhausen's cubic, for example, has parametric equations that do not involve sine or cosine:

$$x = 3a(t^2 - 3)$$
$$y = a(t^2 - 3)$$

The miniprogram called TSCHIRNHAUSEN therefore employs a parameter t that runs from a minimum value to a maximum value, both determined by screen size. The 150-by-200 screen mentioned above, for instance, will accommodate the curve from $t = -4.4$ to $t = +4.4$ when a is equal to 1. No digital computer can vary the parameter t continuously through such a range of values; instead it must increase t by increments small enough to give the impression of continuity. The chalk must not squeak on the board. Because this particular board has 200 points horizontally, a reasonable step size for t must be obtained by dividing the range of values for t, namely 8.8, into 200 equal steps. The calculation yields .044. On the other hand, the curve is not traced out evenly. Some parts are drawn faster than others, resulting in separation of points. Fortunately computation of this kind is so cheap (and fast) that we can drop the step size to .01 in a perfectly cavalier fashion:

```
input a
for t ← −4.4 to +4.4 step .01
    x ← 3a(t² − 3) + 100
    y ← at(t² − 3) + 75
    point (x,y)
```

Another simple way to improve the smoothness of the curves involves the use of line segments. TSCHIRNHAUSEN and any of the other curve-drawing programs described here can be modified so that each time a new point is obtained a line-drawing command joins it to the point previously plotted. The coordinates of the old point are then replaced by those of the new. To the eye even a coarsely polygonal curve may look graceful.

In either version of the program one can add a new outer loop that varies the constant *a* from .1 to 2 in steps of .1. In this case the invisible professor will draw a family of 20 beautifully nested cubic curves that would make Tschirnhausen proud.

The hippopede, first investigated by the Greek philosopher Proclus in about A.D. 475, has two forms. It can appear as an 8 lying on its side or it can assume a dumbbell shape, depending on the values of its two constants, *a* and *b* (*see* right half of illustration on page 270). The parametric equations are only slightly complicated:

$$x = 2\cos(t)\sqrt{ab - b^2\sin^2 t}$$
$$y = 2\sin(t)\sqrt{ab - b^2\sin^2 t}$$

The parameter *t* runs from −180 to +180 degrees. A small economy of computation is available in that the same square-root function appears in both equations. As a result the program HIPPOPEDE needs to compute the function only once, store it as a variable called *temp*, and then multiply $2\cos(t)$ and $2\sin(t)$ by *temp*. Here again readers setting up their own invisible professor must consider the step size. Although it depends to some degree on *a* and *b*, the screen size and other factors, a step size of one degree will work well in most cases. Again, different values of the constants *a* and *b* can be tried, anywhere from 1 to 10 with stops either at integer or at fractional values. The wise old Athenian owl will be found staring out from the screen if for each of four curves *a* is set to 20, 25, 30, 40, and 50 and *b* is held at 20.

Spirals, among the most beautiful forms found in nature, are second nature, so to speak, to the invisible professor. It is no surprise that they grow best in the polar medium. A point on the spiral of Archimedes has the polar coordinates (r, θ). The equation is, as mathematicians say, trivial: $r = a\theta$. The angle θ begins at 0 and can run as high as one's screen (and the constant *a*) will allow. Step size can be 1 or less. If *a* is chosen to be .01, the spiral will be tightly wound; at .1 it will be much less so.

The Invisible Professor can also easily handle the famed logarithmic spiral (also called the equiangular spiral for the sake of people who are frightened by the idea of logarithms). The spiral inhabits seashells and the heads of sunflowers. The Invisible Professor uses the polar equation $r = e^{a\theta}$, where the transcendental number e can be taken as 2.7183. The step size used with the Archimedean spiral can be used here, but readers must be warned about the awesome speed with which the exponential function grows: Even when a is equal to .01, the curve does not stay tightly wrapped for long.

There are hundreds of curves in a handy little paperback called *A Catalog of Special Plane Curves*, by J. Dennis Lawrence. The invisible professor will thrive on these forms. For more advanced programmers it is an interesting project to assemble all the curve-drawing programs one can write into a single package that the user can access through a menu.

In some cases it is not necessary to incorporate several distinct programs into a single package. The magic of generalization leads to a single program that generates all the curves involved. It becomes simply a matter of selecting values for various constants that appear in the master formula. The circle, for example, is just one member of a class of forms called the Bowditch curves, or Lissajous figures, that arise from a single parametric equation:

$$x = a \cdot \sin(ct + d)$$
$$y = b \cdot \sin(t)$$

These curves are familiar to owners of cathode-ray oscilloscopes. Electronic signals that vary sinusoidally will produce such curves on the tube.

The constants a and b define a rectangle a units long and b units high. Within this rectangle a Bowditch curve will weave its wild dance. The constants c and d are the ones that make a difference. When d is equal to 0, for example, values for c of 3/5 and 1/4 produce the two curves shown at the right. If c happens to be rational, a Bowditch curve will come back to its starting point, tracing itself for as long as the Invisible Professor does not run out of breath. There is no point in worrying about whether the numbers in one's computer are rational; a digital computer accepts only such numbers. (The foregoing remarks apply when the units of t are radians. To convert the equations into degrees, one must multiply the input of the function *sin* by $\pi/180$.)

If the parameter t starts at 0 degrees, a Bowditch curve begins somewhere on the x axis. In general it weaves back and forth, in and out, before rejoining itself. But how large will t get before that happens? Here

Two Bowditch curves, one of which retraces itself

is a small puzzle for rational readers. For puzzle dodgers, let t get no bigger than 3600 in steps of 1 and stick to rational numbers whose components are small. For the curious, humorous, or simply insane, open-ended adventures are available; exhaust the old professor by setting no upper limit to t. One can then decide, by watching the drawing of the curve in process, how long it takes to rejoin itself. The loop one uses must be mechanically constructed in this case. At the bottom of the loop place a simple GO TO statement that redirects execution to the top of the loop. To save the elderly academician from an eternity at the chalkboard, it would be a kindness to insert an IF statement in the loop, so that if a key is pressed, the program goes to an instruction outside the loop.

Among the factors prompting the Invisible Professor to come out of hiding was a letter from Stanley S. Miller of Concord, Mass. Miller, a management consultant by profession, has fallen in love with the trails left by various functions. It all began with a commercially available program called CURVES, about which I shall have more to say below.

"One late, rather winy evening," he writes, "I hit the wrong button and produced something entirely different from any cycloids I had generated before . . . I thought, at first, that some of the Brie I had been eating had got into my computer, but I ran it through again with different parameters [that is, constants], and produced a close relative." The encounter with serendipity gave Miller a glimpse of the profound power and variety possible with a curve-generating program that is reasonably general. I include a trophy of his hunt opposite. It looks like a three-dimensional net thrown out to ensnare impressionable minds. If the curve needs a name, let it be called Miller's Madness. Its parametric equations have an innocent simplicity about them:

$$x = \sin(.99t) - .7\cos(3.01t)$$
$$y = \cos(1.01t) + .1\sin(15.03t)$$

I have no idea how large t must become to complete the plot. Readers who want to view Miller's Madness on their own computer are advised to use the unending loop described above; the units of t are radians.

When programming MADNESS, the reader may as well make it general by putting constants in front of the four trigonometric functions. This will put a virtually infinite space at their disposal for exploration.

CURVES, the program that inspired Miller, is a highly general program produced by Bridge Software (*see* the List of Suppliers). Filled with

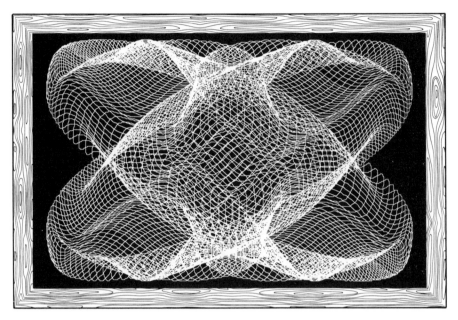

Stanley S. Miller's MADNESS illustrates serendipity in constants

useful options and sophisticated functions, it represents something like the ultimate Invisible Professor. But there is more. Bridge Software also sells a program called SURF, an output sample of which is shown on the next page (upper illustration). Users of this program specify a function of two variables and then watch as the program draws a landscape in three dimensions, complete with mountains, valleys and hidden lines. Neither program is too pricy.

Bridge Software is not the only small company producing mathematical software. For lovers of complex functions, Lascaux Graphics has created a program called $f(z)$. Perhaps a few readers will remember that all the action in the Mandelbrot set took place in the complex plane. The functions produced by Lascaux Graphics map the complex plane onto itself. We cannot visualize a four-dimensional space but we can almost feel a complex function when its effect on the complex plane is clearly seen; a regular polar grid (*see* lower illustration on the next page). Embedded in the plane is transformed by a complex function into something of curvilinear grace, like currents in a mathematical sea. Somewhat more expensive than the CURVES program (*see* the List of Suppliers), $f(z)$ is a

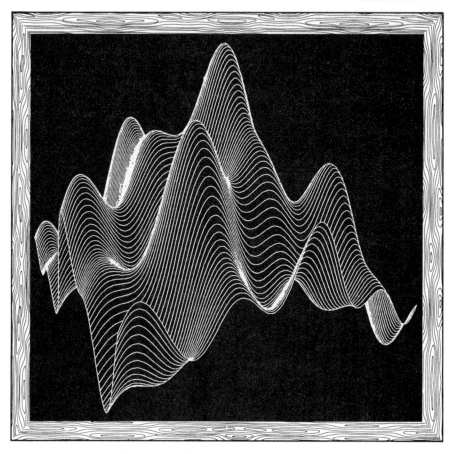

A surface constructed from simple functions

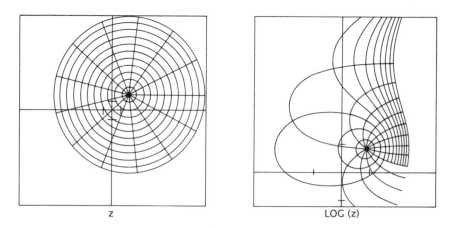

A complex function (*left*) and its logarithm (*right*)

than the CURVES program (*see* the List of Suppliers), $f(z)$ is a bargain for those awaiting initiation into the higher mysteries of the chalkboard.

ADDENDUM

The Invisible Professor appeared to draw a number of classic examples from the infinite variety of trigonometric and algebraic curves. Among the many readers who had made prior acquaintance with the professor in my "Computer Recreations" columns in SCIENTIFIC AMERICAN magazine were some who had interesting comments to make.

Abe Achkinazi of Bell, Calif., has proposed a date between the invisible professor and Lucy, the Hewlett-Packard color plotter in the mathematics laboratory of the California State University at Northridge. The professor might enjoy Lucy's Lissajous figures. Achkinazi has a program that draws straight lines between corresponding points on a pair of such figures. In this way Lucy produces wild curves clad in a kind of moiré sheen.

Tom Dorn of Vancouver, British Columbia, recommends his own program BUMBLEBEE. It incorporates the following parametric equations in which the constant a can be varied:

$$x = 2\sin(at)$$
$$y = e^{t\sin t}.$$

Temple H. Fay of the University of Southern Mississippi finds polar curves, which are plotted in terms of coordinates (r,θ) rather than (x,y), useful in teaching calculus. The professor plots a butterfly with the aid of sine, cosine, and exponential functions:

$$r = e^{\cos\theta} - 2\cos(4\theta) + \sin^5(\theta/12).$$

Commercial and quasi-commercial interest runs rampant in the area of curves. There are products aplenty to aid the amateur charter of curvilinear complexity. For example, David E.-B. Kennedy, a mathematics teacher at the Langley Secondary School in Langley, British Columbia, is enthusiastic about the Casio fx-7000G calculator-plotter. This hand-held marvel displays miniature stepped plots of virtually any function on a 1.5-by-2-inch display.

SPIA, an apparently comprehensive mathematics program, allows users to construct and plot formulas of almost any type. Moreover, it includes special manipulations such as Fourier transforms for those who want to understand signal processing. Interested readers can write to Moonshadow Software, (*see* List of Suppliers).

Finally, I have heard from a shadowy organization called MAL (an acronym for Maths Algorithm Library). An amusing flyer promises MAL-treatment to readers interested in MALfunctions. MALpractice is easy, according to MALadministrator Dr. P. ffyske Howden. Readers should consult the List of Suppliers for the address of MAL.

Battles of the Magi

When magicians do battle, thunderbolts and colored rays fill the air. But in the computer world magicians must be more subtle. Electric charges of mere millivolts suffice to sink ships and overturn empires. To the extent that our modern world depends on the computer, to that very extent it becomes vulnerable (in war or peace) to its productions and disruptions. Two cases in point are cryptology and security. During Word War II primitive computers were employed by both sides to encode messages and to break the codes thus used. Today, computers routinely scramble messages of commercial or military importance. Recently, computer viruses have been released like genies from some electric bottle. They threaten to change the face of computing, driving what were previously "open" systems into fortresses of signs and countersigns. One class of antidotes may lie with the game of Core War. Let us write programs that destroy viruses!

The British mathematician Alan Turing was persuaded by his government to join the war effort at Bletchley Park, a top-secret code-breaking center. The German Enigma machine was daily broadcasting coded messages between U-boats and their bases. How to capture the secret settings of the machine's rotors was the business of the British magi at Bletchley.

Turing, for one, invented a "bombe" that ticked but never exploded. The ticking signaled a logical process of elimination, an embodiment of speeded-up analysis, that ultimately broke Enigma's messages on an almost daily basis. Today the machines are no less logical but are electric instead of mechanical. Many governments and corporations have adopted the so-called DES code, a rather fancy version of the same process used by the Enigma. But is the code secure? Modern magi are divided in opinion.

In Walt Disney's version of the battle between Merlin and his archrival, both hurl thunderbolts and colored rays until imagination finally triumphs: Merlin becomes a virus that infects his rival and kills him. No plaudits, however, to those private persons who, beset by fantasies of secret power, release programs that literally infect computers. Worms and viruses have become household words in a world that depends so heavily on computers. A virus is a program that enters a computer unknown to its user and proceeds to attach itself to other programs resident in the system. It may be a "benign" virus or a killer. Triggered by a certain date or by some other event, the virus may suddenly go on a rampage, destroying valuable files and programs. Nothing is safe!

Some journalists who should know better, but apparently do not, have blamed Core War, a quietly intellectual contest between programmers, for the virus outbreaks. This is like blaming war on sports. But if Core War, the game in which programs battle programs on an equal footing, does not provide a source for viruses, it may provide a defense. When we become expert in the art of seeking and destroying vandalware, we may find that infections become infrequent and weak, hardly worth the effort by technopaths to spread them.

○ 25 ○

The Enigma and the Bombe

What one man can invent another can discover.
—Sherlock Holmes in "*The Adventure of the Dancing Men*,"
by SIR ARTHUR CONAN DOYLE

Was the famous detective's remark an expression of cool confidence in his own cryptanalytic resources or a statement of historic fact? Certainly from the advent of the written word until well into this century codes that some human beings have invented to conceal messages of military or commercial import were indeed discovered by others. Just before World War II the encoding process was mechanized, but that did little to change the situation. To paraphrase Holmes, what one machine can encode another machine can decode.

This chapter, the first of two forays into the arcane world of cryptology, ends with a discussion of such a machine-versus-machine confrontation. On one side is the Enigma machine used by the Axis forces 50 years ago, and on the other is a machine called a Bombe. As we shall see, the Bombe ticked its way to cryptanalytic victory with some help from humans—including Alan M. Turing, one of the founders of computer science. In the next chapter I shall continue the story by relating how computers are currently employed to encrypt and decrypt messages.

The earliest codes converted a message in ordinary language (called the plaintext) into a coded one (known as the ciphertext) by substituting one letter of the alphabet for another. The so-called Caesar code, for example, does this according to a simple numbering scheme. If one numbers the letters of the Roman alphabet (A,B,C . . .) from 0 to 25, one can specify a particular number, say 13, and add that number to the number corresponding to each letter in the plaintext. The sums represent the letters that constitute the ciphertext. If a sum happens to be greater than 25, one must subtract 26 from it in order to get a number between 0 and 25. For example, X (letter number 23) is encoded as K (letter number 10), because $23 + 13 = 36$ and $36 - 26 = 10$.

Julius Caesar is said to have used such a code in case messages from the front fell into enemy hands. One possible plaintext message from the Roman general and its corresponding ciphertext are given below:

> SEND MMCC REINFORCEMENTS
> FRAQ ZZPP ERVASBEPRZRAGF

For such a code system to work the intended recipient of the ciphertext must be supplied with a key. In this case the letter N, which is letter number 13, provides the key. Knowing this letter, the recipient can retrieve the plaintext merely by subtracting 13 from the number corresponding to each letter in the ciphertext.

An unintended recipient of the ciphertext (henceforth known as the code breaker) can attempt to decode it by trying every possible letter key. If he or she attempts to decode Caesar's message by assuming B is the key, the result would be:

> TFOE NNDD SFJOGPSDFNFOUT

Since this makes no sense, the code breaker would try other possible keys until he or she hits on N, which turns the garbled message into plain English.

At first glance it would seem that a computer has no place in decoding messages enciphered with Caesar's code, because it would not be able to discriminate between meaningful and meaningless messages each time a new letter key is tried. Yet a computer can be equipped with a "dictionary" that would at least enable it to determine whether the decoded message contained legitimate words. There is, however, a more powerful code-breaking tool: statistics.

Each letter of a language's alphabet has a typical frequency with which it occurs in text written in that language. For example, the first three letters of the Roman alphabet account for respectively 8, 1.5, and 3 percent of the letters found in ordinary English text. The most frequently occurring letter is E, appearing on average 13 percent of the time. (A complete table of letter frequencies is given in the illustration below.)

In the ciphertext of Caesar's hypothetical message the commonest letter is R, which occurs four times. A decryption program might therefore assume that R stands for E. Since the difference between the numerical values of R and E is 13, the program might further assume that the code's letter key is N.

Such a program would happen to be correct in this case, but largely as a result of luck. In actual practice statistical forces can be fruitfully brought to bear only if the code breaker has gathered a large volume of ciphertext. Beyond identifying the most probable candidate for E, such a program might also hunt for T, A, and O, which are the next most commonly used letters. It might even match the letter distributions of the ciphertext against typical letter distributions to determine the likeliest keys.

Blaise de Vigenère, a French cryptographer of the sixteenth century, complicated the Caesar code by proposing that the key be changed in a periodic manner. When one encodes a message à la Vigenère, one changes the letter key for each successive letter in the plaintext, always running in order through the same sequence of letter keys. In essence the sequence itself is the code's key.

Just for fun, suppose the key sequence happens to be *CLEF*, which corresponds to the number sequence 2, 11, 4, and 5. To encode a message

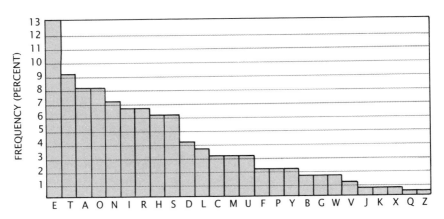

Frequency distribution of letters in typical English text

using this key sequence one would divide the letters of the plaintext message into groups of four and add 2 to the number value of the first letter of each group, 11 to the second, 4 to the third and 5 to the fourth. As in the Caesar code, the resulting sums represent the number values of the letters of the ciphertext. The example below illustrates how a Vigenère code operates on a plaintext to produce a ciphertext:

```
key:         CLEFCLEFCLEFCLEF
plaintext:   SENDINTHECAVALRY
ciphertext:  UPRIKYXMGNEACWVD
```

Enciphered messages can be sent as a continuous string of symbols, as in the preceding example, or in regular blocks. In either case it is assumed that the intended receiver will be able to separate the decoded symbols into proper words.

If the code breaker knows the period of the key (the number of letters in the key sequence) of a Vigenère code, he or she can break it by applying essentially the same method that is applied to crack Caesar codes. The process, however, takes much longer. To decode the Vigenère ciphertext given above, a code-breaking computer program would have to generate four separate letter distributions, one for every fourth letter starting at U, one for every fourth letter staring at P, and so on. The program would then compare each distribution with the standard letter-frequency distribution in order to guess each component letter of the key sequence. In essence the problem boils down to four separate Caesar-code decodings. If the code breaker does not know the period of the key, the exercise takes even more time, because each possible period must be tried. In this case having a computer is definitely an advantage, since it is well suited for such repetitive tasks.

It goes without saying that if one is dealing with short messages or relatively long key sequences, many messages would have to be collected before a successful decoding attack of a Vigenère code could be launched. Conversely, if only short key periods are applied in encoding, messages do not have to be very long before it becomes nearly certain that the plaintext will emerge from the computer.

We shall now skip a multitude of clever coding systems developed between the sixteenth and the mid-twentieth century to arrive at the German Enigma machine, focus of the most intense decoding effort ever undertaken up to that time. The machine was employed by the German armed forces during World War II to encode radio communications (which were themselves transmitted in telegraphic code) between field units and headquarters. Because radio traffic can be intercepted by anyone with a receiver tuned to the proper frequency, the need for encryption is obvious.

The basic Enigma machine consisted of an alphabetic keyboard, three "rotors," a "reflector," and a bank of 26 light bulbs — one for each letter of the alphabet (*see* illustration below). A rotor was a toothed wheel through which ran wires that connected a set of 26 contacts on one side of the rotor with an equal number on the other side. The connections were randomly assigned but fixed. In a given position a rotor would thus represent a particular set of permutations for the 26 possible electrical signals from the keyboard (one for each letter) that might be sent through it. For example, a rotor might send a signal representing the letter *A* to the contact representing the letter *R*, the signal representing *B* to the contact for *D*, and so on. The second rotor, having a different wiring arrangement and set in a different position, took the signal from the first rotor and induced another permutation on it. The last rotor similarly induced a third permutation on the signal.

After a signal had passed through the three rotors, it encountered the reflector: a set of wires that connected each contact with another contact on the back of the third rotor, thus sending the signal back along a different path through the three rotors. In passing from rotor to rotor in reverse order the signal underwent three more permutations. When the

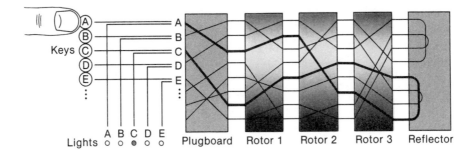

Schematic diagram of the basic Enigma machine

signal finally reemerged from the rotor assembly, it passed directly to a light bulb in the display bank.

A key property of the Enigma machine was that it was self-inverse: if it happened to encode the letter R as Q, it would—in the same state—encode Q as R. The self-inverse property meant ciphertext typed into an Enigma machine would emerge as the original plaintext message if the decoding machine had the same initial state as the encoding machine. As a consequence, encoding and decoding amounted to the same simple operation—as long as the rotors were set in the correct positions. Although it was a tremendous convenience for operators of the machine, the self-inverse property—as we shall see—proved to be a fatal weakness in the Enigma code.

What made the Enigma code so fiendishly tough to second-guess was that the first rotor of the machine rotated one step automatically after a key was pressed. After the keys had been pressed 26 times the first rotor returned to its original position, but then the second rotor moved into a new position. Likewise, when the second rotor had moved 26 times, the third rotor would rotate one step. The assembly of rotors essentially operated like the odometer in an automobile. This mechanism ensured that each succeeding letter of plaintext was encoded by a different letter permutation. In all, $26 \times 26 \times 26 = 17{,}576$ different permutations were used for a given letter before the Enigma machine returned to its original state.

The situation is reminiscent of the older Vigenère code but vastly more complicated. Each letter in a key sequence of a Vigenère code also induces a permutation of the alphabet in the sense that it changes a letter in the plaintext into another, namely the one given by the sum of the numbers corresponding to the plaintext letter and the key letter. A Vigenère code, however, makes use of only as many permutations as there are letters in the key sequence before returning to the same "state." To put it in perspective, the period of the "key" for the Enigma machine can be regarded as 17,576.

It would have been virtually impossible to break the Enigma code if the British cryptanalysts had known nothing at all about the encoding procedure. A statistical attack based on typical letter frequencies in German text would have been useless since a specific letter of plaintext would be encoded as any other letter with almost equal probability. Yet the British were not completely ignorant of how the Enigma machine worked.

Before the war the French intelligence service had obtained copies of instructions for the machine and had passed that information on to the Poles, who made good use of it. By analyzing German radio traffic in the light of the instructions, Polish cryptanalysts managed to deduce the wiring pattern of the three rotors and the reflector. Because the composite permutation comprising the net effect of the three rotors, the reflector and the second pass through the rotors could be readily determined, it was now possible to decode German military messages — if the initial state of the rotors was known. The Polish cryptanalysts in fact were able to ascertain the initial states of the machines from the messages that broadcast, in coded form, the daily rotor settings.

Although the British had learned all of this from the Poles, the information was actually of limited value during the war because, as the war had approached, the Germans made some modifications to their Enigma machines. First, they increased the stock of rotors from three to five. Hence before attempting to decode any intercepted messages it was necessary to determine which three of the five interchangeable rotors were in the machines. Second, some military versions of the machine had a "plugboard" that performed an extra permutation on six or seven pairs of letters before their respective electrical signals entered the rotor system and again after leaving it. The Poles, stretched to the limit of their technical resources, had to give up after these modifications were made.

The British built on the Polish foundation by first assembling a mixed group of cryptanalysts and mathematicians (including Turing) at a Victorian mansion in Buckinghamshire called Bletchley Park. Knowing the Enigma machine's rotor and reflector wirings, the group still had to discover the machine's plugboard wiring. The group based its attack on what is known as the probable-word method.

This method exploits the fact that in some contexts a particular sequence of intercepted symbols almost surely represents a known word. An intercepted ciphertext broadcast from the German naval headquarters, for example, might have had a block of five letters that was interpreted to be — in all likelihood — the encoded version of the German word *U-boot* (an abbreviation for *Unterseeboot*, which means submarine).

Guessing correctly what several ciphertext words were made it possible to work out the plugboard wiring merely by testing all possible wirings and seeing which one yielded the guessed ciphertext-plaintext word pairs.

World War II *U-boots* were equipped with Enigma machines

Yet because there are more than a trillion possible plugboard wirings for seven pairs of letter permutations, Turing realized that only an automated and relatively fast machine could carry out the tests.

Actually it was not surprising that Turing resorted to machines in trying to break the machine-based code. The Poles themselves had already employed electromechanical simulators of the Enigma machine. The simulators ticked from one position to the next, attempting to find which combination of rotors would produce a given permutation. They were called Bombes because of the ticking noise they made.

To unravel the plugboard's wiring a new type of Bombe was therefore constructed. The machine incorporated circuits of relays that tested all possible plugboard combinations for logical consistency. Consider, for example, five Enigma machines that have been numbered 1 through 5 (*see* illustration at right). The machines have consecutive rotor positions in order to simulate the effect a single Enigma machine would have on each letter of a five-letter word. (Remember, we are assuming that the initial rotor positions of the Enigma machine that encoded the word are known on the basis of other intelligence.) Analysts have determined that the five-letter ciphertext word *CZTUC* probably stands for the plaintext word *UBOOT*. What plugboard connections were used in encoding the rest of the day's plaintext?

The Turing Bombe would begin with a hypothesized plugboard wiring, say that C on the input side of the plugboard was passed on as *A* to the

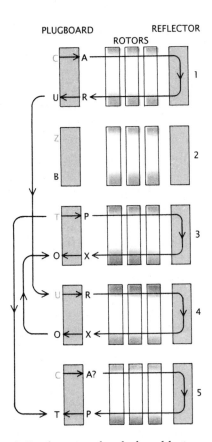

A Bombe traces the plugboard logic

first rotor. Suppose now that Enigma machine 1 transforms the letter A into the letter R. If the probable word is correct, the plugboard must change the R from the machine into a U and, because of the self-inverse nature of the machine, U into R.

That last deduction means that the plugboard for Enigma machine 4 must also change the letter U in the ciphertext word to R. If machine 4 (whose rotor state is shifted three steps in relation to machine 1) converts the R from its plugboard into an X, then the Bombe would instantly deduce that X and O are wired together, since the fourth letter of the plaintext word happens to be O.

That fact can now be exploited in the third Enigma machine, which encodes the third letter of *UBOOT*. If it turns out that machine 3 yields an X only if it receives a P as input, then a plugboard connection between P and T has been established, since T is the third letter of CZTUC.

Because UBOOT happens to end with a T, the Bombe would then arrive at a critical juncture: Will Enigma machine 5 complete the logical loop and transform P to A, so that the plugboard then yields the C that appears in the final position of the corresponding ciphertext word? If not (as was usually the case), the hypothesis that the plugboard linked C with A was eliminated. The Bombe would then tick on to consider the next hypothesis, say that the plugboard links C with B. If that hypothesis too is eliminated, then the Bombe would try C linked to C, and so on. In this way Turing's Bombe would eventually discover the correct plugboard wiring.

The ciphertext word used in the sample is rather short and the Enigma machine's letter permutations were deliberately chosen in such a way that the path analyzed by the consistency test could be neatly traced. In reality longer messages far richer in logical implications were used, so that Turing's Bombe could by sheer deduction discover an entire plugboard wiring. At such a time the ticking would stop, signaling a coming explosion perhaps — but not at Bletchley Park.

The question of plugboard wiring was just part of the cryptanalytic effort undertaken by Turing and his wartime colleagues. The daily initial rotor settings, for example, also had to be determined, as did other features of the Enigma, which I do not have the space to discuss. Suffice it to say that the group at Bletchley Park were kept extremely busy breaking the various versions of the Enigma code employed by the Germans. More important perhaps is the fact that their work, which relied on machines to break the codes generated by another machine, signaled the era of automated logic leading to modern computers.

In the next chapter I shall continue this cryptological theme into the present day. For now let me just say that there are many hobbyists who practice computer cryptology in their spare time. Some have even written programs that simulate the Enigma machine and the British code-breaking effort. I am grateful to Bartosz Milewski of the University of California at Davis for the description of his rather comprehensive code-breaking package called CRYPTO. The package includes a program that breaks one-rotor Enigma codes. Readers interested in CRYPTO can write to Milewski at the address given in the List of Suppliers. Some readers might also want to subscribe to *The Cryptogram*, a newsletter published by the American Cryptogram Association (*see* the List of Suppliers).

ADDENDUM

In "The Enigma and the Bombe" I contended that what one man (or machine) enciphers another can decipher. There is actually one well-known exception to that thesis, which I neglected to mention. A plaintext, or uncoded, message from John C. Shuey, a student in Tacoma Park, Md., reminded me of the so-called one-time pad. A simple version of this encryption system relies on a string of random integers between 0 and 25 to encode each alphabetic character in a plaintext-message string: The ith character of the message string is encoded by shifting it n places along the alphabet, where n is the ith random integer in the encoding string.

Cryptographers call such a string of random integers a pad; it is "one-time" because it is discarded after use. Of course, the receiver of the ciphertext, or encrypted message, must also have a copy of the pad. The code generated in that way is provably unbreakable because the resulting ciphertext does not have the slightest pattern that can be exploited by a cryptanalyst. Shuey himself generates one-time pads from the computer's internal representation of characters.

According to John R. Michener of Princeton, N.J., there are fairly simple encryption algorithms — other than one-time pads — that not only can be run on home computers but also are extremely hard to break. Such algorithms rely on removing redundancies from a message by compressing it to the shortest possible string of bits. The compressed message is then rearranged by a transposition and substitution of the bits. Michener, who has written several technical articles on cryptology, maintains that such a code would be "far too sophisticated for amateur cryptographers (or professionals, if the designer is skilled and careful enough) to have a chance of breaking it."

Several readers alerted me to a couple of important professional publications that may be of interest to readers. the first is a book called *Machine Cryptography and Modern Cryptanalysis* by Cipher A. Deavours and Louis Kruh. The second publication is the quarterly journal *Cryptologia*, of which Kruh is coeditor. Interested readers can subscribe by consulting the List of Suppliers.

· 26 ·

Computers in the Crypt

What was enciphered on a machine might all the easier be deciphered on a machine
—ANDREW HODGES, *Alan Turing: The Enigma*

Until World War II concealment of messages by means of codes and ciphers had been a tedious manual operation. It was during the war that electromechanical machines such as the German Enigma took over. Now computers do the encoding. They swiftly scramble a message in ordinary language (called the plaintext) according to a secret "key" and transmit the scrambled message (called the ciphertext) over telephone or other electronic-communication links. Computers that are supplied with the same key unscramble the ciphertext just as quickly. This, in any event, is the idea behind the Data Encryption Standard (DES), a method of encrypting information issued by the U.S. National Bureau of Standards in 1977 and currently used in commercial and perhaps military communications systems.

In what follows I shall be presenting a complete description of the DES that happens to be its most public appearance to date. I can do so without reservation, because the security of any ciphertext generated by the DES depends entirely on keeping its associated key secret. Yet recent developments in cryptology, the science of making and breaking codes and ciphers, have centered on keys that are partly public and partly private: A private key is buried in a well-known problem the public cannot solve.

Regardless of what is allowed to be common knowledge and what is kept secret, any computer-based cryptosystem is built around an encoding and decoding algorithm. The encoding algorithm of the DES was originally designed at the IBM Research and Development Corporation. Like the Enigma machine described in the last chapter, the DES employs a sequence of scrambling operations that individually are rather simple but collectively are complicated. In the Enigma machine the component operations were effected by mechanical wheels; in the DES they are executed by either software "modules" or microchips.

Because computers are involved in the encryption process, the symbols that are scrambled are not alphabetic letters (as in the Enigma code) but bits, or binary digits. The DES handles only one string of 64 bits at a time. Hence in order to apply the algorithm one must first translate the plaintext message into 64-bit strings. Almost any convention for turning a message in ordinary language into a string of bits is appropriate. For example, since five bits suffice to count to 31 in base 2, the base-2 representations of 0 through 25 can be chosen to stand for 26 different alphabetic characters. Such a scheme would allow 12 contiguous letters of English to be represented as a 64-bit string (with four bits left over).

A plaintext message being encoded by the DES can be visualized as a river that divides and redivides in an extremely complicated manner. Indeed, the best way to keep track of the individual operations is to follow them on a flow chart (*see* illustration on the next page). Individual modules are like waterfalls, churning the code waters to an almost unbelievable degree. Each 64-bit string of plaintext encounters three types of modules on its rocky ride to the output channel: permutation, left-shifting, and substitution modules. The operations done by each type of module can be summarized neatly in tables.

A permutation table indicates how the order of a string's bits is to be altered by a given permutation module. A simple example shows how to read such tables. Suppose a permutation module operates on the binary string 1011 according to the following (horizontal) table: 3 1 2 4. This means the string's third bit goes to the first position, its first bit goes to the second position, its second bit goes to the third position, and its last bit stays in the last position. Hence by applying the table the number 1011 is permuted into 1101.

The DES employs several different permutation tables: the so-called initial permutation table (IP), the E bit-selection table (E), a pair of permuted-choice tables (PC1 and PC2), the permutation table (P), and

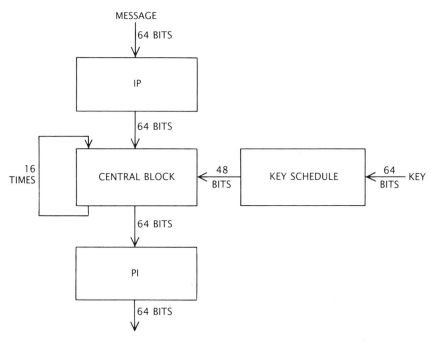

The Data Encryption Standard (DES) in outline

finally the inverse permutation table (PI). These tables are listed in the illustration on the facing page.

Some of the tables do not contain 64 entries, because their input or output strings have fewer than 64 bits. The E bit-selection module, for example, accepts a 32-bit string and expands the string to 48 bits. An inspection of the corresponding table reveals, not surprisingly, that some entries appear more than once. The permuted-choice modules, PC1 and PC2, have the opposite effect: They shrink the strings that pass through them. Accordingly some entries are missing in the corresponding tables.

Home encrypters can transfer the tables, as well as the DES itself, to their computers, but they will have to do so without much advice from me. Since space is short, I have only enough room to mention that assignment statements to be used with permutation tables will have the form

$$T(k) \leftarrow MP(k)),$$

IP	E	PC1	PC2	P	PI	
58	32	57	14	16	40	1
50	1	49	17	7	8	2
42	2	41	11	20	48	3
34	3	33	24	21	16	4
26	4	25	1	29	56	5
18	5	17	5	12	24	6
10	4	9	3	28	64	7
2	5	1	28	17	32	8
60	6	58	15	1	39	9
52	7	50	6	15	7	10
44	8	42	21	23	47	11
36	9	34	10	26	15	12
28	8	26	23	5	55	13
20	9	18	19	18	23	14
12	10	10	12	31	63	15
4	11	2	4	10	31	16
62	12	59	26	2	38	17
54	13	51	8	8	6	18
46	12	43	16	24	46	19
38	13	35	7	14	14	20
30	14	27	27	32	54	21
22	15	19	20	27	22	22
14	16	11	13	3	62	23
6	17	3	2	9	30	24
64	16	60	41	19	37	25
56	17	52	52	13	5	26
48	18	44	31	30	45	27
40	19	36	37	6	13	28
32	20	63	47	22	53	29
24	21	55	55	11	21	30
16	20	47	30	4	61	31
8	21	39	40	25	29	32
57	22	31	51		36	33
49	23	23	45		4	34
41	24	15	33		44	35
33	25	7	48		12	36
25	24	62	44		52	37
17	25	54	49		20	38
9	26	46	39		60	39
1	27	38	56		28	40
59	28	30	34		35	41
51	29	22	53		3	42
43	28	14	46		43	43
35	29	6	42		11	44
27	30	61	50		51	45
19	31	53	36		19	46
11	32	45	29		59	47
3	1	37	32		27	48
61		29			34	49
53		21			2	50
45		13			42	51
37		5			10	52
29		28			50	53
21		20			18	54
13		12			58	55
5		4			26	56
63					33	57
55					1	58
47					41	59
39					9	60
31					49	61
23					17	62
15					57	63
7					25	64

Permutation tables employed by the DES

where the array M holds the bits of the string to be permuted, the array P contains the table, T is a temporary array, and k counts off the new bit positions. In this way the computer can be programmed to place the P(k)th entry of M in the kth position of T. Once all entries in T have been made, M can be set equal to T.

The DES locks messages into ciphertext with a secret key: an arbitrary 64-bit string the DES user supplies to the so-called key-schedule module at the beginning of the encoding process. The key can be thought of as a 64-bit tributary river that narrows to 56 bits in the PC1 module, divides into two 28-bit streams that then come together at the PC2 module and join the main message river sequentially as 16 48-bit rivulets — one for each major iteration of the DES.

While they are in the key schedule, the two 28-bit streams also encounter crosscurrents that shift their bits to the left. As can be seen in the table opposite (above) in the first, second, ninth and 16th iteration the DES calls for shifting the bits of the two strings to the left by one bit. Otherwise the strings are shifted to the left by two bits. The illustration shows expanded versions of the central block and the key schedule.

Such left shifts are easy to program. The 28 individual bits of a key segment are assigned bit by bit to a temporary array in such a way that the ith element of the temporary array takes on the value of either the $(i + 1)$th or the $(i + 2)$th bit of the segment. Of course, the last element (or two) of the temporary array must be set equal to the first bit (or two) of the key.

The DES also incorporates eight substitution modules, each of which converts a six-bit string into a four-bit one. The bits of the number undergoing conversion tell one which row and column indexes to look up in the corresponding tables: The first and last bits determine the row index, and the middle four bits determine the column index (*see the table on the facing page*). For example, the six-bit number 111010 yields the row index 10 (the outside bit) and the column index 1101 (the inside bits). These binary numbers represent respectively the decimal numbers 2 and 13. The entry in table S1 for row 2 and column 13 is the decimal number 10. In binary form 10 happens to be 1010, which would be the output of the S1 module if it had the string 111010 as input. (Most home cryptologists will probably need two conversion procedures in order to change a binary number to a decimal number and to do the reverse.)

So much for the bits and pieces. How do they all fit together? A 64-bit string enters the IP module and is permuted as the module's correspond-

The Left-shift Table (*top*) and Substitution Tables (*bottom*)

ITERATION NUMBER	1	2	3	4	5	6	7	8	9	10	11	12	13	14	15	16
NUMBER OF LEFT SHIFTS	1	1	2	2	2	2	2	2	1	2	2	2	2	2	2	1

	ROW	COLUMN															
		0	1	2	3	4	5	6	7	8	9	10	11	12	13	14	15
S1	0	14	4	13	1	2	15	11	8	3	10	6	12	5	9	0	7
	1	0	15	7	4	14	2	13	1	10	6	12	11	9	5	3	8
	2	4	1	14	8	13	6	2	11	15	12	9	7	3	10	5	0
	3	15	12	8	2	4	9	1	7	5	11	3	14	10	0	6	13
S2	0	15	1	8	14	6	11	3	4	9	7	2	13	12	0	5	10
	1	3	13	4	7	15	2	8	14	12	0	1	10	6	9	11	5
	2	0	14	7	11	10	4	13	1	5	8	12	6	9	3	2	15
	3	13	8	10	1	3	15	4	2	11	6	7	12	0	5	14	9
S3	0	10	0	9	14	6	3	15	5	1	13	12	7	11	4	2	8
	1	13	7	0	9	3	4	6	10	2	8	5	14	12	11	15	1
	2	13	6	4	9	8	15	3	0	11	1	2	12	5	10	14	7
	3	1	10	13	0	6	9	8	7	4	15	14	3	11	5	2	12
S4	0	7	13	14	3	0	6	9	10	1	2	8	5	11	12	4	15
	1	13	8	11	5	6	15	0	3	4	7	2	12	1	10	14	9
	2	10	6	9	0	12	11	7	13	15	1	3	14	5	2	8	4
	3	3	15	0	6	10	1	13	8	9	4	5	11	12	7	2	14
S5	0	2	12	4	1	7	10	11	6	8	5	3	15	13	0	14	9
	1	14	11	2	12	4	7	13	1	5	0	15	10	3	9	8	6
	2	4	2	1	11	10	13	7	8	15	9	12	5	6	3	0	14
	3	11	8	12	7	1	14	2	13	6	15	0	9	10	4	5	3
S6	0	12	1	10	15	9	2	6	8	0	13	3	4	14	7	5	11
	1	10	15	4	2	7	12	9	5	6	1	13	14	0	11	3	8
	2	9	14	15	5	2	8	12	3	7	0	4	10	1	13	11	6
	3	4	3	2	12	9	5	15	10	11	14	1	7	6	0	8	13
S7	0	4	11	2	14	15	0	8	13	3	12	9	7	5	10	6	1
	1	13	0	11	7	4	9	1	10	14	3	5	12	2	15	8	6
	2	1	4	11	13	12	3	7	14	10	15	6	8	0	5	9	2
	3	6	11	13	8	1	4	10	7	9	5	0	15	14	2	3	12
S8	0	13	2	8	4	6	15	11	1	10	9	3	14	5	0	12	7
	1	1	15	13	8	10	3	7	4	12	5	6	11	0	14	9	2
	2	7	11	4	1	9	12	14	2	0	6	10	13	15	3	5	8
	3	2	1	14	7	4	10	8	13	15	12	9	0	3	5	6	11

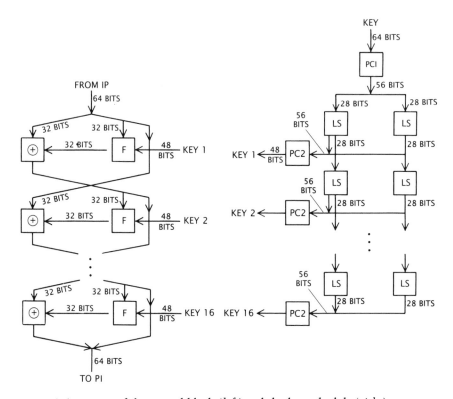

Expanded versions of the central block (*left*) and the key schedule (*right*)

ing table describes. It then passes on to the central block, where the main encoding algorithm scrambles it hopelessly in a kind of recirculating eddy, before it passes on to the PI module, where it is permuted according to a table that happens to be the inverse of the IP table.

The central block takes as input not only the output of the IP module but also the 48-bit keys (numbered from 1 through 16) that are derived in the key-schedule module from the supplied 64-bit key. The same basic operations are carried out in the central block 16 times, but each time with a different 48-bit key. Specifically, the 64-bit string from the IP module is split into right and left 32-bit halves. A copy of the right half is then blended with key 1 in the so-called F module. The result is added modulo 2 to the left half. (Modulo-2 addition is like ordinary addition except that 1 plus 1 equals 0.) The 32-bit sum and the original 32-bit right half then change places for the next iteration (with key 2 this time), the sum becoming the right half of a 64-bit string and the right half becoming the left half. At the completion of 16 such blending-and-swapping iterations the two 32-bit strings are put together once again into a 64-bit whole.

The F operation deserves a diagram of its own (*see* illustration below). A copy of the right half of the current 64-bit string enters the E bit-selection module, where it is expanded into 48 bits. It is then added modulo 2 to the 48-bit key appropriate for the current iteration number. Thereafter the 48 bits are separated like so many rivulets into eight equal parts of six bits each. The parts flow through the substitution modules S1 through S8, where each is reduced to four-bit numbers. Hence when the eight rivulets rejoin as one stream, the overall size of the string has shrunk to 32 bits. At this point the P module scrambles the string once again.

If the reader has been brave enough to keep up with the discussion, he or she might be wondering how one could possibly recover the plaintext message from the ciphertext after all the turbulent mixing the plaintext goes through in the DES. Is it as difficult as making water run uphill? Actually that is the trick: Run the main operations of the central block backward. After directing a 64-bit string of ciphertext through the IP module (as one does when encrypting), have the string retrace the 16

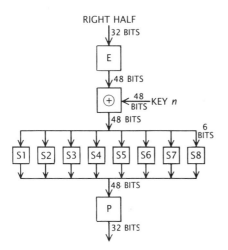

Expanded version of the F module

iterations in reverse order—from the bottom of the central block's blending-and-swapping cascade to the top. Keys 1 through 16 must also be fed into the key schedule in reverse order. After another permutation by the PI module the original message should gush like a geyser.

Is the DES really secure? Some critics say it is not. Even before the standard was issued, Whitfield Diffie and Martin E. Hellman of Stanford University warned that the DES was vulnerable to a brute-force crypto-logical attack by a well-funded organization, one able to build parallel-processing computers that can test 10 billion keys per second.

The need to distribute secret keys among senders and receivers of messages is another weak spot in the DES; it makes it easier for an unfriendly agent to somehow get a copy of the key and use it to decode messages. For this reason Diffie and Hellman proposed 12 years ago that "public" keys be distributed among the members of a communication network.

The public-key distribution scheme depends on a very large prime number, p, and a base number, a. The number a is deliberately chosen so that a^n modulo p, where n equals 0, 1, 2 . . ., gives all the integers between 1 and $p - 1$. All members of the communication network know the numbers p and a, and each member must submit a key that will be listed in a network directory. Member i, for example, selects a personal "half key," x_i, which she locks in a safe. She then computes the number k_i given by the equation

$$k_i = a^{x_i} \text{ (mod } p)$$

and sends it in to be published in the directory under her name. The same thing is done by each member.

If member j wishes to communicate secretly with member i, he looks up k_i in the directory, then uses his own private half key, x_j, to compute the combined key, k_{ij}, by raising k_i to the power of x_j modulo p. In other words,

$$k_{ij} = k_i^{x_j} \text{ (mod } p).$$

Knowing that member j has sent her a message, member i similarly computes the key k_{ji} by raising k_j to the power of x_i modulo p. Readers might enjoy confirming that both members in fact are using the same key, that is, k_{ij} equals k_{ji}.

An inquisitive outsider might break into a public-key system by solving the discrete-logarithm problem with reasonable speed. If the number y in the formula

$$y = a^x \;(\text{mod } p)$$

is called a discrete power of a, then x could be called the discrete logarithm of y base a. The discrete-logarithm problem simply asks us to find x, given y, a, and p.

Is there no method faster than simply trying all possible values of x, raising a to that power modulo p each time, and then comparing the result to y? Theorists think there is not, but no one has been able to prove it. If the discrete-logarithm problem turns out to be as intractable as it seems, then a rather large value of x, say one that is a few hundred digits long, should discourage computational interlopers.

Diffie and Hellman expanded their public-key distribution scheme into a public key cryptosystem by envisioning a special kind of function called a trapdoor one-way function. Here is how the system works. Member i of a communication network selects an arbitrary random integer, k_i, as her private key but publishes in a public directory her special encoding algorithm, E_i. She also formulates another algorithm, D_i, for decoding, which she keeps secret as well. Member j does the same thing, publishing his encoding algorithm, E_j, but keeping his special number, k_j, and his decoding algorithm, D_j, secret.

Later, when member j wants to send a confidential message to member i, he simply looks up her encoding algorithm, E_i, in the public directory and applies it to encode a plaintext message m. In short, he transmits the ciphertext y, where

$$y = E_i(m).$$

It is now a simple matter for member i to decode the message by using her own secret algorithm, D_i, on y.

Such a cryptosystem depends critically on encoding algorithms that compute "one-way" functions, so that knowing E_i makes it no easier to find D_i. The system sounded marvelous, even though no functions were known to be one way at the time Diffie and Hellman proposed it.

That was when the RSA cryptosystem came on the scene. RSA stands for Ronald Rivest, Adi Shamir, and Leonard Adleman, who in 1978 developed what is still voted as the public-key cryptosystem most likely to succeed. In the RSA cryptosystem each member of a communication network selects two prime numbers and an encoding exponent. Member i, for example, selects the prime numbers p_i and q_i as well as an encoding exponent, e_i. She publishes the product $n_i = p_i \times q_i$ and her encoding algorithm, which converts a numerical message m as follows:

$$E_i(m) = m^{ei} \ (\mathrm{mod} \ n_i).$$

Member i also formulates her private decoding algorithm,

$$D_i(x) = x^{d_i} \ (\mathrm{mod} \ n_i).$$

As it happens, the algorithm D_i exactly undoes the work of the algorithm E_i. The two algorithms are used precisely in the manner envisioned by Diffie and Hellman in their public-key cryptosystem. Why does it work? How does member i find the number d_i?

The magic number d_i is easy to compute when one knows both the numbers e_i and $f_i = (p_i - 1) \times (q_i - 1)$. To find it, one solves the modular equation $e_i \times d_i \ (\mathrm{mod} \ f_i) = 1$. In other words, the product of d_i and e_i must be equal to the sum of a multiple of f_i and 1. Additionally, e_i must be relatively prime to f_i: the two numbers must have no common divisor except 1.

Hence when member i receives a message encoded in her own algorithm E_i, she receives in effect a message m in the form

$$m^{e_i} \ (\mathrm{mod} \ n_i).$$

If she now raises this expression to the d_i power, she forms

$$m^{e_i \times d_i} \ (\mathrm{mod} \ n_i).$$

The new exponent of m, $e_i \times d_i$, as I mentioned above, is equal to the sum of some multiple of f_i and 1. According to a theorem of Euclid, however, a number raised to the sum of f_i and 1 modulo n_i exactly equals m itself: The plaintext stands naked in the mathematical daylight!

The question of whether the RSA cryptosystem can be broken has an answer similar to that given for the public-key system. If someone develops a really fast factoring algorithm, one that can chop very large numbers quickly into their prime components, there would be little trouble breaking the RSA cryptosystem. As soon as the number n_i is published, the computational interloper simply breaks it into the factors p_i and q_i and finds the related number d_i, with which he or she can decode any ciphertext from member i. Yet theorists believe this kind of factoring may be one of the problems destined to be forever intractable.

ADDENDUM

There are a few self-professed "bit flippers" in the world, readers who keep close watch for the appearance of a project that promises number-crunching complexity equal to their talents. The two-part series on cryptology, which first appeared in the October and November issues of SCIENTIFIC AMERICAN, raised a cheer in this quarter, in particular, the description of the Data Encryption Standard (DES) provided ample grist for a bit flipper's mill. The DES is used not only by commercial institutions but also quite possibly by various military installations around the world. It is long and complicated, but that is just the way Mike Rosing of Darien, Ill., likes it. Eschewing software that is too soft, Rosing writes his own programs in 68000 assembly code, a low-level computer language that lies at the hardware heart of the 68000 microprocessor chip.

Charles Kluepfel of Bloomfield, N.J., wondered what parts of the DES were arbitrary. For example, must the E bit-selection table really have the form I gave in order for a successful data-encryption system to emerge? And what about the substitution tables? Wafting rumors hold that the designers of the DES deliberately included "side doors" in certain parts of the cryptosystem that make it somewhat easier to decrypt DES ciphertext without knowing the original key.

Daniel Wolf of Santa Maria, Calif., has written several programs of interest in assembly code for his 68000-based Amiga computer. Amiga owners may request copies of a cryptosystem based on the famous Enigma machine or on the RSA algorithm. A major virtue of software cryptosystems that are written in assembly language is their blinding speed. Wolf can be reached at the address given in the List of Suppliers.

Still another journal of cryptology, *Cryptosystems Journal*, was brought to my attention by Tony Patti of Burke, Va., who edits and publishes it. The first two issues pursue Patti's goal of describing and distributing state-of-the-art cryptosystems for IBM PC's and compatible computers. Interested readers can get in touch with Patti for further information (*see* the List of Suppliers).

₀ 27 ₀

Core Wars

Two computer programs in their native habitat — the memory chips of a digital computer — stalk each other from address to address. Sometimes they go scouting for the enemy; sometimes they lay down a barrage of numeric bombs; sometimes they copy themselves out of danger or stop to repair damage. This is the game I call Core War. It is unlike almost all other computer games in that people do not play at all! The contending programs are written by people, of course, but once a battle is under way the creator of a program can do nothing but watch helplessly as the product of hours spent in design and implementation either lives or dies on the screen. The outcome depends entirely on which program is hit first in a vulnerable area.

The term Core War originates in an outmoded memory technology. In the 1950's and 1960's the memory system of a computer was built out of thousands of ferromagnetic cores, or rings, strung on a meshwork of fine wires. Each core could retain the value of one bit, or binary digit, the fundamental unit of information. Nowadays memory elements are fabricated on semiconductor chips, but the active part of the memory system, where a program is kept while it is being executed, is still sometimes referred to as core memory, or simply core.

Battle programs in Core War are written in a specialized language I have named Redcode, closely related to the class of programming languages called assembly languages. Most computer programs today are written in high-level language such as Pascal, Fortran, or BASIC; in these languages a single statement can specify an entire sequence of machine instructions. Moreover, the statements are easy for the programmer to read and to understand. For a program to be executed, however, it must first be translated into "machine language," where each instruction is represented by a long string of binary digits. Writing a program in this form is tedious at best.

Assembly languages occupy an intermediate position between high-level languages and machine code. In an assembly-language program each statement generally corresponds to a single instruction and hence to a particular string of binary digits. Rather than writing the binary numbers, however, the programmer represents them by short words or abbreviations called mnemonics (because they are easier to remember than numbers). The translation into machine code is done by a program called an assembler.

Comparatively little programming is done in assembly languages because the resulting programs are longer and harder to understand or modify than their high-level counterparts. There are some tasks, however, for which an assembly language is ideal. When a program must occupy as little space as possible or be made to run as fast as possible, it is generally written in assembly language. Furthermore, some things can be done in an assembly language that are all but impossible in a high-level language. For example, an assembly-language program can be made to modify its own instructions or to move itself to a new position in memory.

Core War was inspired by a story I heard some years ago about a mischievous programmer at a large corporate research laboratory I shall designate X. The programmer wrote an assembly-language program called CREEPER that would duplicate itself every time it was run. It could also spread from one computer to another in the network of the X corporation. The program had no function other than to perpetuate itself. Before long there were so many copies of CREEPER that more useful programs and data were being crowded out. The growing infestation was not brought under control until someone thought of fighting fire with fire. A second self-duplicating program called REAPER was written. Its purpose was to destroy copies of CREEPER until it could find no more and then to destroy itself. REAPER did its job, and things were soon back to normal at the X lab.

In spite of fairly obvious holes in the story, I believed it, perhaps because I wanted to. It took some time to track down the real events that lay behind this item of folklore. (I shall give an account of them below and in Addendum.) For now it is sufficient to note that my desire to believe rested squarely on the intriguing idea of two programs doing battle in the dark and noiseless corridors of core.

In 1983 I decided that even if the story turned out not to be true, something like it could be made to happen. I set up an initial version of Core War and, assisted by David Jones, a student in my department at the University of Western Ontario, got it working. Since then we have developed the game to a fairly interesting level.

Core War has four main components: a memory array of 8000 addresses, the assembly language Redcode, an executive program called MARS (an acronym for Memory Array Redcode Simulator), and the set of contending battle programs. Two battle programs are entered into the memory array at randomly chosen positions; neither program knows where the other one is. MARS executes the programs in a simple version of time-sharing, a technique for allocating the resources of a computer among numerous users. The two programs take turns: A single instruction of the first program is executed, then a single instruction of the second, and so on.

What a battle program does during the execution cycles allotted to it is entirely up to the programmer. The aim, of course, is to destroy the other program by ruining its instructions. A defensive strategy is also possible: A program might undertake to repair any damage it has received or to move out of the way when it comes under attack. The battle ends when MARS comes to an instruction in one of the programs that cannot be executed. The program with the faulty instruction — which presumably is a casualty of war — is declared the loser.

Much can be learned about a battle program merely by analyzing its actions mentally or with pencil and paper. To put the program to the test of experience, however, one needs access to a computer and a version of MARS. The programs could be made to operate on a personal computer. Indeed, documents describing such MARS systems are available for those who would like to set up a Core War battlefield of their own (*see* List of Suppliers).

Before describing Redcode and introducing some simple battle programs, I should say more about the memory array. Although I have noted that it consists of 8000 addresses, there is nothing magical about this number; a smaller array would work quite well. The memory array differs from most computer memories in its circular configuration: It is a sequence of addresses numbered from 0 to 7999 but it thereupon rejoins itself, so that address 8000 is equivalent to address 0. MARS always reduces an address greater than 7999 by taking the remainder after division by 8000. Thus if a battle program orders a hit at address 9378, MARS interprets the address as 1378.

Redcode is a simplified, special-purpose assembly-style language. It has instructions to move the contents of one address in memory to another address, to alter the contents arithmetically, and to transfer control forward or backward within a program. Whereas the output of a real assembler consists of binary codes, the mnemonic form of a Redcode instruction is translated by MARS into a large decimal integer, which is then stored in the memory array; each address in the array can hold one such integer. It is also MARS that interprets the integers as instructions and carries out the indicated operations.

A list of the elementary Redcode instructions is given in the table on the next page. With each instruction the programmer is required to supply at least one argument, or value, and most of the instructions take two arguments. For example, in the instruction JMP −7 the mnemonic JMP (for "jump") is followed by the single argument −7. The instruction tells MARS to transfer control to the memory address seven places before the current one, that is, seven places before the JMP −7 instruction itself. If the instruction happened to be at address 3715, execution of the program would jump back to address 3708.

This method of calculating a position in memory is called relative addressing, and it is the only method employed in Redcode. There is no way for a battle program to know its own absolute position in the memory array.

The instruction MOV 3 100 tells MARS to go forward three addresses, copy what it finds there, and deliver it 100 addresses beyond the MOV instruction, overwriting whatever was there. The arguments in this instruction are given in "direct" mode, meaning they are to be interpreted as addresses to be acted on directly. Two other modes are allowed. Preceding an argument with an @ sign makes it "indirect." In the instruction MOV @3 100 the integer to be delivered to relative address 100 is not the one found at relative address 3 but rather the one found at the address specified by the contents of relative address 3 (*see* the example on page 311). A # sign makes an argument "immediate," so that it is treated

The Instruction Set of Redcode, an Assembly Language for Core War

INSTRUCTION	MNEMONIC	CODE	ARGUMENTS		EXPLANATION
Move	MOV	1	A	B	Move contents of address A to address B.
Add	ADD	2	A	B	Add contents of address A to address B.
Subtract	SUB	3	A	B	Subtract contents of address A from address B.
Jump	JMP	4	A		Transfer control to address A.
Jump if zero	JMZ	5	A	B	Transfer control to address A if contents of address B are zero.
Jump if greater	JMG	6	A	B	Transfer control to address A if contents of address B are greater than zero.
Decrement: jump if zero	DJZ	7	A	B	Subtract 1 from contents of address B and transfer control to address A if contents of address B are then zero.
Compare	CMP	8	A	B	Compare contents of addresses A and B; if they are unequal, skip the next instruction
Data satement	DAT	0		B	A nonexecutable statement; B is the data value.

The Three-Step Mechanism of Indirect Relative Addressing

	GET ADDRESS OF SOURCE		GET DATA TO BE COPIED		COPY DATA TO DESTINATION
412		412		412	
413 DAT 22		418 − 5 413 DAT 22		413 DAT 22	
414		414		414	
415 MOV @3 100		415 MOV @3 100		415 MOV @3 100	
416		416		416	
417		417		417	
415 + 3 418 DAT −5		418 DAT −5		418 DAT −5	
419		419		419	
420		420		420	
•		•		•	
•		•		•	
•		•		•	
514		514		514	
515		515		415 + 100 515 DAT 22	
516		516		516	

as an address but as an integer. The Instruction MOV #3 100 causes the integer 3 to be moved to relative address 100.

Most of the other instructions need no further explanation, but the data statement (DAT) requires some comment. It can serve as a work space to hold information a program may need to refer to. Strictly speaking, however, it is not an instruction; indeed, any memory location with a zero in its first decimal position can be regarded as a DAT statement and as such is not executable. If MARS should be asked to execute such an "instruction," it will not be able to and will declare that program the loser.

The decimal integer that encodes a Redcode instruction has several fields, or functional areas (see table on the next page). The first digit represents the mnemonic itself, and two more digits identify the addressing mode (direct, indirect, or immediate). In addition four digits are set aside for each argument. Negative arguments are stored in complement form: −1 would be represented as 7999, since in the circular memory array adding 7999 has the same effect as subtracting 1.

The instructions making up a simple battle program called DWARF are listed in the table on page 313. DWARF is a very stupid but very dangerous

The Encoding of Redcode Instructions as Decimal Integers

MNEMONIC	ARGUMENT A	ARGUMENT B	OPERATION CODE	MODE DIGIT: ARGUMENT A	MODE DIGIT: ARGUMENT B	ARGUMENT A	ARGUMENT B
DAT		−1	0	0	0	0000	7999
ADD	# 5	−1	2	0	1	0005	7999
MOV	# 0	@ −2	1	0	2	0000	7999
JMP	−2		4	1	0	7998	0000

ADDRESSING MODES: IMMEDIATE   #   0

DIRECT   1

INDIRECT   @   2

program that works its way through the memory array bombarding every fifth address with a zero. Zero is the integer signifying a nonexecutable data statement, and so a zero dropped into an enemy program can bring it to a halt.

Assume that DWARF occupies absolute addresses 1 through 4. Address 1 initially contains DAT −1, but execution begins with the next instruction, ADD #5 −1. The effect of the instruction is to add 5 to the contents of the preceding address, namely the DAT −1 statement, thereby transforming it into DAT 4. Next DWARF executes the instruction at absolute address 3, MOV #0 @ −2. Here the integer to be moved is 0, specified as an immediate value. The target address is calculated indirectly as an immediate value. The target address is calculated indirectly in the following way. First MARS counts back two addresses from address 3, arriving at address 1. It then examines the data value there, namely 4, and interprets it as an address relative to the current position; in other words, it counts four places forward from address 1 and hence deposits a 0 at address 5.

The final instruction in DWARF, JMP −2, creates an endless loop. It directs execution back to absolute address 2, which again increments the DAT statement by 5, making its new value DAT 9. In the next execution

DWARF, a Battle Program, Lays Down a Barrage of "Zero Bombs"

ADDRESS	CYCLE 1	CYCLE 2	CYCLE 9
0			
1	DAT −1	DAT 4	DAT 14
2	ADD # 5 −1	ADD # 5 −1	→ADD # 5 −1
3	MOV # 0 @ −2	MOV # 0 @ −2	MOV # 0 @ −2
4	JMP −2	JMP −2	⌐JMP −2
5		— 0	— 0
6			
7			
8			
9			— 0
10			
11			
12			
13			
14			— 0
15			
16			
17			

cycle a 0 is therefore delivered to absolute address 10. Subsequent 0 bombs will fall on address 15, 20, 25, and so on. The program itself is immobile but its artillery threatens the entire array. Eventually DWARF works its way around to addresses 7990, 7995, and then 8000. As far as MARS is concerned, 8000 is equal to 0, and so DWARF has narrowly avoided committing suicide. Its next missile again lands on address 5.

It is sobering to realize that no stationary battle program that has more than four instructions can avoid taking a hit from DWARF. The opposing program has only three options: to move about and thereby elude the bombardment, to absorb hits and repair the damage, or to get DWARF first. To succeed through the last strategy the program may have to be lucky: It can have no idea where DWARF is in the memory array, and on the average it has about 1600 execution cycles before a hit is received. If the second program is also a DWARF, each program wins 30 percent of the time; in 40 percent of the contests neither program scores a fatal hit.

Before taking up the other two strategies, I should like to introduce a curious one-line battle program I call IMP. Here it is:

$$\text{MOV} \; 0 \; 1$$

IMP is the simplest example of a Redcode program that is able to relocate itself in the memory array. It copies the contents of relative address 0 (namely MOV 0 1) to relative address 1, the next address. As the program is executed it moves through the array at a speed of one address pre cycle, leaving behind a trail of MOV 0 1 instructions.

What happens if we pit IMP against DWARF? The barrage of 0s laid down by DWARF moves through the memory array faster than IMP moves, but it does not necessarily follow that DWARF has the advantage. The question is: Will DWARF hit IMP even if the barrage does catch up?

If IMP reaches DWARF first, IMP will in all probability plow right through DWARF's code. When DWARF's JMP −2 instruction transfers execution back two steps, the instruction found there will be IMP's MOV 0 1. As a result DWARF will be subverted and become a second IMP endlessly chasing the first one around the array. Under the rules of Core War the battle is a draw (*see* illustration at the right). (Note that this is the outcome to be expected "in all probability." Readers are invited to analyze other possibilities and perhaps discover the bizarre results of one of them.)

Both IMP and DWARF represent a class of programs that can be characterized as small and aggressive but not intelligent. At the next level are programs that are larger and somewhat less aggressive but smart enough to deal with programs in the lower class. The smarter programs have the ability to dodge an attack by copying themselves out of trouble. Each such program includes a segment of code somewhat like the one named GEMINI, shown on page 316. GEMINI is not intended to be a complete battle program. Its only function is to make a copy of itself 100 addresses beyond its present position and then transfer execution to the new copy.

IMP vs. DWARF; Who Wins

7978	MOV	0	1	
7979	MOV	0	1	
7980	—	0		
7981	MOV	0	1	
7982	MOV	0	1	
7983	MOV	0	1	
7984	MOV	0	1	
7985	—	0		
7986	MOV	0	1	
7987	MOV	0	1	
7988	MOV	0	1	
7989	MOV	0	1	
7990	—	0		
7991	MOV	0	1	
7992	MOV	0	1	
7993	MOV	0	1	
7994	MOV	0	1	} IMP
7995				
7996				
7997				
7998				
7999				
0				
1	DAT		7994	
2	ADD	# 5	−1	
3	MOV	# 0	@ −2	} DWARF
4	JMP	−2		
5	—	0		
6				
7				
8				
9				
10	—	0		
11				

GEMINI, A Program That Copies Itself To a New Position in the Memory Array

	DAT		0	/pointer to source address
	DAT		99	/pointer to destination address
→	MOV	@−2	@−1	/copy source to destination
	CMP	−3	#9	/if all 10 lines have been copied . . .
LOOP	JMP	4		/. . . then leave the loop;
	ADD	#1	−5	/otherwise, increment the source address . . .
	ADD	#1	−5	/. . . and the destination address . . .
	JMP	−5		/. . . and return to the loop
	MOV	#99	93	/restore the starting destination address
	JMP	93		/jump to the new copy

The GEMINI program has three main parts. Two data statements at the beginning serve as pointers: They indicate the next instruction to be copied and its destination. A loop in the middle of the program does the actual copying, moving each instruction in turn to an address 100 places beyond its current position. On each transit through the loop both pointers are incremented by 1, thereby designating a new source and destination address. A compare instruction (CMP) within the loop tests the value of the first data statement; when it has been incremented nine times, the entire program has been copied, and so an exit from the loop is taken. One final adjustment remains to be made. The destination address is the second statement in the program and it has an initial value of DAT 99; by the time it is copied, however, it has already been incremented once, so that in the new version of the program it reads DAT 100. This transcription error is corrected (by the instruction MOV #99 93) and then execution is transferred to the new copy.

By modifying GEMINI it is possible to create an entire class of battle programs. One of these, JUGGERNAUT, copies itself 10 locations ahead instead of 100. Like IMP, it tries to roll through all its opposition. It wins far more often than IMP, however, and leads to fewer draws, because an overwritten program is less likely to be able to execute fragments of JUGGERNAUT's code. BIGFOOT, another program employing the GEMINI mechanism, makes the interval between copies a large prime number. BIGFOOT is hard to catch and has the same devastating effect on enemy code as JUGGERNAUT does.

Neither BIGFOOT nor JUGGERNAUT is very intelligent. So far we have written only two battle programs that qualify for the second level of sophistication. They are too long to reproduce here. One of them, which we call RAIDAR, maintains two "pickets" surrounding the program itself (*see* illustration on next page). Each picket consists of 100 consecutive addresses filled with 1s and is separated from the program by a buffer zone of 100 empty addresses. RAIDAR divides its time between systematically attacking distant areas of the memory array and checking its picket addresses. If one of the pickets is found to be altered, RAIDAR interprets the change as evidence of an attack by DWARF, IMP, or some other unintelligent program. RAIDAR then copies itself to the other side of the damaged picket, restores it, constructs a new picket on its unprotected side, and resumes normal operation.

In addition to copying itself a battle program can be given the ability to repair itself. Jones has written a self-repairing program that can survive some attacks, although not all of them. Called SCANNER, it maintains two copies of itself but ordinarily executes only one of them. The copy that is currently running periodically scans the other copy to see if any of its instructions have been altered by an attack. Changes are detected by comparing the two copies, always assuming that the executing copy is correct. If any bad instructions are found, they are replaced and control is transferred to the other copy, which then begins to scan the first one.

So far SCANNER remains a purely defensive program. It is able to survive attacks by DWARF, IMP, JUGGERNAUT, and similar slow-moving aggressors — at least if the attack comes from the right direction. Jones is currently working on a self-repair program that keeps three copies of itself.

I am curious to see whether readers can design other kinds of self-repairing programs. For example, one might think about maintaining two or more copies of a program even though only one copy is ever executed. The program might include a repair section that would refer to an extra copy when restoring damaged instructions. The repair section could even repair itself, but it might still be vulnerable to damage at some positions. One measure of vulnerability assumes that a single instruction has been

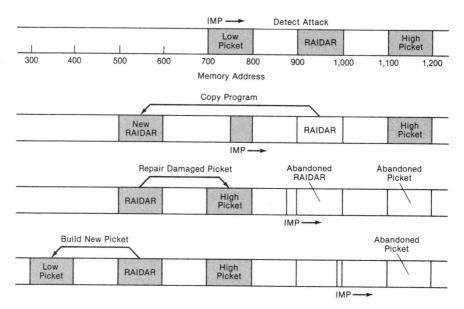

RAIDAR, a sophisticated battle program, eludes the simpler IMP in the memory array of Core War.

hit; on the average, how many such instructions, if they are hit, ultimately cause the program to die? By this measure, what is the least vulnerable self-repairing program that can be written?

Only if reasonably robust programs can be developed will Core War reach the level of an exciting game, where the emphasis is shifted from defense to offense. Battle programs will then have to seek out and identify enemy code and mount an intensive attack wherever it is found.

I may have given the impression that Redcode and the entire MARS system are fixed. They are not. In spare moments we have been experimenting with new ideas and are certainly open to suggestions. Indeed, we have been experimenting so much with new programs and new features that some battles remain to be fought in our own system.

One idea we have been playing with is to include an extra instruction that would make self-repair or self-protection a little easier. The instruction PCT A would protect the instruction at address A from alteration until it is next executed. How much could the vulnerability of a program be reduced by exploiting an instruction of this kind.

Although rules and standards are currently available (see the List of Suppliers) the following rules define the game with enough precision to enable pencil-and-paper players to begin designing battle programs.

1. The two battle programs are loaded into the memory array at random positions but initially are no closer than 1000 addresses.
2. MARS alternates in executing one instruction from each program until it reaches an instruction that cannot be executed. The program with the erroneous instruction loses.
3. Programs can be attacked with any available weapon. A "bomb" can be a 0 or any other integer, including a valid Redcode instruction.
4. A time limit is put on each contest, determined by the speed of the computer. If the limit is reached and both programs are still running, the contest is a draw.

The story of CREEPER and REAPER seems to be based on a compounding of two actual programs. One program was a computer game called DARWIN, invented by Victor A. Vyssotsky of AT&T Bell Laboratories. The other was called WORM and was written by John F. Shoch of the Xerox Palo Alto Research Center. Both programs are some years old, allowing ample time for rumors to blossom. (DARWIN was described in *Software: Practice and Experience*. A vague description of what appears to be the same game is also given in the 1978 edition of *Computer Lib*.)

In DARWIN each player submits a number of assembly-language programs called organisms, which inhabit core memory along with the organisms of other players. The organisms created by one player (and thus belonging to the same "species") attempt to kill those of other species and occupy their space. The winner of the game is the player whose organisms are most abundant when time is called. Douglas B. McIlroy, also of AT&T Bell Laboratories, invented an unkillable organism, although it won only "a few games." It was immortal but apparently not very aggressive.

WORM was an experimental program designed to make the fullest use possible of minicomputers linked in a network at Xerox. WORM was loaded into quiescent machines by a supervisory program. Its purpose was to take control of the machine and, in coordination with WORMS inhabiting other quiescent machines, run large applications programs in the resulting multiprocessor system. WORM was designed so that anyone who wanted to use the occupied machines could readily reclaim it without interfering with the larger job.

One can see elements of both DARWIN and WORM in the story of CREEPER and REAPER. In Core War, REAPER has become a reality. Readers wishing to order a complete Core War system may consult the List of Suppliers.

ADDENDUM

Responses to "Core War" on its initial publication in "Computer Recreations" (SCIENTIFIC AMERICAN, May, 1984), ranged from simple requests for supplementary guidance on the game to descriptions of complete Core War systems already in operation. In between were numerous anecdotes about CREEPER-like programs inhabiting real systems (including worms in Apples), discussions of programs as genes, and speculations about defensive and offensive strategy. Only a few important developments can be mentioned here.

What happens when an IMP runs into a DWARF? One possibility was explained earlier: DWARF transfers control to IMP's code and becomes a second IMP endlessly chasing the first one. Another possible outcome has the opposite effect. Suppose DWARF has just jumped back to its first instruction when IMP copies itself over DWARF's data location. The situation is then as follows:

$$
\begin{array}{llll}
\text{IMP} \rightarrow & \text{MOV} & 0 & 1 \\
\text{DWARF} \rightarrow & \text{ADD} & \#5 & -1 \\
& \text{MOV} & \#0 & @-2 \\
& \text{JMP} & -2 &
\end{array}
$$

Since it is DWARF's turn to execute, it adds 5 to IMP's code, turning it into MOV 0 6. Then IMP executes, copying itself six spaces ahead, well clear of DWARF, which then bombs its next address (specified by the numerical code corresponding to MOV 0 6). On IMP's next turn something curious happens: it executes the first line of DWARF's program, so that for a time the game is played by a "double dwarf" pointlessly shooting up the core array while the object of its attack inhabits its own body and does exactly the same thing!

David Menconi of Milpitas, Calif., a game designer at Atari, Inc., has suggested making this very phenomenon a regular feature of Core War by allowing each battle program to execute in two places at once. Thus even if a program loses one "self," a second self might be able to repair the damage. Edsel Worrell of Bethesda, Md., suggests the somewhat more general scheme of *n* selves, all executing the same program at different addresses.

Robert Peraino of George Mason University wrote a Core War system for the Apple II+ computer, compensating for the machine's small word size by using a two-dimensional array of 2000 by two bytes. Bill Dornfield of AMF, Inc., wrote a complete Core War system in extended BASIC on a Hewlett-Packard 9816/26 desktop computer.

The most impressive system to date was constructed by three graduate students: Gordon J. Goetsch and Michael L. Mauldin of Carnegie-Mellon University and Paul G. Milazzo of Rice University. Mauldin demonstrated the program on a VAX computer in my department at the University of Western Ontario. In an impressive screen display the entire core array is shown, with the position of each contending program marked by a capital letter and the areas affected by the program marked by the corresponding lowercase letter.

Mauldin has invented a battle program called MORTAR that operates like DWARF except that its bombs are directed according to the sequence of Fibonacci numbers (1, 1, 2, 3, 5, and so on, each number being the sum of its two predecessors). Oddly enough, DWARF beats MORTAR 60 percent of the time, but MORTAR invariably kills a three-part self-repairing program called VOTER. On the other hand, VOTER survives attacks by DWARF and regularly defeats it.

Goetsch, Mauldin, and Milazzo have analyzed MORTAR and conclude that if a battle program is longer than 10 instructions, it must be self-repairing in order to defeat MORTAR. No program longer than 141 instructions, however, can repair itself fast enough to survive an attack by MORTAR.

∘ 28 ∘

Attacks of the Viruses

The only truly secure system is one that is powered off, cast in a block of concrete, and sealed in a lead-lined room with armed guards—and even then I have my doubts.
—EUGENE H. SPAFFORD

The knock on the door had a palpable urgency that brought the computer-center director's head up sharply from the pile of papers before him. He grunted loudly and the computer operator entered.

"Something's gone wrong. We have some very weird processes going on. We're running out of memory. I think we've got a virus in the system."

If the center had been equipped with claxons, the director would undoubtedly have set them off.

Such a scene has been played out in one form or another all too often in recent years, and as a result computer viruses have been increasingly in the news. In fact, this department has been cited more than once in connection with the rash of virus outbreaks, probably because it is an instigator of Core War, a game in which computer programs are purposely designed to destroy one another. But, as we shall see, Core War has no direct connection with the infections.

To understand how a computer virus works one must first understand in great detail the system in which it operates. The same thing applies for understanding the operation of worms, logic bombs, and other threats to computer security. This simple observation has two immediate implications. First, journalists are likely to misreport or distort virus news stories for quite innocent reasons: Most reporters are more or less mystified by the internal workings of computers. Second, public descriptions of a computer virus — even fairly detailed ones — cannot be exploited to reconstruct the virus except by someone who has the requisite knowledge of the affected computer system to begin with. A knowledgeable "technopath" who is bent on destroying other peoples's programs and data hardly needs to read a magazine or newspaper article to begin imagining ways to construct a virus. There is consequently no harm in describing how viruses and other destructive programs work. (Indeed, such a description is probably constructive in that it might stimulate efforts to protect computer systems.)

One must distinguish from the start between the two commonest types of malignant program. A virus rides piggyback on other programs; it cannot exist by itself. A worm, on the other hand, can pursue an independent existence, more in the manner of a bacterium. Both kinds of "infection," like all programs, depend on an operating system.

Most readers know that a running computer consists of both hardware and software. In front of me at the moment, for example, is a piece of hardware: an Apple IIc. Inside the machine's memory is software: a program called the Appleworks Word Processor. The program transfers the characters I type on the keyboard into a section of memory reserved by the program for text.

But the word-processing program is not able to run by itself. The program depends on an operating system that, among other things, translates it into a special machine language that enables the hardware to carry out the program's instructions. The operating system for a personal computer normally resides on a disk. To do anything on such a machine (from writing to playing games), the disk operating system (DOS) must first be loaded into the computer's hardware memory. In a home computer the DOS is usually loaded automatically from a disk, which may or may not contain the program one wants to run, as soon as one switches on the computer.

To run a particular program on my personal computer, I must type the name of the program into the computer. The computer's DOS then searches through the disk for a program with that name, loads it into memory and runs it — instruction by instruction — as is shown in the illustration on page 326.

In loading the program the DOS sets aside part of the hardware memory not only for the program but also for the program's "work space." Here the program will store all the values assigned to its variables and its arrays, for example. In doing all of this the DOS is normally careful not to overwrite other programs or data areas, including whatever part of the DOS happens to be in memory. The DOS is equally careful in storing programs or data onto a disk.

Often a programmer may find it necessary to employ the commands the DOS itself uses, which can generally be found in the appropriate manual. Such commands make it possible to write a subprogram that can read files from disk into memory, alter the files and then write them back onto the disk — sometimes with malicious intent.

Here is a sample virus subprogram that does just that. It contains a mixture of pseudo-DOS commands and subroutines: small, internal programs (whose component instructions are kept separate from the subprogram's main body) that carry out specific missions whenever they are called.

this := findfile
LOAD (*this*)
loc := search (*this*)
insert (*loc*)
STORE (*this*)

The subroutine designated findfile opens the directory of executable files, or programs, on a disk, picks a random file name and assigns the name of that file to a variable called *this*. The next line of the program makes use of the pseudo-DOS command LOAD to copy the file into the computer's memory. Another subroutine called search then scans the program just loaded, looking for an instruction in it that can serve as a suitable insertion site for a virus. When it finds such an instruction, it determines the instruction's line number and assigns its value to the variable called *loc*.

At this point the virus subprogram is ready to infect the program it has randomly picked. The subroutine insert replaces the selected instruction with another instruction (such as a call for a subroutine) that transfers execution to a block of code containing the basic virus subprogram, which is appended to the end of the program. It then adds the program's original instruction to the end of the appended subprogram followed by a command that transfers execution to the instruction following the insert in the host program.

In this way when the virus subprogram is executed, it also executes its host program's missing instruction. The execution of the original program can then proceed as though nothing unusual had occurred. But in fact the virus subprogram has momentarily usurped control of the DOS to replicate itself into another program on the disk. The process is illustrated graphically in the illustration on the next page. When the newly infected program is subsequently loaded by the DOS into the computer's memory and run, it will in turn infect another program on the disk while appearing to run normally.

As early as 1984 Fred S. Cohen carried out controlled infection experiments at the University of Southern California that revealed — to his surprise — that viruses similar to the one I have just described could infect an entire network of computers in a matter of minutes. In order to explain the kinds of damage such viruses can do, I shall adapt Cohen's generic virus, writing it in a pseudolanguage.

1234567
main program:
1. infect
2. if trigger pulled, then do damage
3. go to host program

subroutine: infect
1. get random executable file
2. if first line of file = 1234567, then go to 1, else prepend virus to file
subroutine: trigger pulled
subroutine: do damage

Cohen's generic virus is generic in all but its attachment site: Instead of inserting itself in the middle or at the end of the host program, it attaches itself to the beginning. The first line of the virus program is the "recognition code" 1234567. The main program first calls up the subroutine infect, which randomly retrieves an executable file from a disk and checks whether the first line of that file happens to be 1234567. If it is, the program has already been infected and the subroutine picks another program. If the subroutine happens to find an uninfected file, it "prepends" the entire virus program to the target program. This means simply that is places itself at the head of the program and arranges to get

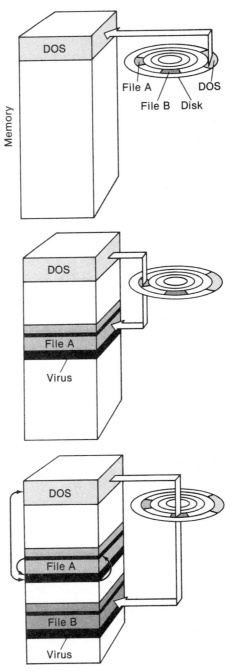

Loading the DOS into memory (*left*) allows a program to be read (*middle*) and a virus (*right*) to replicate itself

itself executed first before transferring control back to the infected program.

The next two subroutines call for a triggering condition and for some damage to be done. The triggering condition might be a certain date reached by the system clock, or perhaps the deletion of a certain employee's name from the payroll file. The damage to be done might be the erasure of all files or, more subtly, the random alteration of bits in just a few places. The possibilities are endless.

Triggering conditions and damage bring us to the edge of moral territory. I think there is no question that willfully perpetrating damage to computer files by means of a virus or other destructive program is a reprehensible act. Computer programs and data are not just impersonal strings of 0's and 1's but also miniature cities of thought. Why would anyone want to destroy the work of another?

Writers of virus programs do so for a variety of reasons. For example, a programmer in a large company might secretly harbor a grudge against the company's management. He might implant a virus for the day his employment is terminated. When that happens, his records will be deleted from the payroll file, triggering the virus. As a result, valuable company data and programs might either disappear or develop serious and costly errors. Replacing faulty data and programs with backups stored on other media might be of no avail, since if the backups were made recently, they too might be infected.

Of course, the kind of destruction just described would ordinarily take place in a multiple-user computer system. The operating system in this kind of computer environment is considerably more complex than a disk operating system for a personal computer. For one thing, the fact that so many users share the same facilities requires an operating system that protects users as much as possible from inadvertent or deliberate interference. Even here, however, viruses are possible, but they require much more sophistication. Usually they exploit a flaw in some part of the operating system—a bug, so to speak—as was evidenced by the "virus" (actually it was a worm) that spread throughout the Internet in fall of 1988.

During the evening of November 2, 1988, someone ran a worm program on one of the several thousand North American computers interconnected through a data-communications network called the Internet. The network connects machines at universities, businesses, government agencies such as the National Aeronautics and Space Administration, and even some military installations. With frightening speed the worm spread to more than 1000 machines during that evening and the next day. As copies of the worm proliferated, operators of individual systems noticed memory utilization soaring and machine response becoming sluggish. The worm did not attack files or other programs, however. It seemed content merely to proliferate throughout as many host machines as possible. Even so, the damage in lost time was immense.

As I mentioned above, a worm is a program that pursues an independent existence within a computer; it moves from computer to computer on its own, leaving duplicates of itself in each machine. The Internet worm consisted of two parts, a vector and a body. Starting from a given host computer, the worm would seek a new host by sending its vector to another computer. Once inside the machine, the vector would establish a communication link through which the worm's body could be sent. Details of this attack were revealed by Eugene H. Spafford of Purdue University in a 40-page document a few weeks after the event. One example of the worm's operation shows the cleverness of its creator.

UNIX, the operating system of choice on many of the Internet computers, allows processes to take place in the computer that are not associated with any particular user. Such independent processes are called demons. One demon, called fingerd (pronounced fingerdee), enables users to get information about other users. Such a service is desirable in a computing environment in which users must share programs and data for research and development purposes.

The worm in its current host computer would send a message to one of the other potential host computers on its list (which was obtained illegally). In requesting the services of the fingerd demon, the worm gave it some information, just as an ordinary user might. But the worm supplied so much information to the demon that the data filled the space reserved for the demon in the computer's memory and overflowed into a "forbidden" area.

The area that was thus overwritten was normally reserved for instructions that fingerd consulted in deciding what to do next. Once inside such an area the worm (whose body still inhabited the original host machine) invoked a so-called command interpreter of the new machine, effectively claiming a small piece of the UNIX operating system all to itself. After the command interpreter was at its disposal, the worm transmitted some 99 lines of source code constituting the vector. On the worm's command, the unwitting potential host then compiled and ran the vector's program, virtually guaranteeing infection.

The vector program hid itself in the system by changing its name and deleting all files created during its entry into the system. After doing that it established a new communication channel to the previous host and, using standard system protocols, copied over the files making up the main body of the worm.

Once inside a new host computer, the worm's main job was to discover the names and addresses of new host machines by breaking into areas reserved for legitimate users of the system. To do so it relied on an elaborate password-guessing scheme that, owing to the carelessness with which most users choose passwords, proved rather successful. When it had a legitimate user's password, the worm could pretend to be the user in order to read what he or she may have had in the computer's memory and to discover the names of other computers in the Internet that it could also infect.

According to Spafford, most of the UNIX features (or "misfeatures," as he calls them) that allowed the worm to function as it did have been fixed. Yet the fact has not allayed his worries about computer security, as the quotation at the beginning of this article reveals. Perhaps he was thinking of Cohen's theoretical investigation of viruses, which might apply to worms just as well.

If technopaths insist on vandalizing computer systems, it may be time to form a Center for Virus Control. During the Internet worm crisis teams at the University of California at Berkeley and a few other Internet stations were able to capture copies of the worm, analyze its code and determine how it worked. It would seem reasonable to establish a national agency that would combat computer viruses and worms whenever and wherever they break out—particularly if computer infections are destined to increase. Although the Internet experience hinted at the horrors that may still come, it also showed the efficacy of an organized resistance against them.

Cohen has established that it is impossible to write a computer program that will detect every conceivable virus, even though a defense can be constructed against any given virus. On the other hand, for any such defense there are other viruses that can get around it. According to Cohen, this ominous state of affairs might subject future computing environments to a kind of evolution in which only the fittest programs would survive.

The situation is reminiscent of Core War, the computer game I described in Chapter 27 (*see* also SCIENTIFIC AMERICAN, March, 1985, and

January, 1987). But a Core War program does not bully innocent systems. It picks on someone its own size: another Core War program. The two programs engage in subtle or blatant conflict in a specially reserved area of a computer's memory called the coliseum. There is no danger of a Core War program ever escaping to do damage in the real world, because no Core War program or anything like it would ever run effectively in a normal computing environment. Core War programs are written in a language called Redcode that is summarized in the table below.

Perhaps a simple example of such a program will serve to introduce the game to readers not already familiar with it. Here is a program called DWARF that launches a 0-bomb into every fifth memory location:

$$
\begin{array}{ll}
\text{DAT} -1 & \\
\text{ADD \#5} & -1 \\
\text{MOV \#0} & @\ -2 \\
\text{JMP} -2 &
\end{array}
$$

A Summary of Core War Instructions

INSTRUCTION	EXPLANATION
DAT B	A nonexecutable data statement; B is the data value.
MOV A B	Move contents of address A to address B.
ADD A B	Add contents of address A to address B.
SUB A B	Subtract contents of address A from address B.
JMP B	Transfer control to address B.
JMZ A B	Transfer control to address A if contents of address B are zero.
JMN A B	Transfer control to address A if contents of address B are not zero.
DJN A B	Subtract 1 from contents of address B and transfer control to address A if contents of address B are not zero.
CMP A B	Compare contents of addresses A and B; if they are equal, skip the next instruction.
SPL B	Split execution between next instruction and the instruction at address B.

The memory coliseum that all Core War programs inhabit consists of several thousand addresses, or numbered memory cells, arranged in a long strip. The instructions that make up DWARF, for example, occupy four consecutive addresses in the coliseum, say 1001, 1002, 1003, and 1004.

The DAT statement serves to hold a value that will be used by the program (in this case −1) at the address 1001. The ADD statement adds the number 5 to the location that is −1 units away from the ADD statement. Since the ADD statement has address 1002, it adds 5 to the number stored at the previous address, namely 1001, changing the −1 to a 4. The MOV command moves the number 0 into the memory cell referred to by @ −2. Where is that? The address if found by referring to the DAT statement two lines in front of the MOV command. There one finds the address where the program will put the number 0. The final command, JMP, causes execution of the DWARF program to jump back two lines, to the ADD command. This begins the process all over again.

The second time around, DWARF will change the contents of the DAT cell to 9 and then deliver a 0 to that memory address. If an enemy program happens to have an instruction at that address, it will be rendered inoperable and the program will perhaps "die" as a result.

In this manner DWARF goes on dropping 0-bombs on every fifth location until it reaches the end of memory — but memory never ends, because the last address is contiguous to the first. Consequently DWARF's bombs eventually begin to fall nearer and nearer to itself. Yet because DWARF is only four instructions long and the number of memory cells is normally a multiple of 10, DWARF avoids hitting itself and lives to fight on — albeit blindly and rather stupidly.

Over the past few years Core War has evolved into a rather sophisticated game with numerous strategies and counterstrategies. There are programs that spawn copies of themselves, that launch hordes of mindless one-line battle programs and that even repair themselves when they are hit.

The International Core War Society, which currently has its headquarters in Long Beach, Calif., and branches in Italy, Japan, Poland, the Soviet Union, and West Germany, organizes annual tournaments in which a programmer's skills are put to the test. Readers interested in joining a Core War chapter should contact William R. Buckley at the address given in the List of Suppliers.

In the 1987 tournament the Japanese entries gave the North American warrior programs a run for their money. The winner of a more recent tournament, held December, 1988, in Los Angeles, was a program from the Soviet Union called, oddly enough, COWBOY. Written by Eugene P. Lilitko of Pereslavl-Zalesky, a small city northeast of Moscow, COWBOY appeared to watch for "bombing runs" by enemy programs, to move itself out of harm's way and then to retaliate massively. Lilitko won the first prize of $250. The second prize of $100 went to Luca Crosara of Pistoia, Italy. The third prize of $50 was won by Douglas McDaniels of Alexandria, Va.

In closing I quote Spafford once again: "Writing and running a virus is not the act of a computer professional but a computer vandal." Let those who would even contemplate such an act try Core War instead.

I should like to thank Cohen, Spafford, and John Carroll, a computer-security expert at the University of Western Ontario, for help with this chapter.

ADDENDUM

The subject of "Attacks of the Viruses" was vandalware: malicious programs that replicate themselves and do damage to benign software. The plague of such computer "viruses" and "worms" continues. Rumors of a new virus that attacks spread-sheet programs have been circulating. Virus expert Harold J. Highland, who edits the journal *Computers and Security*, calls the new infection a macrovirus, because it consists of special commands called macros.

Reports of a macrovirus would be difficult to track down, because it would strike corporations that are reluctant to release details to the public. Every time a user runs an infected program, the virus would call up a work sheet from memory at random, alter the numerical content of a single cell by a small amount, and put the altered work sheet back in memory. The damage such a virus can do is potentially great, since small changes in data can go unnoticed for months, significantly affecting the results of the spreadsheet calculations.

In spite of such rumors, Tom Pittman of Spreckels, Calif., thinks I overreacted. According to Pittman, one must be careful to distinguish between useful and destructive viruses. The difference may be semantic. There are certainly useful programs that lead a viral or even wormlike existence. They have jobs that range from file compression to input scanning, but they are not normally called viruses or worms.

Edwin B. Heinlein of Mill Valley, Calif., would press for the establishment of a Center for Computer Disease Control modeled after the Centers for (Human) Disease Control in Atlanta. Such a center would be part of a broader effort for studying and categorizing viruses and for drawing up new laws pertaining to the reporting of incidents and the punishment of offenders. The research undertaken in such an effort might also yield new filters and virus-detection schemes.

Further Readings

1 Mandelbrot Magic

Hoffman, Dean, and Lee Mohler. *Mathematical Recreations for the Programmable Calculator*. Hasbrouck Heights, N.J.: Hayden Book Co., 1982.

Mandelbrot, Benoit B. *The Fractal Geometry of Nature*. New York: W. H. Freeman and Company, 1983.

Robert, François. *Discrete Iterations*. Translated by Jon Rokne. New York: Springer-Verlag, 1986.

2 Visions of Julia

Peitgen, Heniz-Otto, and Peter H. Richter. *The Beauty of Fractals*. New York: Springer-Verlag, 1986.

3 Mandelbrew and Mandelbus

Peitgen, Heniz-Otto, and P. H. Richter. *The Beauty of Fractals*. New York: Springer-Verlag, 1986.

Gleick, James. *Chaos: Making a New Science*. Viking Penguin, 1987.

The Science of Fractal Images. Edited by Heinz-Otto Peitgen and Dietmar Saupe. New York: Springer-Verlag, 1988.

4 The Strange Attractions of the Chaos

Crutchfield, James P., J. Doyne Farmer, Norman H. Packard, and Robert S. Shaw. "Chaos." SCIENTIFIC AMERICAN, December, 1986, 46–57.

Hughes, Gordon. "Henon Mapping with Pascal." *Byte* 11, no. 13 (December, 1986): 161–192.

5 Catching Biomorphs

Pickover, Clifford A. "Biomorphs: Computer Displays of Biological Forms Generated from Mathematical Feedback Loops." *Computer Graphics Forum* 5 (1986): 313–316.

Pickover, Clifford A. "Mathematics and Beauty: Time-Discrete Phase Planes Associated with the Cyclic System." *Computers and Graphics* 11, no. 2 (1987): 217–226.
Pickover, Clifford A. *Computers, Pattern, Chaos, and Beauty.* New York: St. Martin's Press, 1990.

6   Vehicles of Thought

Bullock, Theodore Homes, Richard Orkand, and Alan Grinnell. *Introduction to Nervous Systems.* San Francisco: W. H. Freeman and Company, 1977.
Kandel, Eric R. "Small Systems of Neurons." Scientific American, September, 1979, 66–76.
Braitenberg, Valentino. *Vehicles: Experiments in Synthetic Psychology.* Cambridge, Mass.: The MIT Press, 1984.

8   Atomic Computers

Drexler, K. Eric. "Molecular Engineering: An Approach to the Development of General Capabilities for Molecular Manipulation. *Proceedings of the National Academy of Sciences of the United States of America* 78, 9 (September, 1981): 5275–5278.
Drexler, K. Eric. *Engines of Creation.* New York: Anchor Press, 1986.
Feynman, R. *Miniturization.* Edited by G. H. D. Gilbert. New York.
Preuss, Paul. *Human Error.* New York: Tor Books, 1987.

9   Paradoxical Gold

Read, Ronald C. *Tangrams — 330 Puzzles.* New York: Dover Publications, Inc., 1965.
Augenstein, B. W. "Hadron Physics and Transfinite Set Theory." *International Journal of Theoretical Physics* 23, no. 12 (1984): 1197–1205.
Wagon, Stan. *The Banach-Tarski Paradox.* Cambridge: Cambridge University Press, 1985.

10   Fractal Mountains and Graftal Plants

Cook, Robert L., Thomas Porter, and Loren Carpenter. "Distributed Ray Tracing." *Computer Graphics* 18, no. 3 (July, 1984): 137–145.

De Panne, Michiel van. "3-D Fractals." *Creative Computing* 11, no. 7 (July, 1985): 78–82.

11   Hodgepodge Reactions

Dewdney, A. K. *The Armchair Universe.* New York: W. H. Freeman and Company, 1988.
Wright, Robert. "Did the Universe Just Happen?" *The Atlantic*, April, 1988, 29–44.

12   The Demons of Cyclic Space

Toffoli, Tommaso, and Norman Margolus. *Cellular Automata Machines.* Cambridge, Mass.: The MIT Press, 1988.
Fisch, Robert, Janko Gravner, and David Griffeath. *Cyclic Cellular Automata in Two Dimensions.* Ted E. Harris Festschrift. Cambridge, Mass: Birkhäuser, Boston: in press.

13   Slow Growths

Mandelbrot, Benoit B. *The Fractal Geometry of Nature.* New York: W. H. Freeman and Company, 1982.
Sander, Leonard B. "Fractal Growth." Scientific American, January, 1987, 94–100.

14   Programmed Parties

Hall, E. T. "The Effects of Personal Space and Territory on Human Communication." In *Nonverbal Communication in Human Interaction*, edited by Mark L. Knapp. New York: Holt, Rinehart and Winston, 1978.
Modern Computer People. Mountain View, Calif.: Activision, 1985.

15   Palmiter's Protozoa

Dawkins, Richard. *The Blind Watchmaker.* New York: W. W. Norton & Company, 1987.
Artificial Life: The Proceedings of an Interdisciplinary Workshop on the Synthesis and Simulation of Living Systems Held September, 1987, in Los Alamos, New Mexico. Edited by Christopher G. Langton. Reading, Mass.: Addison-Wesley Publishing Company, 1989.

16   *Mazes and Minotaurs*

Bulfinch, Thomas. *Bulfinch's Mythology*. Carlton House, 1936.

Hofstadter, Douglas R. Gödel, Escher, Bach: An Eternal Golden Braid. New York: Basic Books, 1979.

Walker, Jearl. "The Amateur Scientist." SCIENTIFIC AMERICAN, June, 1986, 120–126.

17   *People Puzzles*

Goffman, Erving. *The Presentation of Self in Everyday Life*. Garden City, N.Y.: Doubleday & Company, 1959.

Shasha, Dennis. *The Puzzling Adventures of Dr. Ecco*. New York: W. H. Freeman and Company, 1988.

18   *Panning for Primes*

Bell, Eric Temple. "The Queen of Mathematics." In *The World of Mathematics*, edited by James R. Newman. New York: Simon and Schuster, 1956.

Dudeney, Henry Ernest. *Amusements in Mathematics*. New York: Dover Publications, 1970.

Pomerance, Carl. The Search for Prime Numbers. SCIENTIFIC AMERICAN, December, 1982, 135–147.

Peng, T. A. "One Million Primes Through the Sieve." 10, no. 11, (Fall, 1985): 243–244.

19   *Trains of Thought*

Dudeney, Henry Ernest. *Amusements in Mathematics*. New York: Dover Publications, 1970.

Van Rooten, Luis d'Antin. *Mots d'Heures: Gousses Rames. The d'Antin Manuscript*. Baltimore: Penguin Books, 1980.

20   *Prosodic Programs*

Hayes, Brian. "Computer Recreations: A Progress Report on the Fine Art of Turning Literature into Drivel." SCIENTIFIC AMERICAN. November, 1983, 16–24.

21   The Martian Dictionary

Brady, J. M. The Theory of Computer Science: A Programming Approach. Chapman and Hall, 1977.

The Official Scrabble^R Players Dictionary. New York: Pocket Books, 1978.

Augarde, Tony, ed. *The Oxford Guide to Word Games.* New York: Oxford University Press, 1984.

23   Balls in Boxes

Artwick, Bruce A. Microcomputer Displays, Graphics, and Animation. Englewood Cliffs, N.J.: Prentice-Hall, 1985.

24   The Invisible Professor

Lawrence, J. Dennis. *A Catalog of Special Plane Curves.* New York: Dover Publications, 1972.

25   The Enigma and the Bombe

Codes, Ciphers, and Computers: An Introduction to Information Security. Hayden Book Company, 1982.

Hodges, Andrew. *Alan Turing: The Enigma.* London: Burnett Books, 1983.

Denning, Dorothy Elizabeth Robling. *Cryptography and Data Security.* Reading, Mass.: Addison-Wesley Publishing Company, 1983.

26   Computers and the Crypt

Data Encryption Standard. National Bureau of Standards, Federal Information Processing Standards Publication 46. Springfield, Va.: National Technical Information Service, 1977.

Diffie, Whitfield. "The First Ten Years of Public-Key Cryptography." *Proceedings of the IEEE* 76, no. 5 (May, 1988): 560–577.

27   Core Wars

Kane, Gerry, and Doug Hawkins Legenthal. *68000 Assembly Language Programming.* Berkeley, Calif.: Osborne–McGraw-Hill, 1981.

Null, Aleph. "Darwin." *Software: Practice & Experience* 2, no. 1 (January–March, 1972): 93–96.

28   Attacks of the Viruses

"Computer Viruses." *Computers and Security* 7, no. 2 (April, 1988): 117–125, 139–184.
Denning, Peter J. "Computer Viruses." *American Scientist* 76, no. 3 (May-June, 1988): 236–238.

Illustration Credits

List of Suppliers

Organizations and suppliers of software, posters, publications, and video-tapes appear below. The entries are organized by "spell." The suppliers for all chapters within a given section are listed together for easy reference. Most items listed below require payment as a condition of shipping. If in doubt, a letter of inquiry will result in further information about conditions of sale or distribution

○ *Spell One* ○ *Conjuring Up Chaos*

Algorithm: a newsletter devoted to recreational programming for both beginning and expert programmers. Frequently contains fractal programming projects and subjects of broader interest.

> Louis Magguilli, Managing Editor
> Algorithm
> 2 Oxford St. W.
> London, Ontario
> Canada N6H 1P9

Amygdala: a newsletter for explorers and afficionados of the Mandelbrot set and other iterated systems.

> Rollo Silver, Editor
> Amygdala, Box 219
> San Cristobal, NM 87564

Art Matrix: a company that produces videotapes, posters, and even tee-shirts, all featuring the Mandelbrot set and related subjects.

> Homer Wilson Smith
> Art Matrix
> P.O. Box 880
> Ithaca, NY 14851

Map Art: a company that produces slides and posters of the Mandelbrot set. One of the chief distributors of the work of Heinz-Otto Peitgen and Gerhard Richter.

> MAP ART
> Forschungsgruppe Komplexe Dynamik
> Universität Bremen
> 2800 Bremen 33
> West Germany

Cliff Pickover: distributes recipes for computing powers of complex numbers. Will also send list of computer graphic publications to anyone who asks. Use self-addressed (stamped if possible) envelope.

> Dr. Clifford A. Pickover
> 37 Yorkshire Lane
> Yorktown Heights, NY 10598

Turing Omnibus: distributes software based on A.K. Dewdney's computer recreations columns, in particular programs that generate Mandelbrot and Julia sets.

> David Wiseman,
> Turing Omnibus, Inc.
> PO Box 1456
> London, Ontario
> Canada N6A 5M2

○ *Spell Two* ○ *Weird Machines*

Joseph A. Coppola: distributes plans for a homemade vehicle constructed from off-the-shelf parts available from local hardware and electronic stores.

> Joseph A. Coppola
> 304 Park St.
> Sherrill, NY 13461

The Foresight Institute: an organization devoted to the exploration of the possibilities and limitations of nanotechnology. The Institute publishes a newsletter that keeps members up to date on current developments.

Dr. K. Eric Drexler
The Foresight Institute
Box 61058
Palo Alto, CA 94306

∘ *Spell Three* ∘ *Deus ex Machina*

Scott Camazine: distributes a diffusion-limited aggregation program, the game of Life, WA-TOR and other recreational software.

Scott Camazine
36 Dove Drive
Ithaca, NY 14850

Cellular Automatist: a newsletter devoted to cellular automata. Theory, experiments, and projects involving all manner of cellular automata are reported.

Rollo Silver, Editor
The Cellular Automatist
Box 219
San Cristobal, NM 87564

Rich Gold: distributes Party Planner, a program that simulates motions of guests at a party as seen from above.

Rich Gold
816 N.Gardner St.
Los Angeles, CA 90046

Dr. David Griffeath: distributes EXCITE!, a PC-compatible modelling environment for cellular automata, featuring rules for "excitable media" such as Cyclic Space and the Belousov-Zhabotinsky reaction.

Dr. David Griffeath
Dept. of Mathematics, Van Vleek Hall
University of Wisconsin
Madison,WI 53706

Life Science Associates: distributors of software that illustrates psychological and biological concepts, including Simulated Evolution, the official version of Palmiter's evolving bacteria program.

Frank J. Mandriota
Life Science Associates, Inc.
One Fenimore Road
Bayport, NY 11705

PIXAR: originator of the PIXAR computer. Currently distributes Mac RenderMan, a program that renders geometrical models. Also distributes videotapes, slides and tee-shirts.

> Lola Gill, Marketing
> PIXAR
> 1001 West Cutting Blvd.
> Richmond, CA 94804

Systems Concepts, Inc: manufacturer and distributor of the CAM-6 cellular automata machine, including user's guide. The book called Cellular Automata Machines (see the bibliography) also describes how the CAM is programmed.

> Systems Concepts, Inc.
> 56 Francisco St.
> San Francisco, CA 94139

Turing Omnibus: distributor of recreational software, including cellular automata such as cyclic space and the hodgepodge machine. For address, see entry in Spell One.

○ *Spell Four* ○ *Puzzling Landscapes*

Algorithm: a newsletter devoted to recreational programming for both beginning and expert programmers. Contains a regular column called Algopuzzles by Dennis Shasha. For address see entry in Spell One.

George A. Miller: distributes a program that generates word ladders between any two given words.

> George A. Miller
> 2426 Bush St.
> San Francisco, CA 94115

Michael Newman: distributes a great variety of poetry processing software, including Orpheus, Nerd, and the Poetry Processing Package.

> Michael A. Newman
> 12 West 68th Street,#2-C
> New York, NY 10023

Rob Pike: distributes a lengthy commentary on deconstructionist philosophy by Mark V. Shaney, the word-scrambling program that makes hilarious sense.

> Rob Pike
> At&T Bell Laboratories
> 600 Mountain Ave.
> Murray Hill, NJ 07974

Word Ways: a journal devoted to word-play and word recreations. It features research on exotic words, lists of unusual words, logology, ladders, anagrams, and much more.

> A. Ross Eckler, Editor
> Word Ways
> Spring Valley Road
> Morristown, NJ 07960

R. K. West Consulting: distributes a variety of recreational and practical software including Cliche Finder (to help avoid cliches), Creativity Package (Thunder Thought, Versifier and other programs), Crystal Ball and Maillist. Free catalog available on request.

> Rosemary West
> R.K. West Consulting
> P.O. Box 8059
> Mission Hills, CA 91346

Carl Wurtz: distributes a program called Quickrhyme that produces a list of Words that rhyme with a given word. Just the thing for traditional poets.

> Carl Wurtz
> "a priori"
> 859 Hollywood Way, Suite 401
> Burbank, CA 91510

The Yates Collection: a list of all known prime numbers having more than a thousand digits. This and other lists and tables may be purchased for a modest price.

> Samuel D. Yates
> 157 Capri-D, Kings Point
> Delray Beach, FL 33445

○ *Spell Five* ○ *Mathemagical Movies*

Lascaux Graphics: distributors of mathematical software, including complex function graphics packages, software to visualize functions of a complex variable.

> Lascaux Graphics, Inc.
> 3220 Steuben Ave.
> Bronx, NY 10467

MAL: distributor of mathematical functions and graphing software. The Math Algorithm Library includes polynomials, plots, eigenvalues, Fourier transforms, and prime number programs.

> P. ffyske Howden,
> Math Algorithm Library
> Con Street
> McLeay Island, Queensland
> AUSTRALIA 4184

The Mechanical Universe: a videotape showing simulations of several physical phenomena, including gas molecules and orbiting planets. Narrated in clear and laconical terms. Can be ordered by writing to the address below or by dialing 1-800-LEARNER.

> James Blinn
> Jet Propulsion Laboratory
> Mail Stop 510-110
> 4800 Oak Grove Drive
> Pasadena, CA 91109

Robert Merkin: distributes SHAKEY, a computer reactor in which the unstable element called gridium can be seen undergoing fission.

> Robert B. Merkin
> 56 Milton St.
> Northampton, MA 0160

Moonshadow Software: distributes mathematical curve-plotting packages. SPIA is a comprehensive mathematical program that constructs and plots formulas.

> Moonshadow Software
> P.O. Box 5974
> Baltimore, MD 21208

○ *Spell Six* ○ *Battles of the Magi*

The Cryptogram: a journal devoted to cryptology and codes. Readers publish codes they have constructed or codes they have cracked. Official publication of The American Cryptogram Association.

> Rebecca W. Kornbluh
> The American Cryptogram Association
> 18789 West Hickory Street
> Mundelein, IL 60060

Crryptologia: the official journal of the American Cryptological Society. Published quarterly, it features articles on codes and ciphers.

> Louis Kruh,
> 17 Alfred Road W.
> Merrick, NY 11566

The Cryptosystems Journal: a journal devoted to cryptology and codes, especially state-of-the-art cryptosystems for IBM PCs.

> Tony Patti
> 9755 Oatley Lane
> Burke, VA 22015

International Core War Society: the official organization that sets and distributes the Core War Standards, organizes tournaments, issues a newsletter, and sells Core War software.

> William R. Buckley, Director
> International Core War Society
> 5712 Kern Drive
> Huntington Beach, CA 92649

Bartosz Milewski: distributes CRYPTO, a program that works like a one- or two-rotor enigma machine to encode private messages.

> Bartosz Milewski
> 13649 NE 12th St, #204
> Bellevue, WA 98005

Turing Omnibus: distributor of recreational programs, including the Core War Coliseum, the ICWS standard development and tournament program. For address, see the entry in Spell One

Name Index

Subject Index